WITHDRAWN

THE
RUSSIAN LANGUAGE
SINCE THE
REVOLUTION

The Russian Language since the Revolution

BERNARD COMRIE

AND

GERALD STONE

1978

OXFORD
AT THE CLARENDON PRESS

Oxford University Press, Walton Street, Oxford OX2 6DP

OXFORD LONDON GLASGOW
NEW YORK TORONTO MELBOURNE WELLINGTON
IBADAN NAIROBI DAR ES SALAAM LUSAKA CAPE TOWN
KUALA LUMPUR SINGAPORE JAKARTA HONG KONG TOKYO
DELHI BOMBAY CALCUTTA MADRAS KARACHI

© *Oxford University Press 1978*

British Library Cataloguing in Publication Data
Comrie, Bernard
    The Russian language since the Revolution
    1. Russian language – History 2. Sociolinguistics
    I. Title II. Stone, Gerald
    301.2'1   PG2087   77–30204
    ISBN 0–19–815648–0

*Printed in Great Britain
at the University Press, Oxford
by Vivian Ridler
Printer to the University*

PREFACE

THE general plan of this book and the Introduction are the result of our joint efforts, but we are individually responsible for the various chapters—Bernard Comrie for Chapters 1, 2, 4, and 6, and Gerald Stone for Chapters 3, 5, 7, and 8.

In the vast majority of cases we have given Russian words in the Cyrillic alphabet. Otherwise, transliterations have been made according to the International System. The phonetic transcriptions follow the system of the International Phonetic Association.

We hope our book will be read not only by students of Russian, and we have therefore given English translations of all the examples where this could possibly be of use to the reader. Translations are not given of those examples where the point being made could only be understood by readers with a knowledge of Russian. Word-stress is not shown except where it is, or might be thought to be, relevant to the argument.

Dates preceding 1(14) February 1918 are given in the Old Style, and from then on, in the New Style.

We wish to record our thanks, for bibliographical advice, to Dr. Ju. A. Bel'čikov, N. I. Formanovskaja, and V. P. Trofimenko.

B. C.
G. S.

June 1976

CONTENTS

LIST OF PHONETIC
SYMBOLS USED

VOWELS

1	a	as in сад
2	ã	nasalized 1, as in Fr. fiancé
3	e	as in лето
4	i	as in кит
5	iᵉ	vowel between 3 and 4, as in весна (see p. 52)
6	ɨ	high central vowel, as in сын
7	ɨᵉ	vowel between 3 and 6, as in жена (see pp. 39–40)
8	ɪ	lowered and retracted 4, as in пестрота (see p. 52)
9	ɨ	lowered 6, as in выше
10	o	as in сон
11	ǫ	raised 10 (see pp. 50–1)
12	õ	nasalized 10, as in Fr. bon
13	œ	front rounded vowel, as in Fr. fleur
14	u	as in зуб
15	y	front rounded vowel, as in Fr. lune
16	ʌ	back half-open unrounded vowel, as in вода
17	ə	central vowel, as in масло

CONSONANTS

18	b	as in банк
19	b̦	palatalized 18, as in бить
20	d	as in дом
21	d̦	palatalized 20, as in дядя
22	f	as in фон
23	f̦	palatalized 22, as in фильм
24	g	as in город
25	g̦	advanced ('palatalized') 24, as in гибкий
26	ɦ	'voiced h', as in бухгалтер (see p. 32)
27	j	as in мой, я ([ja])

28	k	as in кот
29	ķ	advanced ('palatalized') 28, as in кит
30	l	as in лапа
31	ļ	palatalized 30, as in липа
32	m	as in мышь
33	m̦	palatalized 32, as in мило
34	n	as in наш
35	ņ	palatalized 34, as in нет
36	p	as in палка
37	p̦	palatalized 36, as in петь
38	r	as in рот
39	ŗ	palatalized 38, as in редко
40	s	as in сам
41	ş	palatalized 40, as in сеть
42	ʃ	as in шаг
43	ʃ̧	palatalized 42, occurs geminated in щи (Moscow pronunciation) (see pp. 27–9)
44	t	as in там
45	ţ	palatalized 44, as in тетя
46	ts	affricate, as in отец
47	tș	palatalized 46, does not occur in standard Russian
48	ʧ	affricate, as in честь
49	v	as in вы
50	v̦	palatalized 49, as in Вера
51	x	as in холм
52	x̦	advanced ('palatalized') 51, as in хитрый
53	z	as in зонт
54	ẓ	palatalized 53, as in зима
55	ʒ	as in жар
56	ʒ̧	palatalized 55, occurs geminated in дрожжи (OM) (see p. 30)
57	ɣ	voiced 51, i.e. fricative corresponding to 24 (see pp. 30–3)
58	ˈ	placed before stressed syllable of non-monosyllabic word

ABBREVIATIONS

CSR	Contemporary Standard Russian (pronunciation)
L.	Leningrad
M.	Moscow
OM	Old Moscow (pronunciation)
OPb	Old St. Petersburg (pronunciation)
Pb.	(St.) Petersburg
Pg.	Petrograd
RJaŠ	*Русский язык в школе*
RJaSO	*Русский язык и советское общество*
RR	*Русская речь*
SAR	*Словарь Академии Российской*
SCRJa	*Словарь церковно-славянского и русского языка*
SPU	'*Словарь произношений и ударений*'
SSRLJa	*Словарь современного русского литературного языка*
VJa	*Вопросы языкознания*
VKR	*Вопросы культуры речи*

INTRODUCTION

OUR objective in this book is to trace and illustrate the main changes that have taken place in the Russian language since the beginning of the twentieth century, particularly those since 1917. The question might reasonably be asked why the year of the October Revolution, famous in the first place for the initiation of political, economic, and social change, should also be of significance in the history of the Russian language. Our answer would be that language change is dependent, to a considerable extent, on sociological factors, and that in many respects the way in which Russian has changed in the Soviet period is due, directly or indirectly, to the changes in Russian society brought about by the Revolution. Some of the new features of present-day Russian can be attributed quite specifically to new attitudes and institutions. Many others of course would probably have appeared even if there had been no October Revolution.

Whatever the proportion of sociological to purely linguistic factors in the changes which have taken place, however, it is clear that the process of change has been gradual and continuous. There were no developments in the Russian language following 1917 to match in abruptness the rapid political events of that year and the consequent economic and social changes. It is only now, when we can look back over more than half a century of Russian in use in a socialist society that we can see the extent to which it has changed. The inevitable conclusion is that, while it has been gradual, the extent of change during this period has been considerable.

Our impression, however, is that the extent to which present-day Russian differs from the language of the nineteenth century is widely ignored or underestimated, and that consequently many students of Russian mistakenly regard reading the nineteenth-century classics as an appropriate method of acquiring practical language skills. This would seem to suggest that there is a lack of information on the ways in which Russian has changed since the beginning of the twentieth century and, particularly, during the Soviet period. One of our objectives is to provide such information in a systematic way.

For the most part we have dealt with the standard language, though some account has been taken of non-standard varieties,[1] and, in particular, of non-standard features which have either become standard or at least tended to do so. The study of non-standard Russian for its own sake does not come within the scope of this book, but standard and non-standard are not discrete categories and it is thus impossible in tracing change in the standard to ignore the overlap. The standard language itself is in any case not uniform, but its development always tends towards uniformity in certain respects. In so far as changes in the standard depend on some kind of change in attitudes as to what is correct, they are all attributable to sociolinguistic causes. Similarly, decisions as to what is to be codified as standard and attempts deliberately to direct the course of development of the Russian language are sociolinguistic matters. The control, or attempted control, of language development comes under the heading of a particular branch of sociolinguistics called 'language planning'. This has been defined as 'the establishment of goals, policies and procedures for a language community' (Haugen 1969: 701). Similar activities and their study come under the Russian heading of культура речи. For the most part, both language planning and культура речи are concerned with questions of the standard language (Stone 1973: 166–9).

The standard language exists in both spoken and written

[1] We use the term 'standard language' in referring to present-day Russian for what is usually called in Russian литературный язык 'literary language' (less commonly стандартный язык). In speaking of current Russian, the two terms refer to the same thing, although they can be distinguished in speaking of certain other periods and other languages: thus русский литературный язык в эпоху Киевского государства 'the Russian literary language in the period of the Kievan state' (Gorškov 1969) does not imply the existence of a standard language at that time. It should be borne in mind that литературный язык does not refer exclusively to the language of (artistic) literature, nor indeed exclusively to the written language, since one can equally speak of разговорный вариант литературного языка 'the colloquial variant of the literary language', or even литературная речь 'literary speech'. Since the English term 'literary' is inevitably associated with literature, we prefer the term 'standard language'. (On language standardization generally see Ray 1963).

forms. In literate societies educated people use varieties of the spoken standard in certain situations. In some literate societies they use standard varieties in *all* situations. In some European speech communities (in Switzerland, for example, and in some parts of Germany) educated speakers use non-standard varieties in many types of situation, and the use of the spoken standard is restricted. In such communities the distribution of standard and non-standard speech is mainly functional. The Russian speech community, on the other hand, is representative of another type in which the distribution of standard and non-standard is mainly on the basis of who the speakers are rather than of what kind of situation they are in. That is to say, the distribution is mainly social rather than functional. Well-educated speakers of Russian generally aspire to use standard varieties in all situations.[1] Non-standard varieties have low social prestige. Nevertheless, there are many members of the Russian speech community whose speech has local characteristics.

The use of a non-standard variety of Russian can reveal the social, as well as the geographical, origins of the speaker. The Russian speech community, like Soviet society generally, has had and still has a high rate of upward social mobility. This means that there are today many speakers of Russian who aspire to use standard varieties but do so only with varying degrees of success, owing to their early linguistic socialization in non-standard (regional) varieties. Social mobility is an important factor in language change, especially where the distribution of standard and non-standard is mainly socially determined.

Apart from changes in the power and prestige structures, there have been a number of other social developments contributing to linguistic change. These include: the growth of literacy (aided by spelling reform), the introduction of universal education for the masses, the increasing urbanization of the population, and equality of rights for women.

At the time of the 1897 census only 21 per cent of the population of the Russian Empire (excluding children under the age of nine) was able to read.[2] The figure for both sexes (over the

---

[1] This does not, of course, mean that non-standard forms are not used in practice, for instance as a sign of solidarity among certain social groups (such as industrial workers, students).

[2] No question as to the ability to write was included in the 1897 census.

age of nine) in Russia itself was 27 per cent and for European Russia it was 30 per cent. But the disparity between the sexes was considerable: in European Russia only 18 per cent of women could read, as opposed to 43 per cent of men. It should not be forgotten that in many parts of the Empire the situation was far worse: in Central Asia, for example, only 10 per cent of men and 3 per cent of women could read. In Poland, on the other hand, the percentages were higher than average, and they were highest of all in the Baltic States. In Estonia (*Èstlandskaja gubernija*) they reached an astounding 95 per cent for men and 97 per cent for women. This was the only part of the Empire where more women than men were literate. However, the situation in the Baltic States was, of course, totally untypical.

The ability to read was far more widespread in the towns than in the countryside, but in 1897 only 13·4 per cent of the Empire's population lived in towns. Among the *gubernii* of European Russia, that of St. Petersburg had the highest figures: 76 per cent for men and 51 per cent for women—a total of 62 per cent. The Moscow *gubernija* came next with 66 per cent for men and 31 per cent for women—a total of 49 per cent. The rates for the St. Petersburg and Moscow *gubernii* were the highest because they included the two largest towns, where the figures would obviously have been higher still.

It is true that the 1897 figures show that illiteracy was already receding, though slowly, and the proportion of those able to read was higher in the group aged 9 to 49 than in the whole population over 9. But the rate at which it was receding rose with startling rapidity after the Revolution. The figures most often quoted in order to demonstrate the drop in illiteracy during the Soviet period are those for the 9 to 49 age-group of the entire population at the censuses of 1897, 1926, 1939, 1959, and 1970.[1] They provide the following picture:

	Total %	Men	Women
1897:	28·4	40·3	16·6
1926:	56·6	71·5	42·7
1939:	87·4	93·5	81·6
1959:	98·5	99·3	97·8
1970:	99·7	99·8	99·7

[1] The criterion of literacy in the 1970 census was still (as in 1897) the ability to read (*Всесоюзная перепись... 1969: 46, 62*).

No less significant than the total figures are those showing the sudden decrease in the disparity between men and women, on the one hand, and between town and country on the other. The disparity between the sexes had been virtually eliminated by 1959, but the fact that formerly there was such a marked difference leads us to assume that until recently (perhaps still) non-standard speech was more common among women than men. There are no figures to support this, but it seems to be a reasonable assumption.

The separate statistics for town and country show that whereas in 1897 only 23·8 per cent of the rural population could read, by 1959 the figure was 98·2 per cent. And by 1970 it was 99·4 per cent. At the same time there had been a rapid urbanization of the whole population: whereas by 1913 the proportion of town-dwellers had risen from 13·4 per cent (1897) to 18 per cent, by 1970 they were for the first time in a majority (56 per cent).

The rise in the standards of education throughout the population is no less striking than the rise in literacy. In 1897 0·07 per cent of the population had received (or was receiving) a higher education. Those with (or receiving) a secondary education constituted 1·03 per cent. In 1970 the figures (for those aged 10 and over) were: higher education 4·2 per cent, secondary education 44·1 per cent. In education too the disparity between the sexes and between town and country have been greatly reduced. The 1970 census showed that of those aged 10 or over 52·2 per cent of men had higher or secondary education against 45·2 per cent of women. The discrepancy between town and country, however, is still serious; in 1970 59·2 per cent of the town population (in the over-10 age-group) had higher or secondary education, against only 33·2 per cent of the rural population.[1]

These improvements in literacy and educational standards for the population as a whole have meant a corresponding increase in the number of norm-bearers (i.e. those commanding and using the standard language) at the expense of those using only non-standard varieties. The standard language in Russia, as elsewhere, is neither static nor uniform. It is diversified both

---

[1] The statistics on literacy and education quoted here are taken mainly from *Уровень образования...* (1960) and *Численность, размещение...* (1971).

according to function and along the scales of time and space. There is therefore no set of criteria on the basis of which one could set up standard and non-standard as discrete categories. If one considers the question purely in terms of the space scale, however, it is possible to say that at the beginning of the twentieth century the majority of members of the Russian speech community, being illiterate, were users of maximally localized varieties exclusively. The position now, on the other hand, is that only a minority use maximally localized varieties exclusively. These are the informants sought by dialectologists, and as time goes by they are more and more difficult to find. The vast majority make use of the standard written language and include in their spoken repertoires varieties which are localized to a minimal or zero degree.

But it was not just a matter of the formerly illiterate and uneducated majority acquiring standard varieties. If it had been so, the standard itself might have changed very little. But in the new power structure following the Revolution those who spoke or had spoken non-standard varieties and now rose to positions of prestige and power were able to assert the acceptability of many features of their own speech. One might, in fact, have reasonably expected that in a society ruled by the working class, the linguistic norms of the working class would prevail; that the old standard language would be rejected and replaced by a new one based on working-class varieties. In reality, however, things did not go that far, but changes in the social prestige structure did bring about sudden changes in the hierarchy of registers: what had been colloquial became stylistically neutral, and what had been non-standard became colloquial standard.

The legalization of features which had formerly been unacceptable, as well as certain other innovations, came as a shock to those who had been norm-bearers before the Revolution, and they expressed concern. In some *émigré* circles the belief is even now held that the Russian language has been somehow damaged by the Bolsheviks.[1] At the other extreme,

---

[1] This may be seen, for example, in the journal *Русская рѣчь*, Paris, 1958–63, published (in the old orthography) by the Союзъ для защиты чистоты русскаго слова (Union for the Defence of the Purity of the Russian Word).

even in recent years, claims have been made that changes in the standard language did not go far enough, and that Russian still preserves pre-Revolutionary 'class norms' which were 'imposed from above' (see, for instance, Grigor'ev 1961).

An essential prerequisite to a proper understanding of standard Russian within Soviet society is a knowledge of the actual usage of native speakers, in particular of educated native speakers. The traditional way of monitoring actual usage and changes in usage has been to observe the practice of writers. In dealing with earlier periods, this is usually the only way to proceed: this approach has been applied to the Russian language of the nineteenth century, for instance, and changes in the usage of writers noted (Bulaxovskij 1954; Vinogradov and Švedova 1964). It is one of the methods applied by Gorbačevič (1971) in comparing nineteenth-century usage with current usage. However, this approach has a number of drawbacks, so where possible (as in investigations of current usage) other methods should be given preference. One drawback is that editors very often modify an author's text quite considerably before allowing it to be published, so that in many cases the printed texts from which one works have been normalized, representing the editor's conception of the standard language rather than the author's actual usage; typically, one does not also have access to the author's manuscript. Another drawback is that in this way one can monitor the usage of only one social group, namely professional writers and journalists; as we shall see below, and in detail in the subsequent chapters, the reactions of writers and journalists to linguistic variants often differ markedly from those of other sections of the population, tending towards a more conservative assessment of the norm. Finally, in this way one can monitor only the written language, and not usage in the spoken language: even dialogue in novels and drama is only an artistic reflection of the spoken language, and a printed text typically gives no indication of the author's choice of pronunciation variants.[1]

In monitoring current usage, more direct methods of analysis are available, in particular the survey methods familiar from

---

[1] To some extent, verse can give information on the author's choice of stress (from the metre) and pronunciation (from the rhyme); but verse does not correspond directly to anyone's ordinary usage.

sociology, whereby the views of a representative sample of the population under investigation are elicited. A number of sociolinguistic surveys of this kind were carried out in the Soviet Union in the fifties and sixties: the most comprehensive of these is that carried out by the RJaSO team of the Russian Language Institute of the Soviet Academy of Sciences, and it is to this survey that we shall principally refer, although mention will also be made of smaller surveys covering more restricted points of usage.

For practical reasons, the RJaSO team decided against conducting a large series of face-to-face interviews, but rather to rely on answers to written questionnaires: this reduces enormously the amount of time that is actually required to conduct the polling, since it is not necessary to wait for the particular variant in which one is interested to occur spontaneously in speech (and some variants, especially lexical variants, are of very low frequency), although it does bring with it certain theoretical disadvantages that will become apparent below. During the period 1959–64 questionnaires were prepared covering pronunciation, morphology (including stress), word-formation, and vocabulary;[1] these were then distributed to informants during 1963–6 (Krysin 1974: 3). Some of the results of the processing of replies to these questionnaires are incorporated in Panov (1968), and a more detailed and specific analysis of the results of the questionnaires is Krysin (1974), with a briefer account in Krysin (1973). In only a few cases, in particular with the questionnaire on pronunciation, were informants interviewed personally, with a view to assessing whether their actual usage corresponded to their own assessment of their usage as reflected in their replies to the questionnaire (Krysin 1974: 34). Most of the questions in the questionnaires are of the following form: the informant is presented with two or more variants, both of which are known to be used by speakers of the standard language, and is asked sometimes to make an assessment of them and sometimes to indicate which of them he uses (Krysin 1974: 29–31). Although this is a very simple method for the compiler of a questionnaire to use, it has a number of disadvantages which must always be borne in mind when evaluating the results of this survey.

[1] There has been no comparable survey of syntactic usage.

Firstly, it is essential that the informant should understand the question: in most cases this presents little difficulty, with educated informants, although in certain instances, such as questions about details of pronunciation, given that very few of the informants were phoneticians, the formulation of the question so that it is comprehensible to the layman is in itself a formidable task (for discussion of how this and other difficulties were partially overcome, see Panov 1971). Secondly, this technique presupposes that, when asked to do so, the informant can correctly monitor his own usage, i.e. that he will indicate that variant which he actually uses, rather than the variant he would like to think he uses (for prestige reasons); again, in the case of pronunciation, the possibility of a simple error from a non-phonetician is highly probable. This is in fact the main disadvantage of asking informants to monitor themselves, rather than having the linguist register actual usage in one or more situations.[1] To some extent allowance can be made for this factor by including check questions, for instance by having a number of questions, distributed through the questionnaire, asking for essentially the same piece of information: the hypothesis is that the informant will not be absolutely consistent in citing prestige forms that do not correspond to his own usage. Another type of check question consists in giving pseudo-variants, i.e. forms that are known not to occur; if an informant then selects such forms with any degree of frequency, he can be excluded as unreliable (Krysin 1974: 29–31). For the pronunciation questionnaire, an additional check was provided by actually recording some of those who replied to the questionnaire, and comparing their recorded replies with their written replies (though this is still not spontaneous speech). Although the results of this comparison (Barinova *et al.* 1971) demonstrate a high degree of correlation between reported and actual usage, there are many individual cases, particularly involving positional variants, where the discrepancies between the two are significant (ibid.: 342): error rates (difference between percentage of informants claiming to use a given pronunciation

[1] This latter technique is used, for instance, by Labov (1966) in his investigation of New York speech, and by many Western sociolinguists influenced to varying degrees by Labov's work, but only to a very limited extent in the RJaSO survey.

and the percentage of occurrences of that pronunciation in their actual speech) of over 80 per cent were found for ужаснётесь and бог-то, for instance, and error rates above 60 per cent are not infrequent. Finally, since the questionnaire was designed primarily to investigate the usage of speakers of the standard language, only variants that are acceptable within the standard were included, or at least only variants for which a case can be made for considering them normative. In considering the stress of the plural of фронт 'front (military)', for instance, both genitive plural фронто́в (the usual current form, and that recommended by most dictionaries) and фро́нтов (now archaic) were included in the questionnaire, whereas the variation in the nominative–accusative plural фро́нты/фронты́ was excluded because the variant фронты́ is 'clearly non-standard' (явно нелитературное) (Krysin 1974: 230); the result is that, unfortunately, we have no detailed evidence as to how widespread among educated speakers the variant фронты́ actually is. This criterion is not applied with absolute rigour, however, so that the questionnaire does include the stress variants распреде́лит, прибы́л, созда́лось, доску́, and the morphological variants бухгалтера́ 'book-keepers', жгёт 'burns', although the authors explicitly note that they do not claim that these are acceptable within the standard language, but that they only wish to ascertain the reactions of different social groups to the forms (Krysin 1974: 15–16, 232–3).

Another consequence of the fact that this questionnaire was concerned with the standard language is that questionnaires were sent out only to those people who are, or can be considered to be, speakers of the standard language. For practical purposes, this was defined to be those who (*a*) were native speakers of Russian, (*b*) had completed higher or secondary education, and (*c*) were urban residents (Krysin 1974: 17–18).[1] The inclusion of the last two factors follows from the informal

---

[1] In view of the restriction of this Soviet survey to educated people, and of the elicitation techniques used, it is doubtful whether any direct comparison can be made between these results and those obtained by Labov, etc., for the United States, since the latter concentrate rather on non-standard speech, and include spontaneous speech in addition to more controlled registers. Apart from traditional dialect studies, based on the comparative and historical method, research into non-standard Russian has been much neglected.

definition of standard Russian as the language of educated urban residents, in particular those of Moscow, and also serves explicitly to exclude as far as possible non-standard variants that owe their origin to regional dialects (which are most tenacious in the speech of the rural population, and of those who have not undergone complete secondary education). The individual questionnaires were sent out to between 12,000 and 18,000 informants satisfying these three conditions; some 20–30 per cent of the questionnaires sent out were completed and returned, of which a few were rejected on the basis of inconsistencies revealed by check questions (Krysin 1973: 38). For each questionnaire there were thus 3,000 to 4,300 informants, or an estimated 0·01–0·02 per cent of the total population of the Soviet Union satisfying the three criteria given above (Krysin 1974: 31–3). In order to ascertain what correlations exist between various social groups and attitudes to the individual variants, informants were asked a number of preliminary questions about their education, residence, age, etc. The education parameter has been largely dealt with already—all informants had higher or complete secondary education (apart from some comparative material on the pronunciation questionnaire using informants with partial secondary education (Krysin 1974: 21))—although a further classification was made into those with and those without higher education.

Informants were classified regionally into the following groups: Moscow residents; Leningrad residents; Moscow *oblast'* residents; Leningrad *oblast'* residents; North Russian urban residents; South Russian urban residents; Central Russian urban residents; native speakers of Russian resident in the Ukraine; native speakers of Russian resident in the Baltic republics. The initial hypothesis was that residents of Moscow and Leningrad would show minimal influence of regional dialects, while residents of provincial towns would show more influence from the surrounding regional dialects (including South Russian for the Ukraine, North-West Russian for the Baltic), and residents of the Moscow and Leningrad *oblasti* would occupy an intermediate position. In general, these predictions were borne out (cf. the summary table in Krysin (1974: 350), and the more detailed breakdown in the text), suggesting that a dialect-coloured environment tends strongly to favour the choice of that variant which is closest to the form found in the dialect. Although the questionnaire provides information not only on place of longest residence, but also on place where the informant's childhood was spent, where he was educated, and his parents' geographical origin, it was found that the essential factors can be restricted to the place where the informant spent his childhood and to the place of longest residence.

The division of provincial speakers into North Russian, South Russian, and Central Russian in the RJaSO survey follows the division of Russian dialects into northern, southern, and central in Durnovo *et al.* (1914), since the more recent classification of the Russian dialects, based on the results of detailed dialectological surveys and embodied in Avanesov and Orlova (1965), was not available at the time the questionnaires were distributed. The main difference between the two dialect classifications, corresponding in large measure to the retreat of specifically southern or northern dialect features in favour of the more neutral central dialects, has been the tendency for the central dialect area to expand southwards and even more strikingly northwards (see the two maps accompanying Avanesov and Orlova 1965). Thus one feature of the development of the Russian language in the Soviet period, which is rather masked by the material of the RJaSO survey but will be alluded to in the individual chapters below, is the relative tenacity of southern dialect features. Northern dialect features have shown a much greater tendency to recede.

On the parameter of age, the informants were divided into ten-year age-groups (born 1890–9; 1900–9; 1910–19; 1920–9; 1930–9; 1940–9) for some of the questionnaires (e.g. on pronunciation), and into twenty-year age-groups (born before 1899; 1900–19; 1920–39; born after 1940) for the others (e.g. word-formation), depending on the degree of precision required (Krysin 1974: 20–1). The over-all results show that age is an important correlate of choice among different variants. However, there are several exceptions, where there is either no correlation with age, or where one finds a form relatively little used by the oldest informants, relatively frequently used by the middle-aged, and relatively little used again by the youngest. To some extent, the different preferences shown by different age-groups at the present time can be mapped into a diachronic representation: the responses of the oldest informants represent the average stage of affairs when they were younger, while the responses of the youngest informants represent those forms that will become even more frequent, and ultimately predominant. However, there are dangers in making this mapping.[1] For instance, the replies to the questions on pronunciation by even the oldest informants often depart significantly from descriptions of Moscow pronunciation at the beginning of the century, in the direction of being closer to the usage of younger Muscovites. Clearly, as a person grows older he will still interact with younger people, and is likely to adopt some features of their language.

The third factor which proved to correlate highly with choice of variants is the informant's social position (and, to a much lesser extent, the social position of his parents). For this purpose, an over-all classification was made into intellectuals,[2] white-collar workers (служащие), industrial workers (рабочие), and students. Of the total number of 3,000–4,000 informants, 40 per cent were intellectuals, 33 per cent students, 18 per cent white-collar workers, and 9 per cent industrial workers (Krysin 1974: 33). The expectation, borne out in the vast majority of cases by the questionnaire results, was that intellectuals would come closest to the traditional norm and workers least close (even workers who speak the standard language are likely to work together with others who do not), with white-collar workers occupying an intermediate position; students fall rather outside this categorization, since they are mostly distinct in age as well as in social position, and though in many respects close to the intellectuals are also particularly prone to the influence

---

[1] For what has become a classical counterexample to this method, see Denison (1968) on Sauris (N. Italy), where the correlation between age and choice of language in a multilingual community remains largely unchanged over a considerable period.

[2] Here and elsewhere we use 'intellectuals' to translate the terms интеллигенция, интеллигенты, used in Soviet works on sociology (including sociolinguistics) of the Soviet Union, i.e. to refer to employed persons engaged in mental work. The term has thus rather wider reference than English 'intellectual' ('high-brow') usually has. We prefer not to use the term 'intelligentsia', which in English has different overtones from the Russian term, stemming largely from the use of this term with regard to nineteenth-century Russia.

of student slang. For some purposes, a finer sub-classification of some of these groups was used: thus intellectuals and students were subdivided into philologists (филологи, i.e. specialists in language and/or literature) and non-philologists, with the sub-group of writers and journalists being further abstracted from the class of philologist intellectuals. The expectation, again borne out in general, was that philologists would be even closer to the traditional norm than non-philologist intellectuals and students, and that writers and journalists would be closest of all.

In connection with professional and other social groups, we may note that certain professions often adopt linguistic features at variance with general standard usage, particularly with regard to items that are especially frequent in the speech of the professional group concerned. Deviant stresses are particularly common: thus sailors usually say, компа́с (standard: ко́мпас) 'compass', and actors хара́ктерный 'characteristic' (for хара́ктерный). Similar deviations are found in syntax, as in the expression на фло́те, used by sailors for standard во фло́те 'in the navy'. Further examples are given in the relevant chapters.

A number of other factors that might correlate with choice among social variants were considered by the RJaSO team, but only one of these actually figures in the presentation by Krysin (1974), namely the extent to which informants listen to the radio. The expectation seems to have been that frequent listening to the radio, i.e. for the most part to trained speakers from Moscow, would increase the degree of accommodation to the varieties used on the radio. In fact, the over-all result indicated that exposure to broadcasts is not a significant factor: the table in Krysin (1974: 350) shows the radio as relevant only to pronunciation, and even then the plus sign indicating relevance is placed in parentheses. The only feature for which there was a marked correlation with exposure to radio broadcasts is the pronunciation of post-tonic non-high vowels after palatalized consonants, and here the results obtained by the RJaSO team differ considerably from those obtained by other elicitation techniques, as will be seen from the discussion in Chapter 1 on pronunciation. Listening to the radio is essentially a passive occupation—the listener is not required to interact with the radio announcer, indeed it is impossible for him to do so—so that on *a priori* grounds there is in fact little reason to suppose that exposure to broadcasts should significantly affect pronunciation.

In the presentation of results in Krysin (1974), each of the parameters (age, territory, social position) is given separately. This means that it is impossible to ascertain detailed correlations, such as the correlation of different pronunciation variants with Muscovites of different age-groups, or the correlation of different morphological variants with different social groups from southern Russia, i.e. any correlation, which includes more than one of the parameters territory, age, and social position. The presentation of such material would of course have increased the size of Krysin (1974) immensely, and detailed statistical analysis would have been impossible because of the small groups involved, but this does represent one unfortunate limitation on the use to which these data can be put.

The great advantage of the RJaSO survey is the large number of informants, from various social groups, who were covered by the investigation. Most of the other surveys on current usage have had much smaller coverage (typically, the students of the institute where the linguist conducting the survey works). Most of these other surveys concerned pronunciation (including stress), and are discussed in detail in Chapter 1 on pronunciation. In many cases, they differ from the RJaSO questionnaire by simply asking informants how they pronounce a given word, rather than asking them to choose between a limited number of variants, so that the existence of certain widespread but non-standard forms can be ascertained. Particularly interesting from this viewpoint are pronunciation tests where the informant is asked to read a passage, so that he is not aware of the particular points of pronunciation that are being tested (though he may, of course, modify his normal pronunciation in the direction of a more standard pronunciation, simply given the general conditions of a test recording). The most valuable surveys from the viewpoint of monitoring actual usage are those where the informant's attention is completely distracted from the fact that it is his linguistic usage that is being observed. Surveys of this kind are discussed on pages 38–9 (Andreev's test on pronunciation of adjectives in -кий), 163–4 (RJaSO's test on use of masculine or feminine occupation titles), and 91 (RJaSO's observation of the genitive plural of fruit names, etc.).

On the basis of such surveys, it is possible to gain some idea of current educated urban usage. However, this still does not answer the question as to the precise relation between this usage and the norm. We have already seen that in Soviet Russian society there is no great chasm between actual and standard usage, as there is in some societies, and most Soviet normative grammarians in fact agree that the linguistic norm is something objective, immanent in the speech collective (Ickovič 1968: 4–5). In the following discussion, we base ourselves in particular on Ickovič (1968); while not all normative grammarians would agree with all the points made in this study, it is an authoritative work on the theory of normative grammar, and seems to come close on most points to the consensus of opinion among normative grammarians of the Russian language. In addition to actual educated usage, the recommendations of normative handbooks have to be taken into account. If these recommendations were always in accord with one another and with actual usage, there would be no problem; in practice, such recommendations sometimes differ from one handbook to another, and are sometimes at variance with educated usage as elicited, for instance, by the RJaSO survey. In particular, normative handbooks tend to lag behind changes in usage: an especially clear instance of this is the recommendation of many features of the Old Moscow pronunciation by orthoepic handbooks long after it had become a minority pronunciation among educated speakers (see Chapter 1 on pronunciation). This is partly due to the usual conception of the 'modern Russian literary language' (современный русский литературный язык) as the Russian language from Puškin to the present day; this inevitably introduces an element of archaization into the codification of the norms of the modern literary language. Indeed, if one of the social functions of the Russian language is considered to be the provision of cultural continuity between the literature of Puškin's time and the present day, then there is some merit in a relatively conservative attitude towards codification of the norm, to prevent uncontrolled change away from the language of the early nineteenth century. In practice, however, discrepancies between the recommendations of normative grammarians and educated usage are often the basis of criticisms voiced against the recommendations in question; as one example among many, we may note Gorbačevič's criticism (1971: 187–8) of the attempt by Avanesov and Ožegov (1959) to distinguish between such genitive plurals as гренадир and гренадиров 'grenadiers' semantically (collective versus individual plurality). In somewhat similar vein, Panov (1967: 299–300) considers the hardening of word-final soft labials, as in голубь 'pigeon', to be non-standard, and a pronunciation error that orthoepists must do their utmost to combat; but concedes that if in the future this pronunciation does become more widespread, then orthoepists will be forced by changed circumstances to alter their recommendations, allowing the final hard labial as a possibility, perhaps ultimately as the only possibility.

Apart from the general conservativeness of normative grammarians, however, there is another way in which some normative grammarians have attempted to draw a distinction between usage and the standard, i.e. by defining a class of cases where some variant is non-standard irrespective of how widespread it may be. Ickovič (1968: 23–46) makes a distinction between the system of a language—its general principles of organization—and the structure of a language—contingent details of the organization of a language, such as the fact that the verb касаться 'touch' takes the genitive case in contemporary Russian. Ickovič argues that variants may be accepted into the standard language, if they become widespread, provided they do not violate the system of the language, although there is no requirement that they should not introduce changes in the structure of the language (as with касаться + genitive, for earlier касаться до + genitive). In practice, it is not at all easy to see how the distinction between system and structure is to be drawn in all cases. For instance, one of Ickovič's examples (1968: 23–7) of a variant that would violate the system of contemporary Russian is *вы писал 'you were writing', addressing a single person, since a general rule of Russian requires the plural of a past tense verb with subject вы irrespective of whether one or more people is being addressed; however, from a different point of view, this is simply an accident of the structure of Russian, since some other predicates stand in the singular with вы of singular reference (e.g. вы глупый 'you are stupid', with a long form adjective). The clearest examples cited by Ickovič of forms that violate the norm because they violate its system, namely вы писал and прочитающий 'about to read' as a perfective future participle, are not really telling because they also violate current usage: neither of these forms is widespread among educated urban Russians. When applied to examples widespread in current usage, Ickovič's criterion often gives results differing from those of other normative grammarians: thus Ickovič rejects купированный 'consisting of compartments' (said of a train) on the grounds that there is no verb купировать and the only productive model for forming such adjectives is as past participles passive of verbs; Ožegov (1972), however, lists купированный without any qualification. Ickovič (1968: 39) introduces another criterion, namely whether or not the new form serves some function in the language, e.g. by having a meaning distinct from all existing forms. Thus he allows the acceptance of купированный into the standard if, as some linguists have claimed, its meaning differs from that of the more traditional form купейный.[1] Thus the role of the criterion 'corresponding to the system' is at best relative. The great danger of the introduction of criteria other than that of current educated usage is that the definition of the norm is no longer objective, but coloured at various points by the subjective feelings of the individual linguist; compare the disagreement between Ickovič and Ožegov over купированный.

In general, discussions by Russian normative grammarians concern whether or not innovatory forms should be admitted as standard, alongside the traditional standard, and perhaps ultimately replacing it; the objective criterion of correspondence to current educated usage is typically modified in favour of greater adherence to the traditional norm, either explicitly so (e.g. on the grounds of the need for continuity of tradition), or on the basis of more or less subjective additional criteria (conformity with the general organization of the language, semantic need for the new form). Sometimes, though not frequently, one finds a new form being actively encouraged by a linguist. For instance, in Švedova's discussion of new constructions with

---

[1] Ožegov (1972), incidentally, simply defines купированный as synonymous with купейный.

the preposition по, such as инженер по технике безопасности 'safety engineer' (1966: 40–52), there is very little discussion of the status of such constructions relative to the norm, apart from condemnation of blatant tautologies; Popova (1974: 183–4), however, considers that, since these constructions enable a semantic relation to be expressed between the nouns involved without any additional semantic specification, this construction fulfils a real need in the Russian language and should perhaps be positively encouraged ('merits . . . perhaps, gradual tactical codification'). But over all, deliberate attempts to introduce or foster innovatory forms are not characteristic of Russian language standardization in the Soviet Union.

So far there is one question that we have not discussed whose omission could lead to oversimplification, namely the question of different styles, since it is clear that a given form may be more appropriate in one style than in another, indeed that a given form may be completely inappropriate in certain styles while perfectly normal in others. In Soviet normative hand-books lexical items and forms are often accompanied by specification of their stylistic value, implying that such items and forms are not acceptable in all styles. One such qualification, просторечное (cf. просторечие 'popular speech'), indicates that the given form is non-standard;[1] the only reason for including such forms in a normative handbook, apart from the desire to warn people not to use them in the standard language, is that they may appear in literature in dialogue which aims to reproduce popular speech. Another stylistic qualification, устарелое 'archaic', presumably indicates that the form is no longer standard, but must still be known by the educated Russian since it will be found in classical literature. The major division within the standard is between разговорное 'colloquial' and книжное 'learned' (with нейтральное 'neutral' referring to standard forms that are neither specifically colloquial nor specifically learned). These terms are self-explanatory: colloquial forms are acceptable in the informal spoken variety of the standard, but not in writing (except dialogue, or other written styles that deliberately mimic ordinary speech,

---

[1] In view of the difficulty in finding an English equivalent for the word просторечно(е) we have throughout this book retained the Russian term (*prostorečno*).

e.g. personal letter-writing),[1] while learned forms are acceptable in writing, especially artistic literature and rhetorical
prose, but would be out of place in speech (except in such
styles as imitate the written language, e.g. some political
rhetoric, news-reading). Particularly within the written language, further stylistic subdivisions are possible; see, for instance, Vinokur and Šmelev (1968). The following are those
styles that we have found it necessary to refer to in this book;
the list is not claimed to be exhaustive for the language as a
whole: artistic literature (narrative); journalistic and popular
scientific; scientific (i.e. the language of learned non-fiction;
more rigid in Russian than in many other European languages
(Lapteva 1968)); poetic; dialogue (in so far as it approximates
to the colloquial); bureaucratic (the language of official documents, letters, etc.). Just as there have been changes in the
acceptability of various forms into the standard during the
Soviet period, and debates over their acceptability, so too
have there been changes in stylistic value—more colloquial
forms becoming accepted in artistic literature, forms from
higher styles filtering down into speech—and disagreements
over the stylistic values of various forms. Examples of such
changes and disagreements will be found in the individual
chapters. One particularly important channel for the inter-
play between 'higher' (e.g. artistic literature, bureaucratic)
and 'lower' (e.g. colloquial) styles in the early Soviet
period was the rapid development of journalism, of the press
as a mass medium. The need to reach the ordinary people
led to the inclusion of many colloquialisms in this variety of
the standard written language, while by the same token newspapers were for many ordinary people the first and most concentrated contact with the standard written language, leading
to the adoption of features from the written language into
their speech (Kostomarov 1971: 12–13).

[1] It is only quite recently that adequate investigations have been carried
out of the actual speech of educated urban Russians, and the results of such
surveys (e.g. Zemskaja 1973) show that many forms are current that would
hardly be considered standard by normative grammarians, and which are
not usual in literature, even in dialogue. The relation between what normative grammarians call 'colloquial standard' and the colloquial speech of
educated urban Russians will almost certainly require rethinking in the
light of such evidence.

The discussion of social changes that have led to changes in the evaluation of the norm in the Soviet period may be summarized as follows. Although even before the Revolution the Russian language was much less varied geographically and socially than many other European languages, the rigid class structure meant that even relatively slight divergence from the accepted standard could be a mark of social status; this was reinforced by the fact that education, particularly at the higher levels, was available only to the privileged classes. One of the results of the Revolution has been the 'democratization' of the Russian language. On the one hand, the rise to power of new social classes led to the adoption of some features of their speech into the standard; on the other hand, the spread of education led to the adoption of standard features into the speech of those who had previously used non-standard varieties of the language. Over all, the latter has been the more powerful factor: except perhaps for the immediate post-Revolutionary years, there has been no trend to reject the traditional standard as a whole in favour of a norm closer to the actual usage of the working class. The fact that only 9 per cent of the informants for the RJaSO survey were industrial workers probably reflects difficulty in finding speakers of standard Russian among the working class. Non-standard (hence low-prestige) forms are still mainly found among workers, whose social prestige otherwise is high.

1

PRONUNCIATION

AT the beginning of the twentieth century, the standard pronunciation of Russian was considered to be that of educated Muscovites (Košutić 1919: vii; Ožegov 1955: 16). There was considerable interest in phonetics in the late nineteenth and early twentieth centuries, and we are fortunate in having on-the-spot descriptions of this kind of pronunciation, usually referred to as the Old Moscow (OM) pronunciation; of these, the best is usually considered to be Košutić (1919).[1] In addition, we can take advantage of the reminiscences of those who were alive at that time, and of early gramophone recordings, in addition to less satisfactory sources such as rhyme in poetry. One of the main characteristics of OM is that in many respects it diverges from Russian orthography; numerous specific examples are given below, but two examples will suffice for this general introduction: the OM pronunciation of ходят 'they go' as [ˈxoḑut], and the OM pronunciation of тихий 'quiet' as [ˈţixəj]. Although St. Petersburg was the capital of the Russian Empire, and although its pronunciation differed in several respects from that of Moscow, Muscovite pronunciation was nevertheless considered standard.[2]

In the pre-Revolutionary period, the OM pronunciation was transmitted by and large within the family, from generation to generation, so that this style of pronunciation was acquired by the younger generation with little modification, and before spelling was learnt, the idiosyncrasies of OM being able to maintain themselves. After the Revolution, this situation changed radically. The standard language, including standard

[1] A briefer account, restricted to those aspects that distinguish OM from other pronunciations, is given by Ušakov (1968). A short bibliography is given by Kuz'mina (1966: 6).

[2] A short bibliography of works on the Old St. Petersburg (OPb) pronunciation is given by Panov (1967: 295).

pronunciation, was no longer the exclusive property of educated Muscovites, but rather of the whole nation, so that non-OM speakers started adopting the standard pronunciation, at least in part, and in turn influenced it themselves. Many people made their acquaintance with the standard language through its written form, so that there was considerable pressure against characteristic OM pronunciations that contradicted the spelling. Of course, the standard language was spread not only by the written word, but also by broadcasting (Moscow radio programmes were and are broadcast throughout the Soviet Union, in addition to local programmes), so that spelling pronunciations contrary to general principles of the standard language have been unable to make headway, such as *okan'e*, the distinction of unstressed o and a, characteristic of northern dialects.

Nevertheless, the loss of some of the idiosyncrasies of OM has meant that OM can no longer be considered the only norm, nor indeed the preferable norm, for Russian pronunciation, although the force of tradition has meant that certain OM pronunciations now used only by a minority, even in Moscow, are often not considered incorrect in current speech. OM was still promulgated as the norm by Ušakov (1935, 1: xxxi–xxxiv), but his recommendations were already out of touch with changing reality (Shapiro 1968: 3–4). The current standard is often referred to as Contemporary Standard Russian (CSR). The 'best' CSR is still considered that of educated Muscovites (those who do not cling to OM), though it is much more widespread outside this circle than was OM, and is normally insisted on for broadcasting purposes throughout the Soviet Union. OM, or rather many of the features distinguishing OM from CSR, is still maintained with some degree of consistency on the stage, particularly in performances of classical plays (Il'inskaja and Sidorov 1955; Kuz'mina 1963; Kuznecova 1963). The most widely accepted description of CSR is that by Avanesov (1972).[1]

---

[1] This is the latest edition of a work that first appeared in 1950; differences among successive editions reflect the development of CSR. Shapiro (1968: 4–6) accuses Avanesov of being too conservative, but this seems more applicable to the earlier editions, and in general Avanesov is rather liberal in allowing pronunciation variants.

Standardization in pronunciation is much more difficult to enforce than standardization of those aspects of language that are reflected directly in the written language. It is possible for a writer to write standard Russian while using non-standard pronunciations in his speech even when, for instance, reading his works out aloud; thus Gor'kij retained traces of the *okan'e* dialect of his native Nižnij Novgorod. Standard pronunciation is not insisted on as much as the written standard in schools. Ušakov's failure to impose OM must be considered one of the major defeats of normative grammarians of Russian.

Monitoring current pronunciation can in many cases be carried out simply by listening to the normal speech of speakers of the standard language and to recordings of broadcasts, etc. This is the method used by Avanesov, e.g. in Avanesov (1972); as a rough-and-ready method it has obvious methodological drawbacks, although the high degree of correspondence between Avanesov's observations and those derived by more detailed and rigorous techniques is a tribute to Avanesov's skill in using the more informal method. However, for some of the more elusive details of pronunciation, such methods are inadequate, since one needs to work with recordings of a higher quality, such as can really only be obtained in the artificial environment of a phonetic laboratory. Moreover, when it is necessary to survey the pronunciation of a given word or set of words by a statistically significant number of speakers, specially designed questionnaires are often the only way of obtaining the required data within a reasonable period. It is the exception, rather than the rule, that someone devises a test like that described by Andreev (1963), where passers-by were asked the names of various stations, bridges, etc., in Moscow and Leningrad; their attention was concentrated on the informational side of what they were saying, and they were given no indication in advance that the centre of interest was the pronunciation of adjectives in -ский.

The tests that have been carried out under laboratory conditions fall into two main types. In the first, informants are asked to read isolated words, which are then analysed; the defect is that the informant is normally aware of the purpose of the test— it soon becomes apparent what the relevant feature of pronunciation is in a list of words—and he may adjust his pronunciation accordingly if he feels that a certain pronunciation is more correct than the one he normally uses. The advantage is that the recordings of the individual words are particularly clear. Reading whole sentences or connected texts, the second type of test, can often overcome this disadvantage, particularly if the features of interest are sufficiently camouflaged amidst the rest of the text, but has the disadvantage that the forms of interest may not be pronounced sufficiently clearly in the more rapid reading style that characterizes reading of whole sentences or texts. This can partly be compensated for by putting the pronunciation feature of interest in a position that receives maximum prominence; in Russian, this usually means stressed sentence-final position (cf. the use made of this position in the survey of pronunciation of unstressed endings noted below). The general problem of the validity of reading tests in gathering data on pronunciation is discussed by Glovinskaja (1966). In addition to such tests for individual points of pronunciation, noted below, Drage (1968) gives the results of a series of tests in which seventeen informants, either born or living in Moscow, were asked to read a series of short sentences; the results are classified according to speaker, his regional provenance, that of his parents, and his age.

For the pronunciation section of the RJaSO survey, informants were sent a written questionnaire, in which they were asked, for each point, which of a number of variants they used (Barinova and Panov 1971; Barinova *et al.* 1971; Panov 1971; Krysin 1974: 38–155). In addition to the drawback of any method allowing informants to control their responses, this method implies a rather optimistic view of the ability of non-phoneticians correctly to assess phonetic distinctions that are often extremely fine (e.g. between post-tonic [ə] and [ɪ] after a soft consonant, or degree of palatalization in palatalization assimilation); see the criticisms of Bondarko (1973). The RJaSO team, in the publications noted above, admit the unsatisfactory nature of some of their materials. This they tried to rectify to some extent by interviewing some of their informants (Barinova *et al.* 1971). Although informants were still able to control their responses, extreme discrepancies between written and oral replies were noted in many cases, although the RJaSO team concluded that over all the discrepancies were not large enough to invalidate the materials. In addition to other surveys covering specific points of pronunciation and discussed below, we should note the survey carried out by Superanskaja (1959), in which some 700 students in Moscow (not all Muscovites) were asked which pronunciation they preferred for individual words and phrases; by the time of publication, 234 responses had been classified for some points, 150 for others.

In discussing pronunciation, it is important to make clear what style of pronunciation one is dealing with, in particular the speed and degree of clarity of articulation, since certain phonetic processes tend to characterize more rapid rather than slower speech, for instance various kinds of assimilation. Following the terminology of Shapiro (1968: 8–9),[1] we may distinguish an explicit code, with the minimum of assimilation, etc., and usually characterizing speech in more formal situations, and an elliptic code, with the maximum of assimilation, etc., and usually characterizing less formal situations; in practice there is, of course, a continuum rather than a dichotomy. One feature of this distinction between explicit and elliptic codes is that when people are asked which of a number of phonetic variants they prefer, or use, they tend to over-report the more explicit variants; similarly, in reading (especially of word-lists) the percentage of explicit forms is much higher than in ordinary speech. Some of the variants discussed below are subject to the difference between explicit and elliptic codes: thus the pronunciation [ʃʃ] for щ rather than [ʃʧ] is elliptic, as is palatalization assimilation, and the use of unstressed [ɪ] rather than [ə] in inflectional endings after a soft consonant. In surveys carried out to test people's pronunciation of these variants, in each case the more explicit variant was over-reported, irrespective of whether it corresponded to the traditional OM standard (as with [ə] in unstressed endings after a soft consonant) or conflicted with it (as with [ʃʧ] and lack of palatalization assimilation). With most other components of the language, over-reporting from educated Russians is found only in the direction of greater adherence to the traditional standard, and while this is often found with pronunciation where the difference between explicit and elliptic codes is not

[1] See also Panov (1963).

involved, the relevance of this difference must always be borne in mind, as otherwise one could gain the impression that there is often an unexplained tendency to over-report innovatory forms.

One final question to be considered briefly in this introduction, and in greater detail at the end of this chapter, is the motivation for the various changes in pronunciation that distinguish CSR from OM, on the assumption that not all such changes are the result of chance. The factor that is most often advanced is the influence of spelling, given that there are many discrepancies between OM and Russian orthography, many of which have been lost in CSR; a more sceptical attitude towards the relevance of spelling pronunciations is taken by Shapiro (1968: 19). Another external factor that might be considered relevant is the influence of other forms of spoken Russian, in particular OPb, and regional dialects. In addition to such external factors, there are also possible internal factors, of which morphological analogy (the tendency for a given morpheme always to have the same pronunciation) and morphological boundaries (i.e. a tendency for morphological boundaries to be marked phonetically) have been suggested. The possible relevance of these various factors will be discussed in the detailed treatment of the various individual points below, and the various strands drawn together in the conclusion to this chapter.

Pronunciation of щ *and* жж

(i) *Pronunciation of* щ

One of the most striking differences between OM and OPb is that for orthographic щ (e.g. щи 'cabbage soup'), also spelt сч (e.g. счастье 'happiness'), and зч (e.g. извозчик 'cab-driver'), Muscovites at the turn of the century pronounced a long palatalized fricative [ʃʃ], whereas in St. Petersburg the norm was for a single fricative followed by an affricate [ʃʧ]. In the period after the Revolution, the distinction between Moscow and Leningrad pronunciations became less marked. Many linguists—mainly natives of Leningrad, e.g. Černyx, Obnorskij, Bojanus, who are criticized on this count by Panov (1967: 330) —claimed that OM [ʃʃ] had lost its prestige, and that the usual pronunciation of Russians, other than native Muscovites, was the Leningrad [ʃʧ]. Similarly, Jones and Ward (1969: 140) say that 'by and large, at least the younger generation seems to prefer the pronunciation ʃʧ, rather than ʃʃ.' Recent surveys carried out in the Soviet Union indicate that this view is mistaken.

An important factor in the discussion is whether the sound in question occurs across a morpheme boundary after a preposition or prefix, or not:[1] [ʃʧ] is commoner in the former case than in the latter, with intermediate values where the presence or absence of a morpheme boundary is unclear (e.g. счастье 'happiness'). The pronunciation [ʃʧ] is also more common the slower the rate of speech, and informants tend to over-report this variant (Krysin 1974: 96).

We may start with the pronunciation not across a morpheme boundary, looking first at the situation in Moscow. Barinova (1966) reports the results of a survey which consisted of two tests: reading a word-list and reading sentences. In both tests, the overwhelming majority of participants used the long fricative [ʃʃ], particularly in reading the sentences (where greater speed was an added factor), although even in the word-list the majority for the long fricative was quite clear in each case. When the results were broken down according to age-group, it was found that the fricative pronunciation increases in frequency the younger the age-group investigated—precisely the opposite tendency from that suggested by the studies cited above.

Even more interesting is the situation in Leningrad, reported by Ivanova-Luk'janova (1971): for here too, where the sound does not occur across a morpheme boundary, the overwhelming preference was for a long fricative pronunciation, and not for the OPb norm. Of 100 school-children (aged 15–17) interviewed, only 6 used [ʃʧ] in борщ 'beetroot soup', while 94 used the fricative; for щи the figures were respectively 9 and 91, with similar figures for other words tested. The figures were broken down according to whether the informant's parents and/or grandparents were also from Leningrad, and from this it emerged that the affricate pronunciation is more widespread

[1] The morpheme boundary between stem and suffix, e.g. in извозчик, seems to have no effect.

among those who are natives of Leningrad of several generations' standing (the informants themselves were all natives of the
city and had lived there all their lives). Thus even in Leningrad,
[ʃʃ], corresponding to the OM standard, is the more widespread
form among the younger generation; the older Leningrad
form is maintained essentially only among natives of the city
of several generations' standing (коренные ленинградцы), and
even then only rarely.

Current orthoepic handbooks give preference to the long
fricative pronunciation, when not across a morpheme boundary,
although the OPb pronunciation is still admitted as a less
preferred orthoepic variant (Avanesov 1972: 82).

When we turn to the position across a morpheme boundary,
e.g. из чайных чашек 'out of tea-cups', расчищать 'clear up',
the picture is essentially the inverse of that where there is no
internal morpheme boundary, although both variants [ʃʧ] and
[ʃʃ] are still found. Even OM, as described by Košutić (1919:
70), allowed the affricate pronunciation here, particularly in
slow speech, and the tendency has been for this affricate pronunciation to become more frequent (see the statistics in
Barinova 1966: 48–9 and Borunova 1966: 71). In Leningrad,
the predominance of [ʃʧ] across clear morpheme boundaries is equally marked, rather more so, as might be expected,
among natives of several generations' standing, where there is
a greater tendency towards [ʃʧ] anyway (Ivanova-Luk'janova
1971).

The fact that [ʃʧ] is the commoner variant across a morpheme boundary might be thought to indicate that the
Leningrad pronunciation has here won out over the Moscow
pronunciation. We would like to suggest a different explanation. Even at the turn of the century, when OM was effectively
the unchallenged standard in Moscow, we know that [ʃʧ] was
possible across a morpheme boundary (Košutić 1919: 70). The
increase in the incidence of this pronunciation is probably an
internal development within Moscow pronunciation: the presence of the morphological boundary, which is in turn reflected
in the spelling (not щ), is making itself felt phonetically, in that
we clearly have morphologically с or з followed by ч, and the
assimilation is only to [ʃʧ] without the further development
to [ʃʃ].

(ii) *Pronunciation of* жж

In addition to [ʃʃ], OM also has the voiced equivalent, long [ʒʒ]. This sound occurs where in spelling we have the group жж (as in жжет 'it burns', вожжи 'reins', жужжать 'burble'), зж (as in визжишь 'you scream', брызжет 'it splashes', езжу 'I travel'), occasionally also жд (in дожди 'rains', pronounced [dʌˈʒʒi]; the nominative singular дождь is pronounced [doʃʃ] in OM). The sound occurs only within the morpheme; across a morpheme boundary only long hard [ʒʒ] is possible, e.g. сжечь 'burn', с жаром 'with heat'.

The tendency over the twentieth century has been for this pronunciation with long palatalized [ʒʒ] to recede. In the case of дождь and other forms from the same stem, the spelling pronunciation [ʒd] has prevailed, i.e. nominative singular [doʃt], nominative plural [dʌˈʒdi]. Elsewhere, [ʒʒ] has been replaced by and large by the long hard fricative [ʒʒ]. In the survey reported in Barinova (1966: 50–1), there was in nearly all cases a majority for the hard pronunciation among younger speakers—the decrease in the frequency of [ʒʒ] correlating with lower age is quite spectacular. The process has been more rapid with less common words: this suggests that for those younger speakers that have [ʒʒ] at all, this pronunciation is a marked feature of the word, bolstered by hearing and using it frequently. With only two of the words tested, брызжет 'it splashes' and дрожжи 'yeast', was there a (slight) majority among younger speakers (born 1930–49) for the soft pronunciation. Avanesov (1972: 139–40) still recommends the soft pronunciation, which is also the pronunciation required on the stage, but admits that the hard pronunciation cannot be considered incorrect, and that it is replacing the soft pronunciation, which is becoming characteristic rather of OM.

The pronunciation of г

In standard Russian, as in the northern and central dialects, the pronunciation of г is as a velar plosive [g]. In southern dialects, and also in the Ukraine and Belorussia, it is pronounced as a fricative, [ɣ] or [ɦ]. In this respect, the usage of the Orthodox Church quite exceptionally follows the South Russian pronunciation; this is usually attributed to the influence of Ukrainian and Belorussian literary figures in seventeenth-century Moscow, such as Simeon Polockij and Epifanij Slavineckij (Uluxanov 1972: 67). In standard Russian [ɣ] occurs regularly as a result of voice assimilation, e.g. он издох бы [ˈon izˈdoɣ bɨ] 'he would die'; in OM also by dissimilation of r in consonant clusters (see the section on consonant clusters in this chapter).

Although the pronunciation in standard Russian, whether OM or CSR, is with plosive [g], fricative [ɣ] occurs in OM in a few words that have Church Slavonic connotations: бог 'God' ([box], with word-final devoicing), genitive singular бога [ˈboɣə],[1] господь 'Lord', благо 'blessing' (the genitive plural is accordingly pronounced [blax]), and богатый 'rich', also derivatives of these, such as благодарить 'thank'. However, in nearly all cases this OM [ɣ] has been replaced in CSR by plosive [g]. The decline in the influence of the Church pronunciation is clearly a contributory factor. Thus Avanesov (1972: 81) says that this fricative pronunciation has been retained only partially, and then only in the speech of the older generation. This conclusion is borne out by the pronunciation of the Moscow students investigated by Superanskaja (1959: 160).

In these cases, the fricative pronunciation is now archaic, and is characterized as such by current dictionaries. To this general trend away from the fricative pronunciation there are a few exceptions. Even in CSR, бог is pronounced [box], although the oblique cases are now usually pronounced with [g]. In the interjection господи! the fricative pronunciation has proved more stable, although the plosive pronunciation is also possible. Thus Avanesov and Ožegov (1959) label the fricative pronunciation as archaic in nearly all cases, but for господи!, though recommending plosive [g], they say [ɣ] is permissible in current usage. The greater tenacity of [ɣ] in interjections is probably connected with the 'expressive' use of the non-standard pronunciation [ɣ] noted by Reformatskij (1966), for instance in the interjection [ɣusʲ] for гусь 'goose' used as an insult.

[1] This applies strictly only to the Christian God; other gods are often referred to by the same word with plosive [g] in OM, particularly in the plural боги and invariably in the exclusively pagan feminine богиня 'goddess'.

The use of [ɦ] in standard Russian is rather different. It is used in some interjections and onomatopoeic words, and in foreign names (Avanesov 1972: 82). In addition, it occurs in some loanwords, mainly Western European loans, e.g. бухгал-тер [buˈɦaltɪr] 'book-keeper', where the [ɦ] pronunciation is more or less *de rigueur*. It is also the recommended pronunciation in another German loanword, бюстгальтер [bˌuzˈɦalˌtɪr], according to Avanesov and Ožegov (1959), and a few others. However, in the survey carried out by Glovinskaja (1971: 62), 38 people out of 41 pronounced [g] in бюстгальтер, as opposed to only 10 out of 41 in бухгалтер. Panov (1967: 333) considers бухгалтер the only word where this pronunciation is now obligatory.

Although this book is concerned mainly with the development of standard Russian, it is worth digressing for a moment to consider the pronunciation of г in South Russian (and similarly, Russian as spoken in Belorussia and the Ukraine, whether by Russians or by Belorussians and Ukrainians). The main point to notice is the surprising stability of the fricative pronunciation despite the influence of the standard language. Even in the speech of intellectuals from the South, fricative [ɣ] is often retained—indeed it is often the only southern dialect feature retained in what is otherwise standard Russian. So tenacious is the fricative pronunciation, at least in the speech of those that remain in the South, that Parikova (1966: 129–30) goes so far as to consider this one feature of a South Russian variant of the standard language. She goes on to say that 'complete command of the pronunciation of plosive г in the conditions of a South Great Russian linguistic environment is a happy exception, rather than a usual occurrence'. While continued residence is a potent factor in the retention of fricative [ɣ], it is by no means a necessary factor, since the fricative pronunciation is retained by many southerners who leave the area where [ɣ] is autochthonous. The whole question is discussed by Pen'kovskij (1967), who adopts a strongly normative position: southerners must be taught to use [g] correctly, the only problem is how. One of the problems he faces is that many southerners are simply unaware that their pronunciation differs from that of the standard. Pen'kovskij (p. 69) quotes the case of a Russian student from Vinnica (Ukraine) taking an examination in dialectology in Vladimir, who answered correctly that fricative [ɣ] characterizes southern dialects, then said that in her own speech she used only 'plosive [ɣ] [*sic!*] in accord with the literary norm'. In fact, she had usually used [ɣ], occasionally [g]. Moreover, it is not that southerners find physical difficulty in pronouncing the plosive sound: [g] occurs in their Russian speech in much the same situations as [ɣ] or [ɦ] in standard Russian, namely as a result of voice assimilation, in interjections and onomatopoeic words, and in loanwords. Southerners rarely carry over fricative [ɣ] to completely foreign languages: Pen'kovskij (p. 63) mentions a teacher from Mglin (Brjansk *oblast'*) whose Russian has only [ɣ], but whose English has only [g]. Many southerners who do make the attempt to adopt the standard pronunciation pronounce [g] perfectly in certain phonetic environments, but retain [ɣ] (presumably unconsciously) elsewhere, especially between vowels. Clearly, the basic conclusion is that many people are not sufficiently aware of their own pronunciation to rid themselves of this regional feature, particularly in so far as the pressure to adopt plosive [g] is minimal or non-existent for most of them, particularly if they remain in the South. Indeed southerners may even take a certain pride in their local [ɣ] (Kogotkova 1970: 122).

The difference between the status of *okan'e*, the most characteristic feature of northern dialects, and *γakan'e*, the most characteristic feature of southern dialects, is aptly summed up by B. V. Gornung («Ответы на вопросник»... 1965: 212): '. . . while *okan'e* has almost died out among speakers of the literary language, fricative r, on the other hand, is found even among natives of northern Russia, who are apparently abandoning plosive r as a "dialectism" '.

Consonant clusters

The pronunciation of consonant groups in Russian involves a number of peculiarities, and here we are unable to go into all the details, particularly as a more detailed treatment of these problems is already available in English (Drage 1968: 355–73). We do wish, however, to draw attention briefly to some of the ways in which the pronunciation of consonant clusters differs between OM and CSR.

(i) г, к, ч *before a plosive*

In OM, к and г are regularly pronounced as fricatives ([x] and [ɣ] respectively) before plosives, as in кто 'who', к кому 'to whom', тогда 'then', pronounced [xto], [x kʌˈmu], [tʌɣˈda]. In the vast majority of words, this pronunciation is now archaic, and apart from the speech of the oldest Muscovites is non-standard (Avanesov 1972: 146). There are, however, a few exceptional words where the older fricative pronunciation is still required by the current standard, and is usual in practice (Drage 1968: 371), namely: the adjectives лёгкий 'light' and мягкий 'soft' and their derivatives, like лёгче 'lighter', смягчить 'soften'. The plosive pronunciation here is considered non-standard. The masculine short form adjectives лёгок and мягок are pronounced with [g], since the consonant is not before a plosive.

The pronunciation of что 'what' as [ʃto] is part of the same phenomenon—an affricate is pronounced as a fricative before the plosive [t]—and here the fricative pronunciation is the only one sanctioned by the standard language (Avanesov 1972: 145) in the nominative–accusative, although [t͡ʃto] is sometimes heard; other forms have [t͡ʃ], since there is no immediately following plosive, e.g. genitive чего. The group чт is pronounced as written in other words.

(ii) *Pronunciation of* чн

In earlier periods of the language for which we have evidence, in Moscow the group чн in non-learned words was pronounced [ʃn], and was in fact often spelt шн. In the vast majority of these words this pronunciation has now been replaced by [t͡ʃn]. Among the few words where the fricative pronunciation is still required (Avanesov 1972: 143) are конечно 'of course' (though not the etymologically related adjective конечный 'final, finite' and its derivatives), скучный 'boring', яичница 'fried eggs', прачечная 'wash-house', and women's patronymics in -ична, e.g. Ильинична. In addition, there are some words where the older pronunciation is still permissible (Shapiro 1968: 30). Even for some of the words where the older pronunciation is still required by orthoepists, the younger generation, according to the results of the survey by Superanskaja

(1959: 159), sometimes shows a preference for the other pronunciation.

(iii) *Loss of consonants in clusters*

All styles of modern Russian have at least a tendency to drop certain consonants in consonant clusters, although this phenomenon is rather more frequent in OM than in CSR. Thus Avanesov (1972: 149) considers the pronunciation of поездка 'journey' as [pʌˈjeskə] to be either OM, or colloquial, while as the current standard he recommends [pʌˈjestkə]. In practice, several other factors intervene: for instance, such consonants are more likely to be dropped in familiar words than in rare, learned words, and of course are more likely to be dropped in rapid than slow, careful speech. Further details are given by Ganiev (1966) and Drage (1968: 372–3).

(iv) *Palatalization assimilation*

In combinations of consonants of which the last is soft (palatalized), earlier consonants in the group are often palatalized by assimilation. The rules determining whether or not assimilation may or must take place are complex, depending basically on the place and manner of articulation of the consonants involved, but also partly on morphological position, stress, and morphological parallelism (Drage 1967a: 142), also on the individual word in certain cases. Assimilation is also more likely in rapid speech, and informants tend to over-report non-assimilation. Recommendations as to the standard are given by Avanesov (1972: 109–28), though many of the generalizations suggested by Avanesov are called into question by the results of the survey reported by Drage (1967a). Over all, there has been a tendency for palatalization assimilation to decrease during the present century, so that many assimilations that are normal in OM are not part of the CSR standard. Fuller details are given by Drage (1967b), who compares the pronunciation of his readers with descriptions of Russian pronunciation in the late nineteenth and early twentieth centuries; the data are summarized according to the consonant groups involved, some of the more striking changes being as follows (in each case, the consonant in italics is normally soft in OM, and is hard for the majority of Drage's informants):

dental plosives before labials, e.g. затмение 'eclipse', Дмитрий, *твердый* 'hard', ме*д*ведь 'bear' (but, exceptionally, the д of две 'two (feminine)' is still soft for the majority of informants, 14 out of 17; cf. a similar observation in Avanesov 1972: 111); р before labials, e.g. ско*р*бь 'grief'; р before dentals, e.g. че*р*ти 'devils'; labial fricatives before velars, e.g. де*в*ки 'girls'. Instances of an increase in the soft pronunciation are quite exceptional, e.g. пре*ж*де 'before', з*д*ешний 'local' (Drage 1967*b*: 202), in the first of which the soft pronunciation is that of the majority (16: 1), although ш and ж are normally said to be invariably hard in native words (Avanesov 1972: 87). Although many instances of palatalization assimilation have been lost in CSR, the phenomenon is still very much alive in certain consonant groups, e.g. all informants had soft [ş] before soft labials in *с*вет 'light', *с*мерть 'death', *с*пина 'back'.

The reflexive particle

In OM the reflexive particle, though written -ся or -сь, is pronounced with hard [s], with one rather strange exception: end-stressed gerunds have obligatorily soft [ş], e.g. боясь [bʌˈjaş] 'fearing', but собираясь [səb̦iˈrajəs] 'intending'. In current usage, the palatalized pronunciation of the reflexive particle is widespread, and where the particle occurs after a vowel this is by far the most prevalent pronunciation in contemporary educated usage; cf. the results reported by Superanskaja (1959: 159) from her survey of Moscow students. The older pronunciation is still retained by the majority of theatres. Indeed Panov (1967: 322) notes that some actors, in trying to maintain OM here, overdo it by pronouncing forms like боясь with hard [s].

After consonants the pronunciation of the reflexive particle in current usage is more complex, and the best approach is to summarize the recommendations of Avanesov (1972: 163–5), which give an indication of the general tendencies (see Table 1). Where Avanesov recommends only the soft pronunciation, the hard pronunciation is still possible in OM, and required on the stage.

The results of the survey reported in Drage (1968: 374–5) agree over all with these recommendations: hard pronunciations predominated in: заботиться 'to worry', несся 'he rushed', трясся 'he shook', though also in гордимся 'we pride ourselves' and, surprisingly, началась 'she began'; hard and soft were about equal in помылся 'he washed', остановился 'he stopped'; while the soft pronunciation predominated in начался 'he began' (for those informants who used end-stress; for those who used initial stress, на́чался, the figures were equal) and сгустились 'they thickened'.

TABLE I. *Pronunciation of the reflexive particle after a consonant*

Participle	Soft	*Examples* оставшихся
Imperative		
in a soft consonant	Soft	двинься, заботься
in a hard consonant	Preferably hard	режься
Past tense		
in с, з	Hard	несся
in other consonants	Preferably hard	ушибся, боялся
Present tense		
in шь	Preferably hard	видишься
in м	Either	беремся
in т	Hard	несется, несутся*
Infinitive		
in чь	Preferably hard	стричься
in ть	Hard	учиться*

* In infinitives (but not imperatives) in -ть, and in present-tense forms in -т, the final т, whether hard or soft in the non-reflexive form, combines with the reflexive particle to give -[ttsə], i.e. an affricate with a long stop component.

Adjectives in -гий, -кий, -хий

Since end-stressed adjectives with a stem-final velar have -[oj] in the masculine singular nominative long form, e.g. дорогой 'dear', морской 'marine', плохой 'bad', one would expect such adjectives with stem-stress to end in -[əj], and this is in fact the pronunciation in OM, despite the spelling in -ий, e.g. строгий 'strict', звонкий 'sonorous', тихий 'quiet'; the spelling is in fact taken from Church Slavonic. Rhymes with this pronunciation were the norm in the nineteenth century, as in the following well-known stanza from Lermontov's *Парус* (1832), where the spelling одинокой is often used to ensure the correct pronunciation:

> Белеет парус одинокий
> В тумане моря голубом!..
> Что ищет он в стране далекой?
> Что кинул он в краю родном?..

Only occasionally are examples of the pronunciation with final -[ɡ,ij], -[ḳij], -[x,ij] found, this being characteristic rather of OPb at the turn of the century. Košutić (1919: 83–4) notes the -[ɡ,ij], etc., pronunciation in St. Petersburg, but considers it non-standard.

In the first edition of Avanesov's handbook on standard pronunciation, published in 1950, only the older pronunciation was considered correct. However, by 1961 the same author (1961: 10) acknowledged that the spelling pronunciation, i.e. [ˈstroɡ,ij], [ˈzvonḳij], [ˈṭix,ij], was more widespread. In this we do, incidentally, seem to be dealing unambiguously with a spelling pronunciation, since on the basis of morphological parallelism we would expect the OM pronunciation. In the current edition of Avanesov (1972: 155), the newer pronunciation is that recommended for most purposes. The OM pronunciation is still recommended for the stage, and is insisted on by many theatres; otherwise, unless it is used as a deliberate archaism, the older pronunciation is considered by Avanesov to be either high style, or non-standard (it is the usual pronunciation in dialects, without spelling influence). It is interesting to observe that as the newer pronunciation has spread in the 'middle', neutral style, the older pronunciation has come to characterize equally deliberately elevated and non-standard speech.

When the pronunciation of these adjectives was tested by Superanskaja (1959: 159), the overwhelming majority of informants preferred the newer forms. This test suffered from the disadvantage that those asked were aware of the purpose of the inquiry, and were therefore on their guard against giving pronunciations they considered incorrect, even if these were their normal pronunciations. A rather different experiment is reported by Andreev (1963): the data here were obtained by asking passers-by of various age and social groups for the names of railway stations (e.g. Ленинградский вокзал), bridges (e.g. Кировский мост), streets (e.g. Ленинский проспект) in Moscow and Leningrad. Those asked were not told that the investigator was interested in pronunciation. Of 2,280 subjects (1,378 in Moscow, 902 in Leningrad), only 3, in Moscow, used the pronunciation in -[kəj], the three being a woman caretaker (сторожиха) in her late fifties, a nun (*sic!*) in her eighties, and a 'famous linguist of the older generation'. When subsequently asked specifically about the pronunciation of these adjectives, only six informants insisted that only the older pronunciation is correct, and five of these used the -[ķij] pronunciation regularly in ordinary conversation; the sixth, perhaps not surprisingly, was the aforementioned linguist.

The orthographic difference between masculine nominative singular трудный 'difficult', синий 'blue', and feminine oblique singular трудной, синей, is likewise due to Church Slavonic spelling conventions. While some speakers of CSR distinguish them in pronunciation (-[ij] versus -[əj], -[ij] versus -[ɪj]), most speakers of CSR, like speakers of OM, have no distinction, often with -[əj]/-[ɪj] and -[ij]/-[ij] and intermediate pronunciations in free variation.

A similar change has taken place in the pronunciation of verbs in -ивать after a velar consonant, e.g. натягивать 'stretch', помахивать 'wave', помалкивать 'keep quiet'. In OM these are pronounced with hard velars: [nʌˈt̪agəvət̪], etc.[1] Nowadays the usual pronunciation follows the spelling (Superanskaja 1959: 159).

Pretonic ша, жа

Normally, immediately pretonic a after a hard consonant is pronounced [ʌ], as in вода 'water'; after a soft consonant it is pronounced [iᵉ], e.g. гляди 'look'. In OM, after ш and ж, both hard, immediately pre-tonic a is pronounced not [ʌ], but [ɨᵉ], i.e. the retracted equivalent of [iᵉ],[2] e.g. жара 'heat', шаги 'steps'.

In current usage, this pronunciation is, for most words, archaic. The usual pronunciation of such words is with [ʌ],

---

[1] No difference is usually made in pronunciation between the unstressed verbal endings -ывать and -овать, both pronounced -[əvət̪] (Avanesov 1972: 165).

[2] In Old Russian, ш and ж were soft (Kiparsky 1963: 154).

corresponding both to the spelling, and to the general rule for pronouncing unstressed a after a hard consonant (see Superanskaja (1959: 160)). Significantly, in such cases the older standard is no longer insisted on even on the stage, except as a deliberate stylistic effect in the speech of certain characters. I. P. Kozljaninova, an elocutionist at the Moscow Theatrical Institute, writes in «Современное сценическое произношение» (1967: 44) that even on the stage the older pronunciation is now definitely considered archaic.

Although the change in pronunciation noted above has taken place for most words, there are still a few that resist. Thus Avanesov (1972: 63–4) considers only the [iᵉ] pronunciation correct for жалеть 'pity' and related words, including к сожалению 'unfortunately', and for жакет 'ladies' jacket', жасмин 'jasmin', жавель 'liquid bleach', бешамель 'Bechamel sauce', and end-stressed forms of лошадь 'horse', e.g. genitive plural лошадей. The results of Superanskaja's survey (1959: 160) indicate that this does reflect current pronunciation, since a large number of informants (for some words, the majority) have [iᵉ] in such words, despite having [ʌ] usually. This illustrates an important principle of linguistic change: it is not always the case that all words containing a given sound change at precisely the same rate: often the behaviour of individual words is idiosyncratic. The figures quoted in Panov (1968, 4: 35–6) suggest that, whereas the [iᵉ] pronunciation is on the decrease for the majority of words, it is on the increase for some, especially those noted in this paragraph.

In OM, proper names with immediately pre-tonic ша were exceptional in the other direction, with the vowel [ʌ] rather than [iᵉ]; Avanesov (1972: 64) notes that D. N. Ušakov, perhaps the staunchest defender of OM, pronounced his own name [uʃʌˈkof].

After ц, also historically a soft consonant, the [iᵉ] pronunciation occurs only in oblique forms of двадцать 'twenty' and тридцать 'thirty' (Avanesov 1972: 64), in both OM and CSR. We may also note here that in forms of the verb целовать 'kiss' where the це- is the immediately pre-tonic syllable, in OM the usual pronunciation was [tsʌ]-, i.e. [tsʌˈluju] (occasionally even written цалую) for CSR [tsiᵉˈluju] (Avanesov 1972: 65; Krysin 1974: 110–11).

Unstressed endings

In general, the rules of Russian that specify the pronunciation of unstressed vowels operate irrespective of morphological or other grammatical criteria. With certain inflections, however, this regularity is not maintained, especially in the case of unstressed a and o after soft consonants, the precise nature of irregularities differing somewhat between OM and CSR. Since only inflectional endings are involved, there is clearly some interference from morphological factors, and we shall see below that the pronunciation of these endings is in fact conditioned by additional morphological criteria, especially in OM.

(i) *Second conjugation verb forms in unstressed* -ят, -ящий

The clearest such difference between OM and CSR concerns the pronunciation of the unstressed ending of third-person plural present verbs of the second conjugation, e.g. хо́дят 'they go'. Where this ending is stressed, as in сидя́т 'they sit', OM and CSR agree in having [ṣiˈd̞at]; хо́дят, however, is pronounced [ˈxod̞ut] in OM (Košutić 1919: 93), with the first conjugation ending, whereas CSR has [ˈxod̞ət]. The same applies to present participles active, e.g. сидя́щий 'sitting' with [a] in OM and CSR, стро́ящий 'building' with [u] in OM, [ɪ] in CSR.

As late as the mid-thirties, Ušakov (1935–40, 1: xxxiv) admitted only the OM pronunciation of such verbal forms. But by the late forties, Avanesov (1947*a*: 5) noted that the new form [ˈxod̞ət] was more widespread, and from its first edition (1950), his *Русское литературное произношение* calls the OM forms archaic, while the CSR forms are recommended as the current orthoepic standard. The older form is now used for deliberate stylistic effect, as when Ju. Kazakov (quoted in Gorbačevič 1971: 96) has one of his characters say: у вас там, в Москве, небось босиком не ходют 'where you live, in Moscow, I don't suppose people go round barefoot'; the spelling ходют implies that the author is contrasting this with the standard pronunciation. At present, the older pronunciation is still to be met from older Muscovites. Elsewhere, Avanesov (1972: 159–60) now considers it non-standard; it is more likely with verbs that are themselves non-standard or colloquial, and is more likely with the third-person plural than with the participle (which is in any case a more literary form).

Many Russian dialects have a distribution of -[ut] and -[at]/-[ət] which does not correspond to that of the written language, i.e. to the difference between first and second conjugations, especially when the endings are unstressed (Bromlej 1973). Forms like [ˈxoɟut] are common in the dialects of the Moscow area, as is the inverse phenomenon, stem-stressed first conjugation forms like [ˈplaʧət] for плачут 'they weep'. The latter forms are not infrequently to be heard from educated Muscovites (Panov 1968, 3: 142); in the RJaSO survey, 32 per cent of informants gave the non-orthoepic pronunciation for борются 'they fight'.

(ii) *Feminine accusative singular adjectives*

In OM, particularly in rapid speech, the unstressed feminine accusative singular adjective ending was often pronounced -[əju]/-[ɪju], e.g. добрую [ˈdobrəju] 'good', синюю [ˈsʲinʲɪju] 'blue' (Košutić 1919: 100). Avanesov (1972: 157–8) specifically warns against this pronunciation, and insists on [ˈdobruju], [ˈsʲinʲuju] in CSR. He does not mention the possibility of the other pronunciation in OM, and considers this pronunciation to be a dialect feature among standard Russian speakers.

(iii) *Unstressed* a, o *after soft consonants*

The data for other unstressed endings, with the vowels a and o after soft consonants, are taken for the most part from Kuz'mina (1966), who gives the results of a reading test using 100 Moscow students aged from 18 to 27 (all born in Moscow, with parents born in Moscow), showing how many used [ə] and how many [ɪ] in individual forms. The forms to be tested were given sentence-finally, phrase-finally (but not sentence-finally), and phrase-medially. The results of this test show that the pronunciations [ə] and [ɪ] are most consistently distinguished sentence-finally, and the discussion is based on this position; phrase-medially, there is a greater tendency for [ɪ] to be used in all cases, and more generally the incidence of [ɪ] is higher the more rapid the speech. The data obtained in this way were then compared with descriptions of OM, in particular Košutić (1919: 88, 93–6, 100, 111). The results are summarized in

Table 2, which gives the majority pronunciation for each position.

In order to ascertain which particular vowel's unstressed version we are dealing with, the morphological form in question is compared with an equivalent form with stress on the ending.

TABLE 2. *Pronunciation of post-tonic* a, o *after a soft consonant and morpheme boundary*

			OM	CSR
V‡	a	дыня 'melon'		
		по́ля 'field (genitive)'		
		кры́лья 'wings'	[ə]	
		по́мня 'remembering'		[ə]
		рва́лся 'tore (reflexive)'	(hard [s])	
	o	по́ле 'field (nominative)'	[ə]	
Vj	a	си́няя 'blue (feminine)'		
	o	си́нее 'blue (neuter)'	[ɪ]	[ɪ]
		си́ней 'blue (feminine oblique)'		
VC′	a	приоса́нясь 'dignified'	(hard [s])	
		ды́нями 'melons (instrumental)'	[ə]	[ɪ]
	o	е́дете 'you travel'	[ɪ]	
VC°V	a	го́нятся 'they chase (reflexive)'	[u]	
	o	си́нему 'blue (non-feminine dative)'	[ɪ]	[ɪ]
		си́него 'blue (non-feminine genitive)'		
VC°‡	a	ды́ням 'melons (dative)'	[ə]	
		ды́нях 'melons (prepositional)'		[ə]
		го́нят 'they chase'	[u]	
	o	мо́рем 'sea (instrumental)'	[ə] (nouns)	
		сту́льев 'chairs (genitive)'		[ɪ]
		си́нем 'blue (non-feminine prepositional)'	[ɪ] (non-	
		ки́нем 'we shall throw'	nouns)	

Key: V = vowel, C° = hard consonant, C′ = soft consonant other than [j], ‡ = word-boundary.

Thus in дыня ['din̦ə], a nominative singular of the second declension, we have the unstressed ending -a, cf. простыня́ 'sheet'. Usually, this corresponds to the spelling, but not invariably so; in nominative–accusative по́ле we have unstressed o (cf. ружьё [ruʒ'jo] 'gun'), while in prepositional singular по́ле we have e (cf. ружье́ [ruʒ'je]). (In the old orthography they are distinguished as по́ле and по́лѣ respectively.)

When the unstressed vowels a and o are not in inflectional endings, they are pronounced [ɪ] after soft consonants in both

OM and CSR, e.g. случай [ˈsluʧıj] 'chance', вынес [ˈvin̡ıs] 'carried out'. For a few words, e.g. занял '(he) occupied', занят 'occupied', сегодня 'today', the statistics are not systematic, but show a tendency towards the [ə] pronunciation, perhaps because of uncertainty as to where the morpheme boundary lies.

If we look at the predominant pronunciation of the endings in question, a number of unusual features emerge. One is that a and o, unstressed, are distinguished in pronunciation: in OM before a soft consonant, partly also before a word-final hard consonant; in CSR before a word-final hard consonant. The second is that, in OM, not only is the morphological information that the vowel is in an ending relevant to its pronunciation, but also the particular part of speech, in that o is pronounced [ə] before a word-final hard consonant in nouns, but [ı] in other parts of speech.

Further to the first of these two features, it is often claimed (e.g. Shapiro 1968: 40; Avanesov 1972: 70) that in nominative–accusative поле CSR tends towards the pronunciation [ı], the same as the prepositional, and different from the [ə] pronunciation of word-final unstressed -a. But the results reported by Kuz'mina contradict this. The pronunciation [ˈpol̡ə] was used by 98 of the 100 informants sentence-finally, 79 phrase-finally, and 64 phrase-medially—the highest figure for [ə] of any of the word-forms tested (Kuz'mina 1966: 16). The figures broken down according to age-group equally fail to show any over-all trend towards [ı] here (Panov 1968, 4: 52).

With regard to morphological criteria, we may note that the relevance of such criteria has been reduced in CSR. The only morphological information relevant is whether or not the vowel is in an inflectional ending, and even this only word-finally or before a word-final hard consonant. The tendency for OM [ə] to be replaced by [ı] means that in CSR the general rule that unstressed a and o are pronounced [ı] after a soft consonant has widened its sphere of applicability to encompass many of the classes of forms that were exceptions in OM.

Although we have taken OM as our point of departure, OM is itself the result of historical development, and we have some indications of the pronunciation of these endings in the preceding period. Košutić (1919: 100) gives only the [ı] pronuncia-

tion for синего, синему, синем in OM, but notes that the [ə]
pronunciation occurred in non-standard Moscow speech even
after having been lost in the standard language. Shapiro (1968:
17–18) assumes, but unfortunately does not substantiate, an
earlier form (which he identifies, rather simplistically, with
OM) where post-tonic a and o are always pronounced [ə] after
soft consonants, even in stems (e.g. вынес). Extrapolating from
the data available, we may hypothesize that OM (as described
by Košutić) and CSR are two intermediate stages on a development from consistent [ə] to consistent [ɪ] for unstressed a and o
post-tonically, intermediate stages that demonstrate the complexity of this change.

In fairness, we should point out that some other investigators
have failed to note the [ə]/[ɪ] distribution claimed by Kuz'mina:
Thelin (1971: 104–22), using a small number of informants
and spectrographic analysis; Bondarko and Verbickaja (1973),
although the latter tests speakers' ability to *perceive* the distinction, rather than to produce it; Krysin (1974: 111–16),
although the author notes that the RJaSO survey techniques
are particularly unreliable here, and it is doubtful whether the
results show anything more than a tendency to over-report the
more explicit variant [ə].

Loanwords

Loanwords in Russian, and in particular loans from Western
European languages in the nineteenth century, often originated
in the speech of members of the gentry and intelligentsia who
were familiar with the pronunciation of the language in question, and attempted to retain something of the original pronunciation when using the word in Russian, even where this
meant contradicting the normal rules of Russian pronunciation.
Writing in 1931, Polivanov (quoted in Glovinskaja 1971: 87)
noted that in the following loanwords, the retention of the non-
Russian nasalized and front-rounded vowels was obligatory in
the speech of the pre-Revolutionary intelligentsia: [õ] in бомонд
'beau monde', лонгшез 'deck-chair'; [ã] in шансонетка 'music
hall song', рандеву 'rendezvous; [œ] in бретёр 'swash-buckler',
блеф 'bluff'; [y] in ревю 'revue', парвеню 'upstart', and меню
'menu'. In Glovinskaja's survey of the speech of the contemporary

Soviet intelligentsia, of 41 informants only 17 retained the foreign pronunciation in бомонд, 8 in ревю and парвеню, 7 in бретер, 4 in лонгшез, шансонетка, and меню, 3 in рандеву, and 2 in блеф (Glovinskaja 1971: 87–8). Clearly, there is a marked trend away from the pronunciation that retains elements of the foreign pronunciation that conflict with the usual rules of Russian pronunciation.

(i) *Unstressed* [o]

In the speech of the pre-Revolutionary intelligentsia, many foreign words were pronounced with retention of unstressed [o]. This particular tendency has decreased considerably during the present century. Writing in 1915, Černyšev (quoted in Gorbačevič 1971: 94–5) said that in educated speech бокáл 'goblet', вокзáл 'railway station', комáнда 'command', костю́м 'suit' should be pronounced with unstressed [o]. Nowadays, this pronunciation for these words is either archaic or affected—it is used, for instance, by actors portraying aristocratic ladies in productions of the Moscow Arts Theatre (Gorbačevič 1971: 95). There do remain some words where the older pronunciation is still required, or at least preferred, by current orthoepic dictionaries, although in practice their recommendations are often not adhered to. Thus Avanesov and Ožegov (1959) recommend the pronunciation of поэ́т 'poet' with unreduced [o], allowing the variant with vowel reduction as a permissible variant; according to the survey reported in Glovinskaja (1971: 95), all forty of her informants had a reduced vowel. Moreover, the authoritative dictionaries do not always agree with one another. Avanesov (1972: 167) lists both портвéйн 'port (wine)' and фойé 'foyer' as words where the pronunciation with un-reduced [o] is to be preferred, although the reduced vowel is permissible. Avanesov and Ožegov (1959) allow only the un-reduced vowel in фойе, while the absence of any remark on the unstressed vowel of портвейн should imply that the only admissible pronunciation is with the vowel reduced. Glovin-skaja's informant responses were, for портвейн: 1 non-reduced, 42 reduced, and for фойе: 3 non-reduced, 32 reduced (Glovin-skaja 1971: 95).

One reasonably common loanword with unstressed o is шоссé '(surfaced) highway'. Here, Avanesov and Ožegov (1959) allow only the pronunciation with unreduced [o], while Avanesov (1972: 167) allows [ʃʌsˈse] as a permissible variant. Normally, after [ʃ] and [ʒ] stressed o (often written ë) becomes [iᵉ] (written e) when unstressed, e.g. женá 'wife' (cf. plural жёны); both pronunciations given so far for шоссе make it an exception to this rule. However, among Glovinskaja's informants, 4 had unreduced [o], 9 had [ʌ], while 18 had [iᵉ]/[i]. It seems that in this respect even the updated version of Avanesov's handbook is behind the current pronunciation trend.

(ii) *Consonants before* e

Another feature of foreign pronunciation often carried over into loanwords is the retention of a hard (non-palatalized) paired consonant before e. One might expect that this relic of foreign pronunciation would also tend to disappear with time, particularly as Russian spelling does not normally make use of the special letter э to mark the hardness of the preceding consonant in such words. And indeed, a number of words that would once have been permissible with a hard consonant are now admissible only with a soft consonant, unless deliberate affectation is intended, e.g. текст 'text', профессор 'professor', музей 'museum'.

However, this tendency has not proved nearly so strong as that against unstressed [o]. This leads to interesting results in words that have both unstressed o and a consonant before e, e.g. сонéт 'sonnet'. One possible pronunciation is with unreduced [o] and hard [n]: [soˈnet]. Another is with reduced o and soft [n̩]: [sʌˈn̩et]. Yet another is with reduced o but hard [n]: [sʌˈnet]; this is the form recommended by Avanesov and Ožegov (1959). The fourth logical possibility, unreduced [o] but soft [n̩] is a contradiction in terms, since reduction of unstressed o is far commoner than palatalization of consonants before e in foreign words, so that the pronunciation [soˈn̩et] is effectively excluded (Halle 1959: 73).

Table 3, based on the material in Glovinskaja (1971: 93–4), gives some of the results of a survey on whether Russians pronounce hard or soft consonants before e in loanwords. Three possible pronunciations are distinguished: hard, medium, and soft. From the data given by Glovinskaja, the author notes a

TABLE 3. *Pronunciation of consonants before* e *in loanwords*

	Hard	Medium	Soft	Avanesov and Ožegov
агре́ссор 'aggressor'	59	1	29	*soft (not hard)
атеи́ст 'atheist'	83	0	7	hard
ателье́ 'studio'	41	0	0	hard
бандеро́ль 'wrapper'	37	1	3	*soft (not hard)
бутербро́д 'open sandwich'	37	0	4	hard
бухга́лтер 'book-keeper'	0	0	40	soft (not hard)
бюстга́льтер 'brassiere'	28	0	12	hard
ге́тто 'ghetto'	23	21	46	soft
декаде́нт 'decadent'	30	0	1	*soft (not hard)
декаде́нт	20	4	16	*soft (not hard)
ко́декс '(legal) code'	40	0	0	hard
ко́фе 'coffee'[1]	0	6	31	soft (not hard)
ко́фе[1]	6	19	71	
купе́ 'compartment'	37	4	0	hard
купе́йный ' „ (adjective)'	11	2	28	*hard
медресе́ 'madrasah'	24	0	1	hard
медресе́	21	2	3	hard
медресе́	7	2	31	*hard
меню́ 'menu'	2	3	37	soft
моде́ль 'model'	40	0	0	hard
парте́р 'ground floor'	35	0	0	hard
резюме́ 'résumé'	14	6	14	*hard
сви́тер 'sweater'	37	0	2	hard
се́кс 'sex'	22	2	16	(not given)
сексуа́льный 'sexual'	15	1	26	soft
соне́т 'sonnet'	32	3	5	hard
теа́тр 'theatre'	0	0	43	soft
те́зис 'thesis'	36	1	3	hard
тенде́нция 'tendency'	40	0	0	hard
тенде́нция	39	0	1	hard
фоне́тика 'phonetics'	40	0	0	hard
фонети́ст 'phonetician'	42	0	0	hard
шоссе́ 'highway'	41	0	1	hard

* We have marked with an asterisk those cases where the pronunciation recommended does not correspond to the largest figure in Glovinskaja's study (for резюме an equal number of informants had hard and soft м; note that Avanesov and Ožegov recommend hard м but soft р).

number of statistical tendencies, in particular: (1) dental consonants are more likely to remain hard than labials, which are in turn more likely to remain hard than velars; (2) a hard

[1] This word was tested on two different occasions, whence the two entries in the table.

consonant is more likely to be retained if it immediately pre-
cedes the stressed vowel than if it occurs earlier in the word;
(3) the hard pronunciation is commoner in words of medium
frequency than in words of very common or very rare occurrence. The last point is perhaps rather surprising at first sight,
but not entirely unexpected: very common words naturally
fall under the general rule palatalizing consonants, in so far as
they come to be felt as part of the native vocabulary; words in
which the consonant remains hard are marked items, and
words of infrequent occurrence are unlikely to be well enough
known for the average native speaker to have assimilated the
irregular pronunciation. One further generalization, not mentioned by Glovinskaja, is that the hard pronunciation is less
common with derived words with native suffixes than with the
simple word, cf. секс and сексуальный and, even more clearly
since there is no stress difference, купе and купейный.

In addition, in Table 3, we have added the recommendations
of Avanesov and Ožegov (1959). In the vast majority of cases,
their recommendations agree with the most widespread usage
recorded by Glovinskaja—surprisingly so, given that Avanesov
and Ožegov (1959) is based not on informant-polling, but on
intuitive and rough-and-ready methods. Where the consonant
in question is a labial (купейный, медресе, резюме), Avanesov
and Ožegov appear to tend towards a norm with more hard
consonants than the general trend of informant responses, but
in fact they are hesitant about the phonetic status of these
labials (681–2), and suggest that the orthoepic pronunciation
is rather half-soft (medium). In the other examples, and in
several other words noted by Glovinskaja (1971: 91), the
recommendations given by Avanesov and Ožegov (1959)
differ from majority usage in over-recommending the soft
pronunciation, i.e. in suggesting that these words are more
assimilated to the native pattern than in fact they are. Clearly,
the hard pronunciation of consonants before e is coming to be
felt more and more an integral part of the Russian sound
system.

The difference between the fate of unstressed [o] and that of
hard consonants before e gives a clear indication of the two
ways in which the Russian language has been 'democratized':
in the first case, the non-popular pronunciation has tended to

be lost, while in the second case the non-popular pronunciation has been adopted by a much wider section of the social spectrum.

Miscellaneous

(i) *Soft* ρ *between* e *and* a *hard consonant*

In older stages of the language, soft [ɹ] was used in many words, between e and a hard consonant, where CSR has hard [r]. Occasionally, the soft pronunciation was indicated in spelling, as on the Bronze Horseman monument to Peter the Great (Петру перьвому) in Leningrad. In OM of the turn of the century, this pronunciation was still usual for certain words, at least among the older generation. Košutić (1919: 158) notes верх 'summit', церковь 'church', четверг 'Thursday', and points out that in some other words the soft pronunciation had recently been ousted by the hard, e.g. зеркало 'mirror', первый 'first', стерва (term of abuse, originally 'carrion'). Avanesov (1947*b*: 152) notes that L. Tolstoj pronounced первый with soft [ɹ].

In CSR, the pronunciation is with hard [r] in all these words, although церковь is rather more complex. The main text of Avanesov (1972) does not mention this word in this connection, but the index gives it with soft [ɹ]. Professor Avanesov kindly informs us that церковь is the only word in this class where he considers soft [ɹ] preferable, although hard [r] is widespread.

(ii) *Pronunciation of* их, им, ими

In OM, the oblique forms of the third-person pronoun их, им, ими were pronounced with initial [ji], the only words to be so pronounced. Avanesov (1972: 92) notes this pronunciation, but considers it definitely archaic or non-standard in CSR. Drage (1968: 379–80) reports that of his seventeen informants, only one used the initial [j], and then only in one of four different test sentences with these words.

(iii) *Pronunciation of* солнце *'sun'*

In the word солнце the л is silent, in both OM and CSR. However, in OM the pronunciation of the stressed vowel is much closer than usual (symbolized [ǫ]) (Trubeckoj 1958: 56).

In this pronunciation, the quality of stressed o is closer before
л, as [ǫ], so the OM pronunciation of солнце retains a trace of
the 'silent л' which is pronounced in other derivatives from the
same stem, e.g. солнечный 'solar'. In CSR, there is no such
marked difference of quality between stressed o before л and
elsewhere, and the pronunciation of солнце does not differ
from that of an imaginary word сонце. Since Trubeckoj's
example has become one of the canonical examples of phonological theory, it is worth emphasizing that his argument is
based on data from OM, while CSR does not provide the
relevant data.

(iv) *Word-final palatalized labials*

Many Russians do not distinguish hard and soft labials in
word-final position, pronouncing кров 'roof, shelter' and кровь
'blood' alike with hard [f]. In fact, of all Russian regional
dialects, only some central Russian dialects of the region
around Moscow retain this distinction (Avanesov and Orlova
1965: 88). Loss of the distinction among people who are otherwise speakers of standard Russian is commoner in Leningrad
than in Moscow. Although this pronunciation, on the evidence of
other dialects and Slavonic languages, may be a sign of the way
Russian is developing, it is not admitted as standard at present
(Avanesov 1972: 102–3). Panov (1967: 299–300) considers the
hard pronunciation a serious mistake, to be combated.

(v) *Word-initial и after a hard consonant*

In standard pronunciation, when words beginning with и
occur without pause after a word ending in a hard consonant
(e.g. a preposition), the initial и is pronounced [ɨ], e.g. в
Италию 'to Italy' ([v ɨˈtaḷiju]), unlike Виталию 'Vitalij (dative)'
([v̡iˈtaḷiju]), к Ире 'towards Ira' ([ˈk iɾ̡]), unlike Кире 'Kira
(dative)' ([ˈk̡iɾ̡]). The pronunciation, fairly common nowadays,
of both members of such pairs with [i] (i.e. indiscriminately
[v̡iˈtaḷiju] and [k̡ˈiɾ̡]) is not admitted as standard (Avanesov
1972: 107–8). Avanesov notes further that many Russians
adhere to the norm where the consonant is not velar, but deviate
from it where the consonant is velar: within the morpheme,
[ki] is not, of course, a possible sequence in Russian; within
OM, the same phenomenon was noted by Košutić (1919: 163).

(vi) *Ikan'e and ekan'e*

One aspect of standard pronunciation that has given great difficulty to orthoepists is the pronunciation of pre-tonic e and a (я) after soft consonants, as in леса́ 'forests' and язы́к 'tongue'. The major point at issue is whether unstressed e/a should be pronounced the same as unstressed и (*ikan'e*), or not (*ekan'e*). Avanesov (1972: 66–8) gives as the basic variant of the standard language a form of *ekan'e*, where unstressed e and a are pronounced as a sound in between stressed e and и, symbolized [iᵉ] (immediately pre-tonic), or [ɪ] (elsewhere). He notes, however, that in rapid speech e/a and и are often not distinguished, since unstressed и tends to be lowered slightly, i.e. approaches [e], while unstressed e is raised towards [i], with the possibility of them meeting in the middle. Avanesov criticizes the pronunciation (strong *ikan'e*) where unstressed e/a is pronounced identical to stressed и.

Over all, it seems that Avanesov allows both variants, with some preference for a variety of *ekan'e*, especially in slow, careful speech, i.e. distinguishing преда́ть 'betray' and прида́ть 'impart', леса́ 'forests' and лиса́ 'fox', частота́ 'frequency' and чистота́ 'cleanliness'. The situation is not helped, incidentally, by some confusion in the use of the terms *ikan'e* and *ekan'e*, as noted by Thelin (1971: 68–81), who discusses the range of variants in greater detail. While it is occasionally maintained that the older standard is with *ikan'e*, now being replaced by *ekan'e* (e.g. Gvozdev 1958: 69, and other references cited by Panov 1967: 305), the discussion by Panov (1967: 301–8) and the statistical data given in Panov (1968, 4: 22–30) demonstrate that the current tendency is towards *ikan'e*, replacing the older pronunciation with *ekan'e*.

Conclusions

As noted in the introduction to this chapter, having discussed various changes between OM and CSR, and also changes that are taking place within CSR, it is useful to try to ascertain what have been the motive forces behind these changes, in particular the relevance of spelling pronunciations, other forms of spoken Russian (dialects, OPb), morphological analogy, and morphological boundaries. In many cases, of course, we may expect more than one of these factors to interact.

The influence of morphological boundaries has been advocated in particular by Glovinskaja *et al.* (1971: 21–2), as part of the general movement towards analyticity: the various morphemes are set off more clearly from one another, by giving phonetic expression to the morpheme boundary. Unfortunately, clear instances of the relevance of morphological boundaries are rare (see Bondarko 1973), the best example being the relevance of such boundaries in fostering the pronunciation [ʃʲʃʲ] across a morpheme boundary; although this pronunciation was noted by Košutić, it seems to have become more frequent during the present century. The alleged role of morpheme boundaries in fostering the loss of palatalization assimilation is brought into doubt by the results of Drage's survey (1967a), and also by the extreme degree of over-reporting of lack of assimilation in the RJaSO survey. At best, one can perhaps say that over-reporting of lack of assimilation is more likely where there is a boundary than where there is not. The same would apply to the pronunciation of post-tonic a and o in inflectional endings after a soft consonant, where the discrepancy between the results of reading tests and the RJaSO survey suggests over-reporting in the latter; indeed, the reading tests suggest that these boundaries are tending to be less marked phonetically, as OM [ə] gives way to CSR [ɪ]. The pronunciation of word-initial и as [i] rather than [ɨ] after a hard consonant in non-standard CSR is another instance of the loss of phonetic marking of morpheme boundaries.

There seems to have been little, if any, influence of regional dialects on the development from OM to CSR; indeed, OM is usually closer to regional dialects, especially the central dialects, than CSR is. In particular, there is no tendency for southern dialect forms to penetrate the standard language. On the other hand, southern dialect features, in the speech of those who do not speak consistent standard Russian, are much less susceptible to the influence of the standard than are northern dialect features, so that there is evidence from outside the standard for the greater tenacity of the southern dialects. Slightly more complex is the possible influence of OPb, since in many respects CSR is closer to OPb than to OM (e.g. pronunciation of adjectives in -кий, verbal forms like ходят, the cluster чн). However, in each instance where CSR is closer to OPb than to OM, the CSR pronunciation can be explained by means of spelling pronunciation or morphological analogy, and there is no need to invoke OPb. Indeed, the problem is rather to explain the origin of OPb, given that St. Petersburg was populated primarily from Moscow. A particularly clear case is the pronunciation of adjectives in -кий, where the pronunciation -[ķij] can only be a spelling pronunciation, and is certainly not that of the regional dialects closest to Leningrad. Filin (1973: 5–6) suggests that most of the characteristics of OPb are the result of earlier and more widespread spelling pronunciations there than in Moscow at the turn of the century, and this explanation fits the facts well.

The main difficulty arises in discriminating between the influence of spelling and that of morphological analogy, since in the majority of cases both of these criteria would give the same result: in the tendency not to simplify consonant clusters (which are split up by fugitive vowels in certain morphological forms, and which are present in the spelling), in the pronunciation of immediate pre-tonic ша, жа as [ʃʌ], [ʒʌ] (given the general rule for pronouncing immediate pre-tonic a after a hard consonant, and also the general rule relating the pronunciation of the same vowel stressed and unstressed in related morphological forms), in the pronunciation of ходят as [ˈxodʲət] (the spelling has я, not ю, and verbs of this conjugation with end-stress have -[at]). There is, however, the one clear case of a spelling pronunciation, namely the pronunciation of adjectives in -кий, etc.: this spelling contradicts morphological parallelism (the stressed ending is -[koj]), and also finds minimal support in Russian dialects, none in those of the Moscow or Leningrad area. There are also some minor changes between OM and CSR that seem attributable only to spelling pronunciation (or at least, to this rather than to any of the other factors noted above): the loss of soft [r̩] in words like церковь, the pronunciation of forms of целовать, the loss of initial [j] in их. CSR developments contrary to the spelling are extremely rare: if indeed *ikan'e* is becoming more widespread, then this would be one such example; similarly the hardening of final soft labials. On the other hand, it is difficult to find convincing examples of morphological analogy that are not also cases of spelling pronunciation: perhaps the non-standard pronunciation of verb forms like плачут as [ˈplaʧət], using the second conjugation unstressed ending, if this is not due to the influence of regional dialects on those who otherwise speak near-standard Russian.

Over all, then, the evidence seems to point in the direction of spelling pronunciation as the main (though not the only) factor in the development from OM to CSR. It is interesting to note, moreover, that many of the unstable points in CSR correlate with inexplicitness of the orthography: the pronunciation of [e] or [o] when stressed after soft consonants (the special letter ё being rarely used outside of school-books) (Es'kova 1967); the pronunciation of single or double consonants in loanwords (the orthography has double consonants in many cases where only a single consonant is pronounced) (Glovinskaja 1971: 63–9); the pronunciation of hard or soft consonants before e in loanwords (since the special letter э is rarely used in their spelling, e does not adequately indicate the pronunciation of the preceding consonant) (Glovinskaja 1971: 76–87, 93–4).

2

STRESS

STRESS in Russian is free (i.e. can occur on any syllable in the word) and mobile (i.e. the position of stress can change in the inflection of a word, or between derivationally related words). The rules determining position of stress are complex, and the stress of many individual words and word-forms is simply idiosyncratic. This leads to a certain amount of inconsistency even among native speakers,[1] a factor which is reinforced by the existence of different stress patterns in different regional dialects, and by the fact that stress is not marked in the orthography (except in some school-books). Thus there are variant stresses in current usage, and there have been changes in normative stress between the nineteenth century and the present day.

Since stress is not marked in Russian spelling, our main source of information about stress in earlier periods comes from verse, where the stress of individual words can be deduced from the metrical scheme. In using verse one has, of course, to remember that a poet may use an unusual stress to fit the metre, although such examples are in fact rare in nineteenth-century Russian poetry (Tobolova 1974), and where we find a given stress used consistently by a large number of poets at the same time, we can be reasonably sure that this stress was admissible at that period. In addition to verse, for the late eighteenth and nineteenth centuries there is also the evidence of early normative dictionaries.

For current usage we have, apart from the practice of contemporary poets, evidence from the various surveys: in addition to the RJaSO survey, reported in Krysin (1974: 223–41), these include Kolesov (1967), as well as surveys concerned with

[1] See Nicholson (1968: 130): 'The memory burden which the stress system places on the Russian is often forgotten, although the demonstrable gaps and inconsistencies in the stressing practice of even highly educated native speakers may be in large measure due to this burden rather than to the specific influence of dialect forms.'

particular problems of stress, as noted below. These may be compared with the recommendations of normative dictionaries.

Most often, normative dictionaries qualify all but one of the variants as non-standard, less commonly one of the variants is archaic or permissible, while only occasionally is more than one variant equally recommended. Even here a certain amount of reservation may be expressed, as in Ožegov (1972: 14): 'only in isolated cases are stress variants given as of equal normativity in the literary language (in this case the preferred variant is given first . . . e.g. творóг, -á (-ý) and твóрог, -a (-y)).' Apparently, some variants are more equal than others.[1]

As noted above, there are marked differences in stress patterns between different Russian dialects, in particular between the northern and southern dialect groups, with the northern dialects tending to be more archaic, the southern dialects (and also Ukrainian and Belorussian) more innovatory. This pattern corresponds by and large to the findings reported in Krysin (1974: 236–41), where Russians from the northern dialect area tend to be closer to the traditional standard, and even educated Russians from the southern dialect area (and likewise Russians from the Ukraine and Belorussia) tend to be more innovatory, while those from Moscow, Moscow *oblast'*, and Leningrad (which here goes with Moscow, rather than the surrounding northern dialects) occupy an intermediate position, i.e. are open to some extent to the influence of the newer southern dialect forms.[2]

While there have been changes in the stress of individual words, such as библиотéка 'library' (archaic библиóтека, still to be heard from some older Russians and in *émigré* circles) and творóг (newer variant твóрог), the most interesting area of

---

[1] In the Moscow area, at least, the pronunciation твóрог seems to be much more frequent than творóг 'cottage cheese'.

[2] Recent detailed dialectological work, noted by Krysin (1974: 238) but not taken into account in the RJaSO survey, indicates that the northern dialect area is in fact less homogeneous than this, with archaic stress patterns characteristic primarily of the north-eastern dialects, and the north-western dialects sometimes even more innovatory than the southern dialects (cf. the preponderance of newer stress forms in the speech of Russians living in the Baltic republics). One may hypothesize that the difference between southern and north-eastern informants would be even greater than that between southern and northern informants noted by Krysin.

study from the viewpoint of general tendencies in the development of stress patterns is the interaction of stress variation and (inflectional and derivational) morphology.

Stress levelling in noun declension

With a number of Russian nouns, the stress of the nominative is changed in some or all of the oblique forms. In the singular, the main such change is in the accusative of second-declension nouns: here a nominative singular in -á may correspond to a stem-stressed accusative (e.g. головá 'head', accusative гóлову). In the plural, many nouns have a different stress in the nominative(–accusative) and in the oblique cases, e.g. nominative–accusative гóловы 'heads', genitive голóв,[1] dative головáм. One of the major tendencies in the recent development of noun stress patterns has been to reduce the amount of stress-alternation within the singular and within the plural. Here, as with many recent and current changes in stress, there are two possible factors: first, the internal factor of analogy, i.e. the tendency to reduce the amount of morphophonemic alternation; secondly, the external factor of the influence of southern dialects, which have less morphophonemic alternation than do the northern (especially north-eastern) dialects. In general, it is difficult to separate the two factors, particularly since the current situation in the southern dialects is largely the result of more widespread operation of analogical levelling.

(i) *Accusative singular in* -y

In the standard language there are only some twenty second-declension nouns for which all dictionaries agree on requiring or recommending a stress-shift in the accusative singular to stem-stress (e.g. водá 'water', accusative вóду), plus a small number of words where the stress-shift is qualified as permissible (e.g. полосá 'stripe', accusative полосý and (permissible) пóлосу (Avanesov and Ožegov 1959)); most of these are, however, very common words. In the nineteenth century, there were rather more words in this class, including веснá 'spring', золá 'ashes', избá 'hut', норá 'burrow', овцá 'sheep', росá

---

[1] Where a word has no ending, as with голóв, or nominative singular бегýн (genitive бегунá), end-stress is realized as stress on the last syllable of the word, i.e. голóв, бегýн.

'dew', сохá 'wooden plough' (Vinogradov *et al.* 1960, 1: 200).
An example of nineteenth-century usage here is the first line of
Puškin's poem *Утопленник* (1828):

> Прибежали в избу дети...
>
> Children ran into the hut...

For all seven of these words, Avanesov and Ožegov (1959) give
only the form with end-stress, except that both избý and
избу are given (in that order), the latter presumably under the
influence of literary tradition (Gorbačevič 1971: 73), since it
does not correspond to current usage.

In addition to those words that have clearly gone over to
fixed-stress in the singular, there are a few words in this class
subject to variation. Vinogradov *et al.* (1960, 1: 202) allow, in
addition to the stresses péку 'river', ценý 'price', and зиму
'winter', the newer forms рекý, ценý, and зимý; Avanesov and
Ožegov (1959) give both péку and рекý (in that order), but
condemn ценý, and cite зиму without any comment. Of the
informants polled in the RJaSO survey (Krysin 1974: 232),
36 per cent gave the stress рекý.

(ii) *Oblique plural forms*

End-stress in the oblique cases with stem-stress in the nomi-
native(–accusative) is common in the plural of a number
of types of Russian nouns, in particular those of the second
declension (e.g. губá 'lip', plural гýбы, dative губáм), but also
less commonly with first-declension nouns (e.g. волк 'wolf',
plural вóлки, dative волкáм), and quite commonly with third
declension nouns (e.g. часть 'part', plural чáсти, dative
частя́м). Over the recent history of the Russian language, there
has been a tendency for such stress-shifts to be levelled out,
usually in the direction of the nominative plural,[1] particularly
with second-declension nouns.

In nineteenth-century usage, for instance, земля́ 'land' and
водá 'water' had end-stress in the oblique plural cases, whereas
nowadays these forms have stem-stress. With земля́, the older
stress is still retained in the genitive plural земéль. This is true
of a number of words that seem to have participated in this

---

[1] With masculine nouns of the first declension, however, the reverse
levelling is usual; for instance, the nominative plural волки́ is common as
a non-standard form.

stress change: thus хло́поты 'troubles', dative хло́потам (Ušakov (1935–40) still gives хлопота́м) but genitive хлопо́т, and семья́ 'family', dative plural се́мьям (cf. nominative plural се́мьи), but genitive plural семе́й. Normative dictionaries allow only деревня́м as the dative plural of дере́вня 'village', although дере́вням is frequently heard from educated Russians; the genitive plural is still дереве́нь.

Two words which are subject to variation in this respect in current usage are волна́ 'wave' and стена́ 'wall'. The attitude of normative handbooks to these two words is different, being more liberal in allowing both variants with волна; thus Avanesov and Ožegov (1959) give stem-stress as a permissible variant in the oblique plural cases of волна, alongside the recommended end-stress, but for стена give only end-stressed oblique plural forms. Yet in the practice of contemporary poets, stem-stressed forms are more common with стена than with волна (Gorbačevič 1971: 70–2). Similarly, in the survey reported in Kolesov (1967: 100) preference was for в волна́х (162 informants, with 56 for в во́лнах, and 1 for both), but for в сте́нах (82 informants, with 57 for в стена́х, and 17 for both). In the RJaSO survey (Krysin 1974: 232) only 14 per cent of those replying gave в во́лнах.

While several words of the second declension have lost stress alternation in the plural, at least one word has, exceptionally, undergone the reverse development: де́ньги 'money', dative деньга́м (archaic де́ньгам); the genitive retains the older stress, де́нег.

Some nouns of the third declension have undergone a similar change: thus the traditional stress of the genitive plural of ве́домость 'register' (nominative plural ве́домости) is ведомосте́й, and Avanesov and Ožegov (1959) specifically condemn the newer variant ве́домостей, although in the RJaSO survey (Krysin 1974: 232) the latter form was given by 74·8 per cent of informants. However, there are also some nouns that have gone the other way, such as тень 'shadow', nominative plural те́ни, genitive plural тене́й; те́ней is archaic, though it is retained in the expression ца́рство те́ней 'the kingdom of shades'.

According to Nicholson (1968: 80), end-stress on the oblique plural cases is a southern dialect feature. If this is true in general, it would provide interesting evidence in deciding the relative importance of analogy and southern dialect influence, since analogy would favour stem-stress (like the nominative plural), while southern dialect influence would favour end-stress; in fact, the tendency is towards stem-stress. However, the generality of Nicholson's claim is called into question by the results of the RJaSO survey (Krysin 1974: 264), for в волнах 'in waves' and в реках 'in rivers', where stem-stress is commoner with southern than with northern informants.

(iii) *Stress and number*

The shift from a paradigm like водá–вóды–водáм to водá–вóды–вóдам makes the stress alternation purely a marker of number, rather than a complex marker of number and case; the spread of the nominative plural in -á of masculine nouns, noted in Chapter 3 on morphology, has the same over-all effect; while the shift from the older type дуб 'oak' (genitive singular дýба)–дýбы–дубóв to current дуб–дýба–дубы́–дубóв again increases the number differentiation. Any decrease in number differentiation seems to be incidental, as in the newer variants of the paradigms дерéвня–дерéвни–деревня́м (newer дерéвням), вéдомость–вéдомости–ведомостéй (newer вéдомостей). In a few cases, the introduction of number stress differentiation seems to be taking place piecemeal: thus фронт '(military) front' has stem-stress in the singular, but, as a relatively recent development, end-stress in the oblique plural, e.g. genitive фронтóв; in the standard language the nominative plural is фрóнты, but the form фронты́, completing the pattern of stem-stress in the singular and end-stress in the plural, is common in non-standard Russian (Krysin 1974: 226, 230, 232)—Gorbačevič (1973) allows it as a permissible variant. The general tendency is thus for stress alternation to be lost as a marker of case difference, while there is a secondary, weaker tendency for stress alternation to be extended as a marker of number difference.

Other stress changes in noun declension

Since masculine nouns of the first declension have no ending in the nominative singular, it is not possible to tell from a nominative singular with final stress whether the word is stem-stressed or end-stressed, e.g. жук 'beetle', genitive жукá, but лук 'onion', genitive лýка. A few nouns have changed over the recent history of the language from having stem-stress to having end-stress. For пруд 'pond', Avanesov and Ožegov (1959) allow only end-stress, and specifically condemn genitive прýда, although this earlier stress is the only one admitted by Ušakov (1935–40). Similarly, Ušakov (1935–40) allows only stem-stress on мост 'bridge', characterizing genitive мостá as 'regional'; Avanesov and Ožegov (1959) give both мóста and мостá (in that order); the survey reported by Kolesov (1967: 99) includes у мóста 'by the bridge' and к мосту 'to the bridge', with 198 informants preferring end-stress in the first case (and only 16 for stem-stress), and 152 for end-stress in the second case (with 76 for stem-stress, and 3 allowing both).[1] The word гусь 'goose' is subject to similar variation in the singular, with genitive гýся or гуся́, although Avanesov and Ožegov (1959) specifically condemn the latter variant; Kolesov (1967: 99) found, however, that 146 informants gave гуся́, and only 70 гýся, with 7 allowing both, suggesting that here again normative handbooks and current usage are out of step. Gorbačevič (1971: 68–9) found that all of his informants (more than 40) gave only end-stress for гуля́ш 'goulash', foɪ which Avanesov and Ožegov (1959) allow only genitive гуля́ша.[2]

Prepositions and prefixes

(i) Stress on prepositions

In Russian, a number of combinations of preposition plus noun take the stress on the preposition. In the nineteenth century this practice was much more widespread, and examples are found which would be quite impossible nowadays, such as this one from Griboedov's *Горе от ума*, ΙΙ. 7 (1823–8):

Молчалин нá лошадь садился
Molčalin mounted the horse

[1] The figure of 3 is actually quoted for к мóсту, which occurs twice, but by comparison with the layout of the other entries it seems that the second occurrence of к мóсту is an error for к мóстý.

[2] A particularly complex picture is presented by words in -аж; for details, see Jiráček (1969).

Even in nineteenth-century verse many doublets are found, with the same poet using stress now on the preposition, now on the noun; thus Lermontov uses both на́ берег and на бе́рег 'to the shore', where the traditional standard is the former (Gorbačevič 1971: 86). In current usage, the tendency to replace preposition stress by stress on the noun is continuing; thus Avanesov and Ožegov (1959) allow both на́ берег and на бе́рег (in that order), and Superanskaja (1959: 161) notes that of her informants, 87 preferred на бе́рег, only 27 на́ берег, with 32 hesitating.

With some combinations of preposition plus noun, stress is found on the noun in the literal meaning of the expression, and on the preposition in other meanings. One such example sanctioned by the normative handbooks is за го́родом 'beyond the town' versus за́ городом 'in the suburbs'. For a number of combinations where the traditional standard is with preposition stress, differentiation of this kind is common in practice (Superanskaja 1959: 161–2). For instance, Avanesov and Ožegov (1959) give only на́ стену 'onto the wall', while many of Superanskaja's informants distinguished the literal meaning на сте́ну from лезть на́ стену 'go up the wall', in the sense of 'become irritated'.

Stress on the preposition is more characteristic of the northern dialects than of the southern dialects, so here we have another example of encroachment of a southern dialect feature into the standard language; though here again, the loss of preposition stress also means a reduction in the amount of stress alternation.

(ii) *Stress on verbal prefixes*

Similar to stress on prepositions is stress on the prefix of a number of verbs with monosyllabic roots in the past tense and past participle passive (excepting the feminine form with final stress), e.g. про́дал (feminine продала́, neuter про́дало, plural про́дали) 'sold', cf. дал (дала́, да́ло, да́ли) 'gave'. Although there is some variation even in nineteenth-century literature, for the most part the traditional standard, with prefix stress, was then usual. In current usage, there is a tendency for this to be replaced by stress on the root of the verb, particularly where the meaning of the prefixed verb is literally the sum of the meaning of prefix plus root, e.g. отдать 'give away', but less so where this is not the case (e.g. продать 'sell'), or where the root does not exist as a separate word (e.g. принять 'accept'). Pirogova (1967: 19) describes the result of a questionnaire completed by 75 students, which included the stress of отдал, отдали 'gave away', прожил, прожили 'lived through', and продали 'sold', in all of which the traditional standard is with prefix stress. Root-stress was preferred by 57 informants for отдал, 61 for отдали, 38 for прожил, 45 for прожили, and 34 for продали. Many normative handbooks allow only the traditional standard, although Avanesov and Ožegov (1959) also cite the root-stressed variants of these as colloquial alternatives. *SSRLJa* (1950–65) allows прожил as a colloquial variant, but gives only о́тдал, without comment, although Pirogova's survey suggests that отда́л is in fact more widespread than прожи́л.

Root-stress in such verbs is again a southern dialect feature, which also has the effect of reducing the amount of stress alternation. The results of the RJaSO survey (Krysin 1974: 265) for нали́л 'filled by pouring', отпи́л 'took a sip', при́был 'arrived', за́дали 'set (a task)' show that for each of these items root-stress was reported significantly more frequently by informants from southern Russia than by those from northern Russia.

Other stress changes in conjugation

(i) *Verbs in -ить*

Verbs of the second conjugation with infinitive in stressed -ить either have end-stress throughout the present tense (e.g. говори́ть 'speak', first person singular говорю́, second person singular говори́шь), or have end-stress on the first person singular only and stem-stress on all other forms (e.g. води́ть 'lead', вожу́, во́дишь). In current usage there is considerable variation with a large number of verbs in -ить,[1] and there is a tendency

---

[1] The situation is complicated by the fact that derivatives of verbs need not belong to the same class as the verb from which they are derived: thus сади́ть 'seat' has stress alternation, but сади́ться 'sit' does not; води́ть 'lead' does, but руководи́ть 'control' does not. The fullest account of the stress of verbs in -ить is Voroncova (1959), with numerous examples from nineteenth-century and contemporary verse, and the results of surveys.

for verbs without stress alternation to move into the class of verbs with stress alternation. For instance, Grot (1891–5) cites both дарить 'present' and дружить 'be friends' as having only fixed stress, while allowing both fixed and mobile stress with варить 'cook' and грузить 'load'; in current usage all four verbs are found most often with mobile stress, and this change is reflected in most current normative handbooks. The treatment of дружить in normative handbooks is, however, exceptional: *SSRLJa* (1950–65) describes дружишь as *prostorečno*; Avanesov and Ožegov (1959) describe it as 'permissible'; Ožegov (1972) allows both дружишь and дружишь, in that order; while Ageenko and Zarva (1960), usually conservative in their attitude towards the norm, cite only дружишь, without comment. Of the informants in the RJaSO survey (Krysin 1974: 232), 94·4 per cent preferred дружишь.

Revealing light can be thrown on the normativity of various verbs in -ить with mobile stress by examining the qualifications given to forms with mobile stress in Avanesov and Ožegov (1959). For варить, where nineteenth-century usage allowed fixed stress, mobile stress is given without any comment. For дарить, where Grot (1891–5) allows only fixed stress, mobile stress is recommended, and fixed stress qualified as 'archaic'. For грузить, where nineteenth-century usage allowed both fixed and mobile stress, mobile stress is given, but fixed stress is qualified as 'permissible'. For дружить, where Grot allows only fixed stress, fixed stress is recommended and mobile stress 'permissible'; as noted above, current usage overwhelmingly favours mobile stress. For звонить 'ring', only fixed stress is allowed, and mobile stress is specifically condemned; this verb has become something of a shibboleth with normative grammarians, being one of the most often cited examples of a word which is frequently wrongly stressed, although from the informant responses in Kolesov (1967: 109) it is doubtful whether mobile stress is so widespread with this word (141 informants gave звонит, 53 звонит, 11 both forms); some recent dictionaries permit mobile stress, though only as a colloquial form (*SPU* 1971–2; Gorbačevič 1973).

In such verbs, the northern dialects tend to favour fixed stress,[1] the southern dialects mobile stress (Kasvin 1949). As

---

[1] This feature of the northern dialects seems to be an archaism within

generally with stress, the traditional Russian standard is based on the northern dialects, and the changes that have taken place and are taking place in the stressing of verbs in -ить represent southern dialect influence. The role of southern dialect influence is particularly clear here because the effect of this change is to increase the amount of stress alternation within the paradigm, rather than to reduce it, as has been the case in most of the stress changes examined earlier in this chapter. The southern dialect influence has here been a much more potent factor than analogical levelling.[1]

In addition to this geographical difference, there is also a stylistic difference between fixed and mobile stress: learned words tend to have fixed stress, everyday words mobile stress; in Russian Church Slavonic, the usual rule is for fixed stress, following here, as usually with stress, North Russian. Thus we find contrasts like просветить 'shine through' with mobile stress and просветить 'enlighten' with fixed stress,[2] and изменить 'change' with mobile stress but видоизменить 'modify' with fixed stress.[3]

Similar variation is found with present participles active and past participles passive of verbs in -ить, although over-all end-stress is commoner with these forms than with forms of the present tense (perhaps because the former are more learned forms); for examples, see Kolesov (1967: 111–12), Krysin (1974: 232).

The number of verbs in -ить with mobile stress is also being increased to a lesser extent by the shift of a number of verbs which originally had stem-stress in the infinitive into this class

the Slavonic language-area as a whole; the South Slavonic languages have reflexes of a stress pattern more like that of southern Russian dialects here.

[1] The statistics cited in Krysin (1974: 265) show that in general southerners are more likely than northerners to favour mobile stress, though for the examples cited the difference is not particularly significant.

[2] Other forms of these two verbs also show differences between Church Slavonic and native Russian variants: in the sense 'shine through' the first person singular of the future is просвечу, the past participle passive просвеченный, and the imperfective просвечивать; the corresponding forms in the sense 'enlighten' are просвещу, просвещённый, просвещать.

[3] Fixed stress for видоизменить is given by most dictionaries, although Ageenko and Zarva (1960), surprisingly, give only mobile stress.

(Gorbačevič 1974).[1] In the nineteenth century, for instance, the usual stress was у́дить (у́жу, у́дишь) 'fish', whereas nowadays it is удить (ужу́, у́дишь). For a number of verbs where Avanesov and Ožegov (1959) give only stem-stress, end-stress in the infinitive is in fact common in contemporary speech and verse, e.g. пригубить 'take a sip', принудить 'compel', приструнить 'take in hand'. For the verb искриться 'sparkle', the variant искри́ться is qualified as '*prostorečno*' by *SSRLJa* (1950–65) and as 'permissible' by Avanesov and Ožegov (1959); of Gorbačevič's 258 informants (students at Leningrad State University) only 25 gave the traditional stress и́скриться (Gorbačevič 1974: 11).

(ii) *Reflexive verbs*

In the masculine singular past tense, a number of monosyllabic verbs and their derivatives, and also родиться 'be born' (though only in the perfective aspect) have, in accordance with the traditional standard, stress on the reflexive particle, e.g. начался́ 'began', роди́лся́ 'was born', взялся́ 'set to (work)', обня́лся́ 'embraced'. In nineteenth-century literature this stress was in general adhered to, though there are exceptions, as in Puškin's *Евгений Онегин*, I. ii (1823–31):

> Онегин, добрый мой приятель,
> Роди́лся на брегах Невы...

(Onegin, my good friend, was born on the banks of the Neva . . .)

In current usage, many such verbs have lost the possibility, or at least the requirement, of stress on -ся. Thus обня́лся́ is qualified only as 'permissible' by Avanesov and Ožegov (1959), and given by only 20 per cent of the informants in the RJaSO survey (Krysin 1974: 232). Взялся́ is described as archaic by Avanesov and Ožegov (1959), and in the survey reported in Kolesov (1967: 115) 169 informants gave взя́лся, 19 взялся́, and 8 both forms. Avanesov and Ožegov (1959) list both роди́лся

---

[1] This article also notes a small number of verbs which have undergone the reverse change (e.g. current уско́рить 'speed up' for older уско́рить) and a number of other infinitives where the recommendations of normative handbooks do not correspond to current usage, e.g. ржаве́ть 'rust' (ржа́веть common in contemporary speech and verse), балова́ть 'spoil, pamper' (ба́ловать preferred by 195 of Gorbačevič's 247 informants)

and родился (in that order); of Kolesov's informants (1967: 115), 178 gave родился, 12 родился, 8 both forms (though it is not clear whether these informants distinguished in their replies between perfective and imperfective родиться, since the latter has only родился). Only a few verbs still require stress on -ся, e.g. начался (given by 100 of Kolesov's 194 informants as the only possibility, and as a variant by a further 13).

In the feminine singular of such verbs there is no problem, since stress is on the last syllable in both reflexive and non-reflexive forms (e.g. взяла, взялась). With the neuter singular form and plural form, however, a similar stress alternation exists in the traditional standard, with stem-stress in the non-reflexive (e.g. взяло, взяли), but end-stress in the reflexive (взялось, взялись). Change has been much slower here than in the masculine singular, although here too there has been a tendency to lose the stress alternation by having stem-stress in the reflexive form too; many such forms are given in Avanesov and Ožegov (1959), though usually as permissible (дождались 'waited for', придрались 'found fault'), or colloquial variants (напились 'got drunk', создалось 'was created'). From the informant responses quoted in Kolesov (1967: 114) and Krysin (1974: 232) придрались seems much commoner than придрались, дождались somewhat commoner than дождались, напились and напились about equally common, while создалось is preferred to the traditional form создалось by under 20 per cent of those questioned.

Lack of stress alternation in such verbs is again characteristic of the southern dialects (see the statistics in Krysin 1974: 265).

Stress changes in adjective declension (short forms)

(i) *Feminine singular*

Such forms from non-derived adjectives, and also from adjectives with the suffixes -н-, -л-, -к- preceded by a consonant, usually have end-stress. However, a number of suffixed adjectives are exceptional in having stem-stress; for the most part these are more learned adjectives, though in practice the application of this criterion is rather subjective (Gorbačevič 1971: 79–80), e.g. вечна 'eternal', праздна 'idle'. In a number of cases, however, where normative handbooks recommend, as the only or preferred form, end-stress, in current usage one finds stem-stress very frequently, even as the preferred form (Gorbačevič 1971: 79–81). Thus Avanesov and Ožegov (1959) give only склоннá 'inclined', but of the 222 informants polled by Kolesov (1967: 106), 206 gave склóнна, 15 склоннá, and 1 both forms.

(ii) *Plural*

The traditional rule for such forms in Russian is to have the same stress as the neuter singular short form: жáрки 'hot' (cf. жáрко), хорошú 'good' (cf. хорошó). However, many such adjectives, even within a conservative conception of the standard, allow variants with stem-stress and end-stress. Thus for вóльны 'free' and сúльны 'strong' Avanesov and Ožegov (1959) allow both variants (citing the stem-stressed variant first); for бóдры 'cheerful', гóрды 'proud', and прóсты 'simple' the end-stressed variant is allowed as a permissible alternative; while for крýглы 'round', прямы 'straight', тýги 'tight', and хрáбры 'brave' only the stem-stressed form is given; all of these are adjectives where Šapiro (1952) found preference for the end-stressed variant. Similarly, Kolesov (1967: 105) found that his informants preferred end-stress in all cases examined where the normative handbooks allow alternatives, and even in some cases where they do not (e.g. блúзки 'near'); only with стáры 'old', where Avanesov and Ožegov (1959) give старь́ as permissible, was there preference for the older form стáры.

Stress and derivational morphology[1]

(i) *Nouns in* -граф, -лог, -метр[2]

Nouns with these suffixes started entering Russian from French in the eighteenth century. In the earlier period they almost always followed the French stress pattern, with final stress. During the nineteenth century, particularly towards the end of the century, most words of this group transferred to

---

[1] The general problem of variant stresses in derived words is treated by Red'kin (1966).

[2] See further Superanskaja (1968: 147–61).

having penultimate stress, and most of the numerous new creations connected with technological developments were also given penultimate stress. Grot (1891–5) is the first dictionary to list the penultimate stress variants widely.

Nearly all nouns in -граф, whether referring to people or things, have penultimate stress in current usage, e.g. фото́граф 'photographer', авто́граф 'autograph', пара́граф 'paragraph' although there are a few exceptions like телегра́ф 'telegraph'. For some of these words, however, final stress was widespread, if not the rule, in the nineteenth century: nineteenth-century dictionaries give only автогра́ф, and even *SSRLJa* (1950–65) still gives this as an archaic alternative; фоногра́ф 'phonograph' is not noted in the nineteenth-century dictionaries, and twentieth-century dictionaries all give фоно́граф, but L. Tolstoj's pronunciation фоногра́ф is preserved on the record Голоса писателей.[1]

For nouns in -лог, a distinction must be made between those referring to people and others. For those referring to people, the older standard was for final stress (thus Puškin uses филоло́г 'philologist' and физиоло́г 'physiologist'), whereas in contemporary usage and normative handbooks most have penultimate stress, with the exception of космоло́г 'cosmologist', генеало́г 'genealogist', and минерало́г 'mineralogist'.[2] Grot (1891–5) is the earliest dictionary to list penultimate stress as a regular alternative to final stress (though Dal' (1863–86) gives био́лог 'biologist'), and Ušakov (1935–40) still lists some final stresses as alternatives (e.g. метеоро́лог 'meteorologist').

Words in -лог not referring to humans have been subject to the same tendency, though to a lesser extent, and with many words of this class the stress variants go back two hundred years. Thus nineteenth-century and many twentieth-century dictionaries give both диало́г and диа́лог 'dialogue', which latter Avanesov and Ožegov (1959) consider archaic; диа́лог is apparently cultivated by specialists in literature, as also is occasionally моно́лог 'monologue', for which the dictionaries

---

[1] The word is now archaic, having been replaced successively by граммофон, патефон, and проигрыватель.

[2] The last two exceptionally end in -алог, not -олог. Avanesov and Ožegov (1959) warn against the pronunciation минеро́лог; *SAR* (1806–62, the relevant volume having appeared in 1814) gives минера́лог.

allow only моноло́г (Superanskaja 1968: 153).[1] Катало́г
'catalogue' has been subject to similar variation, though here
it is the stress катало́г that is cultivated by librarians; катало́г
is the only form recognized by Avanesov and Ožegov (1959);
the survey cited by Superanskaja (1968: 153) noted overwhelming preference for ката́лог, though of the informants polled by
Kolesov (1967: 108) 99 preferred ката́лог and 98 катало́г.
Некроло́г 'obituary' is another word where Avanesov and
Ožegov (1959) allow only final stress, but where the survey
reported in Superanskaja (1968: 154) shows overwhelming preference (89·5 per cent of informants) for penultimate stress.

Nouns in -метр, excepting those that are measures in the
metric system, have undergone the same general change: thus
термоме́тр 'thermometer' is given in most nineteenth-century
dictionaries as термоме́тр, while modern dictionaries give only
термо́метр. With the names of measures in the metric system,
however, current normative handbooks allow only final stress
(киломе́тр 'kilometre', миллиме́тр 'millimetre'), although
penultimate stress is common in speech. The famous metal-
lurgist and member of the Academy of Sciences I. P. Bardin,
when asked whether one should say киломе́тр or кило́метр,
replied: 'It depends on the time and place. At a meeting of the
Praesidium of the Academy—киломе́тр, otherwise academician
Vinogradov will curl his face up. But at the Novotul'skij factory,
of course, кило́метр, otherwise people will think Bardin is
giving himself airs' (Kostomarov and Leont'ev 1966: 5).

(ii) *Verbs in* -ировать[2]

In current usage, the overwhelming majority of verbs with
this suffix are stressed -и́ровать, although those in -ирова́ть
include many common verbs, and the partition into two classes
is essentially arbitrary. In the nineteenth century there were
far fewer such verbs, and the majority of such verbs that did
exist were stressed on the last syllable. The shift from final to
antepenultimate stress started in the late nineteenth century,
and the many new coinages resulting from technological

[1] With several words, non-standard stresses are cultivated by certain
professional groups, e.g. ко́мпас 'compass' among sailors, хара́ктерный
'characteristic' among actors (Gorbačevič 1973).
[2] See further Voroncova (1967).

developments generally fell in with the newer pattern. Some idea of the change can be gained by looking at the stress given for буксировать 'tow' in various dictionaries: *SCRJa* (1847) gives only буксировáть; Grot (1891–5) gives both stresses, as does Ušakov (1935–40); Avanesov and Ožegov (1959) give only буксúровать, and specifically condemn final stress.[1]

With many verbs in -ировать, there is variation between final and antepenultimate stress in current usage. One such verb is премировать 'award a bonus to', where nearly all dictionaries allow only премировáть (Avanesov and Ožegov (1959) specifically condemn премúровать), although Gorbačevič (1966) notes that in speech it is the antepenultimate stress that predominates. This latter form is admitted as a permissible variant by Rozental' (1964: 120) (but not in earlier editions of this work), *SPU* (1971–2), and Gorbačevič (1973).

---

[1] Occasionally, the past participle passive may retain the earlier stress even when the other forms have changed, e.g. дистиллúровать 'distil', but дистиллирóванный 'distilled'; see the discussion of verbs in -ить earlier in this chapter.

3

MORPHOLOGY

Gender

THE gender of many Russian nouns has changed in the period since 1917. The largest specific group consists of those affected by the change from masculine to common gender—a change motivated by the new roles of Russian women in Soviet society. This phenomenon is of such proportions that we have allotted a separate chapter to it (Chapter 6).

There have been other kinds of gender-change, however, which have, in addition, involved change of declension. Usually, for a time, two variants of the same word have existed simultaneously, belonging to two different genders and two different declensions. But while the lexical meaning of both variants is the same, they are often distinguished stylistically, socially, or functionally. The standardizing pressures operating in the Soviet period have substantially reduced the number of such variant pairs, establishing as correct only one gender or the other.

Among the nouns whose gender has recently changed a prominent place is occupied by borrowings. In many cases their gender had been unstable ever since they were first borrowed and has only recently been stabilized. In particular, a large number of words which in the nineteenth century were found as both feminine and masculine, are now found in only one or other of these two genders.

In 1915 Černyšev published a list of nouns of unstable gender (1915: 119–41), but his notes describing certain variants as *prostorečno*, 'archaic', 'rare', etc., show that in some cases stability was already very close. A large number of his words are given without comment, however, which means, according to his own statement (1915: 123), that both (or all) forms quoted were at that time equally acceptable. They include the following: бакенбард–бакенбарда 'side whisker', бисквит–бисквита 'sponge-cake', ботфорт–ботфорта 'jackboot', брызг–брызга 'splash', валенок–валенка 'felt-boot', вуаль 'veil' (masculine or feminine), глист–глиста 'worm', дрязг–дрязга 'squabble', жар–жара 'heat', желатин–желатина 'gelatine', жираф–жирафа 'giraffe', жниво–жнива 'stubble', зал–зала 'hall', клавиш–клавиша 'key' (piano), манер–манера 'manner', метод–метода 'method', начал–начало 'beginning', ниш–ниша 'niche', овощ–овощь 'vegetable', округ–округа 'region', плевальник–плевальница 'spittoon', поверток–повертка 'turning', пролаз–пролаза 'dodger', прохлад–прохлада 'coolness', псалтырь–псалтирь 'psalter' (both masculine or feminine), рельс–рельса 'rail', рояль 'grand-piano' (masculine or feminine), санаторий–санатория 'sanatorium', ставень–ставня 'shutter', табурет–табуретка 'stool', щиколоток–щиколок–щиколотка–щиколка 'ankle', эполет–эполета 'epaulet', эстафет–эстафета 'relay-race', ярем–ярмо 'yoke', яства–яство 'victuals'.

By the 1930s things had changed considerably, as can be seen from the entries for these words in Ušakov (1935–40), where we frequently find only one of the two (or more) variants given by Černyšev. By omitting their variants Ušakov gives, for example, exclusive approval to the following: бисквит, вуаль (feminine), желатин, жниво, клавиш, начало, ниша, плевальница, прохлада, щиколотка and щиколка, яство.

By this time, moreover, many pairs of variants were no longer equally acceptable. The following forms, though included by Ušakov, are noted as 'archaic': бакенбард, ботфорта, округа, пролаз, рояль (feminine), санатория, эстафет, ярем. Others are described as *prostorečno*: манер (occurring only in fixed phrases), рельса.

Despite the general move towards stability indicated by these examples, there were still many nouns of unstable gender in the 1930s, some of which have since been stabilized. Several of the unstable nouns in Ušakov are recorded in only one gender in subsequent dictionaries such as Ožegov (1972):

Ušakov (1935–40)	Ožegov (1972)
банкнот–банкнота	банкнот
валенка–валенок	валенок
глюкоз–(чаще) глюкоза	глюкоза
жираф–жирафа	жираф
эполет–эполета	эполета
фильм–фильма	фильм

The pace at which gender changes (i.e. at which one variant supplants another) varies considerably. An example of rapid change is provided by the loanword фильма (from English 'film'), which appeared in Russian in the early 1920s and was soon followed by the masculine variant фильм. Both were in use in the 1920s and 1930s, but even by the end of the twenties the masculine form was predominant (Krysin 1968: 85; Gorbačevič 1971: 156–7). Nearly all recent change has tended to reduce the number of variants; the emergence of new forms in the twentieth century has been a rare occurrence. However, an example is provided by стропá 'sling'; in Ušakov (1935–40) and Ožegov (1972) we find only строп, but nowadays both genders are acceptable as standard (Bukčina 1970; Gorbačevič 1973).

The potential scope for instability appears to be particularly great in the case of masculine and feminine nouns whose nominative singular ends in a soft consonant (i.e. soft stem with ø-ending), for here the synthetic manifestations of gender are restricted to certain oblique cases and to the singular. Nevertheless, here too there has been a movement towards greater stability in the twentieth century. For example, госпиталь '(military) hospital', портфель 'briefcase', профиль 'profile', рояль 'grand piano', which in the nineteenth century occurred as either feminine or masculine, are now only masculine. (The change in gender was in some cases linked to change in stress; see Superanskaja 1965a: 48–9.) Formerly feminine табель is now masculine, except in reference to Peter the Great's табель о рангах 'Table of Ranks'. The gender of шампунь 'shampoo', which formerly fluctuated (e.g. in Ušakov 1935–40), has recently been decreed to be masculine (Ljustrova and Skvorcov 1972: 48; Ožegov 1972). The following, on the other hand, have now been stabilized as feminines, although in the nineteenth century they could also occur as masculines: антресоль 'mezzanine', вуаль 'veil', дуэль 'duel', диагональ 'diagonal', кадриль 'quadrille', мигрень 'migraine', модель 'model' (Superanskaja 1965a: 49–50).

In speech, however, nouns may well occur with a gender other than that prescribed officially, as may be seen from the fact that guides to usage find it necessary to emphasize that портфель, рояль, тигр 'tiger', тюль 'curtain lace', шампунь, etc., are not feminine and that бандероль 'wrapper', мигрень, модель, плацкарта 'reservation in sleeping-car', etc., are not masculine. (Masculine плацкарт is in common colloquial use; cf. Jazovickij 1969: 19; Gorbačevič 1973.)

Mention must also be made of the professional specialization of certain gender variants, e.g. компонента 'component' (mathematics, physics, chemistry—Butorin 1969), желатина (photography—Gorbačevič 1973). Although non-specialist dictionaries give only компонент, желатин, the feminine variants are in no way non-standard but simply restricted to specialist use. Спазм–спазма 'spasm' also shows a rudimentary tendency towards professional specialization as masculine (Gorbačevič 1973).

We have so far dealt mainly with changes in the distribution of masculine and feminine genders. Changes affecting the neuter seem to have been relatively few in number. A few indeclinable loanwords which in the nineteenth century might have masculine (e.g. кашне 'scarf', портмоне 'purse', пальто 'overcoat') or feminine (e.g. шоссе 'highway') gender, have subsequently become neuter. After going through a period in the 1920s and 1930s when they could be either masculine or neuter авто 'car', кино 'cinema', радио 'radio', такси 'taxi', метро 'underground railway' have now settled down as neuters, though the non-standard use of такси as masculine is occasionally encountered even nowadays (Krysin 1968: 81; Gorbačevič 1971: 161 n.; Gorbačevič 1973). Instability acknowledged by normative works is still encountered in виски 'whisky' (masculine or neuter) and динамо 'dynamo' (feminine or neuter). Before rushing to the conclusion that the neuter gender has been resistant to change in the Soviet period, however, we should take a look at the generally somewhat unsteady state of this gender. In some dialects it is absent, in others only weakly represented, and it has been argued that even in the standard language it is in the initial stages of corruption (Mučnik 1963a: 55). Statistics prepared by Mučnik underline its weakness (1963a: 57): of the 33,952 nouns in the modern dictionaries examined 15,600 (46 per cent) were found to be masculine, 13,884 (41 per cent) feminine, but only 4,468 (13 per cent) neuter.[1] Even more ominous is the fact that of the post-1914

---

[1] How nouns of common gender were allocated is not stated.

innovations in Ušakov (1935–40) only 10 per cent are neuter. This appears to indicate a state of general decline.

One aspect of the general weakness of the neuter gender is the tendency for recent borrowings which are neuter in standard Russian to acquire other genders in non-standard varieties. But it is not only the neuter that is involved in such divergences from the standard. The loanwords which came pouring into Russian in the early twentieth century have often acquired non-standard genders in the speech of the people. The feminine appears to have been particularly popular, as may be seen from the following examples occurring in the speech of characters in Soviet literature (Mučnik 1963a: 58 n.): броне-поезда (for бронепоезд 'armoured train'), митинга (for митинг 'meeting'), большевизма (for большевизм 'Bolshevism'), социализма (for социализм 'socialism'), литра (for литр 'litre'). Feminines are also well represented among forms recorded in Jaroslavl' *gubernija* in 1925: кила (for кило 'kilo'), емпа (for ЕПО (единое потребительское общество) 'united consumers' society'), закса (for загс 'registry office') (Seliščev 1939: 68–9). There is a general tendency for borrowings in dialects to be feminine whenever the stem ends in a sonant preceded by another consonant (Seliščev 1939: 77). This explains the gender of социализма, механизма, кадра, литра, метра. The tendency of stem-stressed neuters to become feminine (e.g. for повидло 'jam' to be feminine повидла) is a result of *akan'e*.

Gender confusion also occurs over nouns of common gender ending in -a. Although the latter, according to the codified rules, are masculine when they refer to male persons, agreements such as ты такая большая неряха (with неряха 'sloven' applied to a boy) are not uncommon and, though sometimes condemned (Jazovickij 1969: 20–1), are often approved (Gorbačevič 1973: 515), at least in colloquial Russian (Rozental' and Telenkova 1972: 304).

Compared with the state of affairs presented by Černyšev (1915), the number of nouns of unstable gender in the standard language nowadays is small, especially if we restrict the list to those that are really equally acceptable in all respects. As we narrow the list down we tend to find disagreement between the normative authorities, but differences of opinion are minimal viewed in the light of the over-all state of greater stability already reached.

Nevertheless, in Russian schools, the problem of correcting non-standard genders used by pupils remains. It is sometimes discussed by Soviet teachers in their specialist publications. N. N. Ušakov (1957), for example, records mistakes made in written work by pupils from various areas including the *oblasti* of Moscow, Novosibirsk, Gor'kij. Some of the forms are familiar to those who know the history of the words in question: на сковородке жарилась картофель; лицо закрыто вуалем; тела (singular) потеряла гибкость; etc. The fact that Tolstoj and Turgenev treated вуаль as masculine must be disconcerting to the teacher who has to explain that nowadays it is only feminine. Many of the incorrect formations encountered by teachers have never been used in literature, however, and can only be understood from a knowledge of the pupils' local dialect. (On the problems of Russian teaching in areas where the local system differs from the standard, see Tekučëv 1974: 157–72.)

Gender and declension of acronyms and stump-compounds

Our attention so far has been directed to the gender of nouns which were already in existence at the time of the Revolution and also that of a few post-1917 borrowings. The picture has been one of accelerating standardization. We turn now to the question of certain post-1917 innovations which Russian has formed from its own resources.

The gender of stump-compounds[1] has posed no special problems. They acquire the gender appropriate to their form: собес is masculine (though социальное обеспечение 'social security' is neuter), зарплата (заработная плата) 'wages' is feminine, ликбез is masculine (though ликвидация безграмотности 'abolition of illiteracy' is feminine). Acronyms,[1] on the other hand, have introduced new problems to the gender system. Those in which the names of the letters are retained (e.g. МТС [emte'es] (машинно-тракторная станция) 'machine and tractor station', ЦК [tse'ka] (центральный комитет) 'central committee') are indeclinable—just as the names of

[1] For definitions, see p. 100.

letters in other circumstances are indeclinable—and take their gender from the central noun of the phrase for which they stand. Hence, МТС is feminine; ЦК is masculine. Declined forms (e.g. в эмтээсе) are nowadays possible only in non-standard Russian, though in the 1920s they might also be encountered, rarely, in literary usage (Seliščev 1928: 159, 165; Alekseev 1961: 67–8; Mučnik 1964: 168).

It is possible for the other main type of acronym, i.e. that in which the sounds of the letters are pronounced, to take its gender in accordance with the same principle. It is thus possible for ГЭС [ges] (гидроэлектростанция) 'hydro-electric power station' and НОТ [not] (научная организация труда) 'scientific organization of labour' to be feminine, for МИД [m̡it] or [m̡id] (министерство иностранных дел) 'ministry of foreign affairs' to be neuter, and for РОНО [roˈno] (районный отдел народного образования) 'regional department of popular education' to be masculine. There are, however, conflicting tendencies. Conflict arises from the fact that acronyms, having their own morphological propensities, tend to acquire a gender appropriate to their form, and this may be different from the gender of the central noun of the phrase for which they stand. Since acronyms constitute a fair proportion of all Soviet neologisms, the amount of new instability they have introduced (measured in numbers of words) may even outweigh the movement towards stabilization in the gender of other words. For example, ЖЕК [ʒek] (жилищно-эксплуатационная контора) 'housing office', has the appearance of a masculine noun of the same type as дом, стол, etc., and this word is in fact very often used in the same way, being declined ЖЭКа, ЖЭКом, etc. On the other hand, контора is feminine. Consequently, ЖЭК may alternatively be feminine, in which case it is not declinable. This particular word remains unstable to the present day, but many acronyms of this type have stable gender, especially those that were formed during and immediately after the Revolution. At that time new acronyms came into wide use so quickly that often their users had never heard the phrases from which they were derived. In those circumstances gender could be determined only on morphological grounds. Therefore КЕПС [k̡eps] (Комиссия по изучению естественных производственных сил России) 'Commission for the Study of the Natural Productive Forces of Russia', for example, was masculine and declined: Поэтому монографическое изучение, предпринятое КЕПС'ом,[1] более чем своевременно... (*Печать и революция*, 1923, 4: 184). Like many other institutions of the 1920s, КЕПС has long since been defunct and forgotten, but other acronyms of that time have survived and acquired stable gender:

(i) The gender of НЭП (Новая экономическая политика) 'New Economic Policy', which dates from 1921, fluctuated for a year or two between masculine and feminine before settling down as a declined masculine. It is attested (declined) in a letter from Lenin to Molotov dated 23 March 1922 (Panov 1968, 3: 62).

(ii) The word вуз (высшее учебное заведение) 'institution of higher learning' has existed as a declined masculine since the early 1920s. In its early years it was not always declined, however, though non-declension would be impossible nowadays:

Наибольшее число стипендий русским учащимся в В.У.З Германии выдается организацией: ,,Europäische Studentenhilfe''.

(*Печать и революция*, 1923, 2: 262)

Основная цель его — объединение разрозненных действий отдельных ВУЗ'ов, рабфаков и организаций в области издательской деятельности...   (ibid. 3: 304)

In the 1920s there was much inconsistency in the morphology of acronyms. It is not unusual to find discrepancies on one and the same page in publications of that period. Nevertheless, the main tendency then was for acronyms ending in a consonant to become declined masculines.

Declinability is correlated with the question of gender: the declension of feminines or neuters ending in a hard consonant would conflict with the existing declensional system. It is said that there are certain acronyms which must be feminine because of the gender of the underlying phrase and that to treat them as masculines (and thus to decline them) is *prostorečno* (see Gorbačevič 1971: 164, and particular entries in Gorbačevič 1973). This is true, for example, of ГЭС (гидроэлектростанция) 'hydro-electric station', and ООН (Организация объединен-

---

[1] In quotations from sources of the 1920s we reproduce the apostrophe and full stop used with acronyms (cf. p. 212).

ных наций) 'United Nations Organization'. Despite the efforts of editors and language planners to establish order, however, disorder persists. A new case is that of the name for the Pacific railway link, now under construction—Байкало-Амурская магистраль 'Bajkal-Amur main-line'—abbreviated as БАМ [bam]. Despite the fact that магистраль is feminine, БАМ is usually masculine and declined. But in *Вечерняя Москва* for 28 September 1974 we find, in addition to declined forms, the following: Москвичи призывают отлично обслуживать стройки БАМ.

The only type which cannot, whatever its gender, decline (in standard Russian) is that ending in a vowel, e.g. РОНО (see above), ГАИ (Государственная автомобильная инспекция) 'state automobile inspection', including a few of a mixed type composed of both syllables and initials such as сельпо (сельское потребительское общество) 'village consumers' society' (real meaning 'village shop'), самбо (самозащита без оружия) 'unarmed self-defence'. Despite their absolute indeclinability, however, there is much uncertainty as to gender: РОНО fluctuates between masculine and neuter, ГАИ and самбо between feminine and neuter.

These problems have evolved, together with the acronyms themselves, in the Soviet period, and there are no signs of any language planning initiative to settle them. There is not even consistency between various normative works. For example, НОТ (see above) is masculine in Ušakov (1935–40) and Ožegov (1972), but feminine, or 'colloquially' masculine, according to Gorbačevič (1973).

Particularly significant is the fact that even acronyms which by either criterion are masculine (like МХАТ (Московский Художественный академический театр) 'Moscow Arts Theatre', СЭВ (Совет экономической взаимопомощи) 'Council of Economic Mutual Aid', ОВИР (отдел виз и регистрации иностранцев) 'aliens office') frequently appear undeclined both in print and in standard speech. It is surmised that they would be declined even less in print, were it not for the vigilance of editors (Panov 1968, 3: 63). However, the fact that non-declension has now been given a degree of official approval (Gorbačevič 1973: 516–17 and entry under СЭВ) means that editors, too, are now less likely to insist on declension.

The appearance of a class of words of masculine gender fitting the masculine declension pattern yet not declined is a development with serious implications. It is best interpreted as a form of hyper-correction (comparable to the non-declension of эхо—see pp. 84–5). There will always be a tendency for all acronyms ending in a consonant to be treated equally, owing to their paradigmatic relationships.

Indeclinable nouns

The most distinctive feature of grammatical change in Soviet times has been the growth of analyticity—the increasing tendency for the grammatical meaning of words to be expressed by their context rather than their form. An obvious aspect of this tendency is the growth of indeclinability among nouns. With the increase in the number of indeclinable nouns since the Revolution growing account has to be taken of them in describing the morphological system. In the nineteenth century they were so few in number as to be merely peripheral to the system as a whole. That is now no longer the case.

A large proportion of indeclinables are borrowings of neuter gender, like депо 'depot', фото 'photo', бюро 'office, bureau', пальто 'overcoat', which have nothing in their structure to prevent them being declined, as may be demonstrated by comparing them with such declined nouns as вино 'wine', нутро 'interior', лето 'summer'. Their non-declension is a convention. Some, but not many, were borrowed as long ago as the eighteenth century, including депо and бюро. The habit of not declining them grew up in the first half of the nineteenth century among the upper class, but declined forms too, such as на бюре, на фортепиане are attested from that period (Bulaxovskij 1954: 81). Only certain members of the intelligentsia and upper class, owing to their knowledge of Western languages, were conscious of the foreign origin of these words, and it was only in upper-class circles that they were not declined (Kudrjavskij 1912: 93, quoted Panov 1968, 3: 49; Karcevskij 1923: 55; Superanskaja 1965b: 119). But even the educated strata did not consistently observe non-declension (Černyšev 1915: 116). Even as late as 1934 N. S. Trubeckoj (born Moscow 1890, emigrated 1919) stated that for his generation (and, presumably, for his class) declension was normal though 'somewhat *prostorečno*' (Trubeckoj 1934: 37, quoted Mučnik 1964: 164).

The vast majority of the population were ignorant of the Western languages from which these words came, and, on the rare occasions when they knew and used such words, they declined them. At the time of the Revolution non-declension of neuter loanwords had acquired prestige among the ruling class, but to the illiterate masses it was unknown or (if known) incomprehensible. It would therefore have been quite possible in the early years of Soviet power to codify declension of these words as standard, approximating Russian practice to that of most other Slavonic languages. Only a small minority of the population would have been offended.

After 1917, however, non-declension continued its progress under the impetus of the pre-Revolutionary prestige structure. And so, when in the 1960s, as part of the RJaSO project, a survey was carried out in which 1,500 Russians were asked: 'Do you accept the possibility of declining . . . nouns . . . of the type пальто, депо?' only 3 per cent said 'Yes'. The actual text of the replies received indicates that most of the informants were quite indignant at the thought of declining (Panov 1968, 3: 50–5).

Nevertheless, declined forms of these words may still be heard in Russia, though more commonly in the country than in the towns. (We are, of course, not speaking of their use by speakers of standard Russian for humorous or ironic effect.) The assumption made in Panov (1968, 3: 50) that even the 3 per cent who said 'Yes' do not actually use declined forms tells us more about the social make-up of the sample than about the survival of declension among the population as a whole. In any case, the RJaSO survey was not aimed at non-standard Russian.

Mučnik draws the following conclusions from the survey: 'In the modern Russian language без ведро and без пальта are to an equal degree impermissible infringements of the grammatical norms' (Panov 1968, 3: 55). But there is, in fact, an important difference, for без ведро is not recognizable as any kind of utterance known to the Russian speech community. There is no question as to whether ведро is declinable or not (and no surveys have been thought necessary to test public opinion on that point). On the other hand, the question whether пальто (and other similar neuters) should decline or not is a real one, for declined forms, though non-standard, do occur, however much displeasure they may cause (Čukovskij 1963: 23–7; Timofeev 1963: 158–60). They occur, moreover, in literature, both in the speech of characters (to convey social information) and (rarely) for expressiveness in the author's own words (Mučnik 1964: 178). The indeclinable plural бигуди 'curlers' shows a tendency to decline, even in print, e.g. бессонная ночь с бигудями на голове 'a sleepless night with your hair in curlers' (quoted from a provincial newspaper by «Заметки крохобора», 1976).

We have so far considered only those indeclinable borrowings whose structure is such that they might decline but for the prescriptive rule which says they may not. There are also some borrowings which simply do not fit into the Russian morphological system, such as такси 'taxi', рагу 'ragout', конферансье 'master of ceremonies', мадам 'madam', виски 'whisky', меню 'menu'. There are some which are placed outside the system by their stress only, e.g. ателье 'studio, workshop', желе 'jelly', портмоне 'purse'. (Declined soft-stem neuters, except those ending in -ьё, are virtually all stem-stressed in the singular.)[1] In the nineteenth century and earlier, loanwords which did not immediately fit into the system were adapted to make declension possible, producing such forms as желей (masculine), мадама (feminine) (Černyšev 1915: 116–17). The same, or similar, processes operated, and probably continue to operate, in non-standard varieties, but there is a dearth of information on what happens to indeclinables in non-standard Russian, apart from the fact that the пальто type declines like other neuters. Panov (1968) and Mučnik (1964) only give examples from fiction and poetry, including бюро, пианино, and танго as declined feminines, такси declined as a plural, etc.

The emphasis on non-declension has had an interesting secondary effect on the morphology of эхо 'echo', which, in the singular, was until recently nearly always declined. In recent times (contrary to the advice of dictionaries) it has

[1] Such exceptions as житиé, бытиé are very distinctly Church Slavonic.

shown a tendency not to decline (Panov 1968, 3: 47 n.; Vomperskij 1964). The results of hyper-correction are also seen in the non-declension of declinable acronyms (see p. 81) and in reluctance in scientific texts and the press to decline new technical terms and personal names (Superanskaja 1965*b*: 119). Planned language change (i.e. the decision taken by nine-teenth-century grammarians not to decline the пальто type) has led to new planning problems. Mučnik appositely describes indeclinables as 'an open flank in the Russian declensional system (which on the whole is synthetic) for the penetration of analytical elements' (Panov 1968, 3: 45).

Another case of hyper-correct non-declension is that of the word товарищ when used as a woman's title, e.g. говорят о товарищ Яковлевой. This usage is condemned by normative works (e.g. Jazovickij 1969: 94–6), but is encountered in both speech and writing. According to some informants, other titles such as профессор, when applied to women, are also occasion-ally affected in the same way in speech.

Declension of personal names

The majority of Russians have surnames which in their masculine nominative singular form end in -ов, -ев, -ин, or -ский and are therefore consistently declined according to established paradigms. In the use of most other surname types, however, there is considerable inconsistency. This affects the names of some Russians, other Soviet citizens, and foreigners. Theoretically, all names which fit into the morphological system are capable of being declined, but in practice they are sometimes undeclined. Resistance to declension is particularly strong among bearers of surnames which have appellative homonyms, e.g. Жук (жук 'beetle'), Крыса (крыса 'rat'), and, being motivated by the desire to distinguish the name from the appellative, is accepted by some guides to usage (Ljustrova and Skvorcov 1972: 55). However, the non-declension of various other declinable names may sometimes be seen, especially in the press, e.g. ...наградил Коровкевич Николая Владими-ровича (*Вечерняя Москва*, 6 October 1954). But it is a practice that is censured by (among others) Superanskaja (1965*b*: 121, whence this example is taken). A reader's letter to *RR* (1967,

4: 85) drew attention to the inscription Академику Вильямс В. Р. on a monument in Moscow—an error which would logically lead to the erroneous conclusion that Vil'jams was a woman. On the other hand, there is a firmly established tradition of not declining French surnames ending in -á, such as Дюма́ 'Dumas', Золя́ 'Zola', etc., and despite the fact that there is nothing in their form to prevent declension this is approved.

The question of inconsistencies in the declension of surnames (of which a good over-all view is given by Superanskaja 1965*b*) cannot be overlooked in the general discussion of increasing analyticity. Particular attention must be given to the surnames of Ukrainian origin ending in the suffixes -ко and -енко. There are three possible declension patterns: (i) like neuters ending in -o (as in Ukrainian), (ii) like feminines and masculines ending in -a (the result of *akan'e*, though those with stressed ending such as Франко́ are included), (iii) undeclined. Type (i) is rarest and although used, for example, by Čexov in *Дуэль* (1891), was already considered abnormal by Černyšev (1915: 85–7). The main problem, both in Černyšev's time and subsequently, has been fluctuation between declension and non-declension, and although he considered either expedient acceptable, prescriptive works have sometimes insisted on declension. The RJaSO survey conducted in the 1960s showed an overwhelming majority (about 95 per cent) in favour of non-declension, increasing from approximately 90 per cent in the oldest age-group to approximately 96 per cent in the youngest. The breakdown by profession showed more resistance among writers and journalists (11 per cent favouring declension) than in any other professional group (Krysin 1974: 194–6). Although these figures are based not on objective observation but on the subjects' assessment of their own behaviour, they cast serious doubt on Superanskaja's assertion that the declined forms are colloquial and the undeclined forms characteristic of the official style (Superanskaja 1965*b*: 126–7). Officialdom's preference for undeclined forms (both of these and of all types of name whose declension might lead to muddle) is well known and understandable. Owing to the difficulty or impossibility of deducing the nominative from an oblique case, it is only reasonable to use undeclined forms of unusual names in official

documents. But the tendency not to decline names ending in
-ко, -енко appears to be general.

Declension of place-names

With the exception of those ending in -о, such as Глазго
'Glasgow', Токио 'Tokyo', Сан-Франциско 'San Francisco',
foreign place-names are traditionally regarded as declinable if
they conform to the existing declension patterns. Non-declension
incurs disapproval, but in the case of certain morphological
types it is quite clearly increasing (Kalakuckaja 1970: 233–42).

Among Russian place-names those with the suffixes -ово,
-ево, -ино, such as Шереметьево, Щелково, Пушкино, behave
inconsistently, but it is only in Soviet times that they have
developed a tendency not to decline. Černyšev remarks on
certain particularities of such names, but does not mention
the possibility of not declining them (1915: 185). Instructions
issued by the authorities during the Second World War for-
bidding the declension of place-names in dispatches and documents to avoid confusion left a deep and lasting effect. During
the war undeclined forms were used in the press (Mirtov 1953:
105), and although normative works did not accept it, the
tendency not to decline them grew.[1]

The survey conducted by the RJaSO team to test the preferences of Russians on this point produced figures of 31·9 per
cent in favour of non-declension and 61·9 per cent in favour
of declension. These figures relate to test sentences including
the names Большево and Щелково. In the case of the place-
name Пушкино, however, 72 per cent favoured non-declension.
All the names tested showed increasing support for non-
declension in each succeeding age-group, so that whereas, for
example, only 27·2 per cent of the age-group born before 1909
used the undeclined dative of Щелково, it was used by 39·5 per
cent of those born after 1939 (Panov 1968, 3: 60–1). These
figures show the rapid growth of a feature which before the
Revolution was unknown and which, until recently, was rejected by all normative works. The 1970 Academy Grammar

[1] For non-declension of place-names when accompanied by a generic
appelation in apposition, e.g. город Москва, see pp. 113 ff.

acknowledges the tendency of such names to be undeclined (Švedova 1970: 377).

Changes in case endings

(i) *Masculine genitive singular*

The principal function of the morpheme -у in the masculine genitive singular is to indicate the partitive, e.g. ...две чайные ложки сахару; дайте нарзану! But it is also used in certain other contexts, e.g. из лесу, со страху, ни разу. In 1915 Černyšev observed that -а was replacing -у (1915: 27), and during the Soviet period this tendency has continued. The use of -у has become increasingly rare, and some instances in nineteenth-century literature would not be acceptable in present-day Russian, e.g. болит от морозу лоб (Gogol', *Шинель*; quoted in Gorbačevič 1971: 171). Even by Černyšev's day there was much fluctuation, and there are today many environments where -а is acceptable, but would not have been in the nineteenth century. Despite the decline of this distinction popular normative guides continue to insist on its observation (Jazovickij 1969: 21–2; Gorbačevič 1971: 172 n.).

Statistical analysis of texts of various kinds shows a rapid falling off of -у forms among partitive genitives between 1900 and the 1960s (Panov 1968, 3: 177–200). General decline, but at a slower rate, is indicated by the results of a self-assessing survey, although comparison of the survey data with that collected by objective observation of the forms used by customers in food shops suggests that some Russians may consciously prefer -а forms yet unconsciously use -у (Panov 1968, 3: 190–200; Graudina 1966).

In addition to partitives, texts from the early twentieth century contain prepositional constructions such as для запаху, вместо сахару, до пару. This type was described by Černyšev, though he already regarded the -у genitive with для and у as archaic (1915: 20). By the 1930s such constructions had disappeared (Panov 1968, 3: 182).

Even in fixed phrases -а is replacing -у, so that nowadays we encounter both без спору and без спора 'indisputably', со страху and со страха 'from fear', etc. The -у type is most stubborn of all in partitive constructions with diminutives, e.g. хотите чайку? 'Would you like some tea?' (from чаёк diminutive of чай 'tea'). Чаёк is one of a small and dwindling number of words which as yet cannot take their partitive genitive in -a (Gorbačevič 1973: 512).

(ii) *Masculine prepositional singular*

The prepositional singular ending for the majority of masculine nouns is -e, but after the prepositions в and на certain masculines take the ending -ý (always stressed), e.g. в углý 'in the corner', на берегý 'on the bank'. There are also some nouns which after these prepositions may take either -e or -ý.

Some of the words which at the beginning of the twentieth century could take either ending can now take only one or the other. There has been a movement towards greater uniformity, as may be seen by comparing the words quoted by Černyšev as taking either ending (1915: 30–3) with those in modern guides to usage (such as Gorbačevič 1973). Whereas at the time of the First World War ад 'hell', берег 'bank', год 'year', дым 'smoke', лес 'forest', остров 'island', сад 'garden', снег 'snow', угол 'corner' (among others) could take either -e or -y (though in most cases one was already more common than the other), the present-day standard is: в аду, на берегу, в году, в дыму, в лесу, на острове, в саду, в снегу, в углу.

Not surprisingly, some of the words which were unstable in 1915 are still unstable, e.g. в отпуске and в отпуску 'on leave' are both acceptable still. Sometimes there is disagreement as to the present standard: the information on порт 'port' and пруд 'pond', for example, in Gorbačevič (1971: 176) and Gorbačevič (1973) is conflicting. Even new instability has arisen in a few cases: в цехе and в цеху 'in the shop', в мёде and в меду 'in honey' (formerly only в цехе, в меду).

The RJaSO survey included the prepositional singular of мед, отпуск, снег, and цех, and recorded that (in locative contexts) almost no one favoured в снеге (less than 3 per cent). The picture produced by the other words shows, broadly speaking, that the younger the speakers the less likely they are to use the -ý forms (Krysin 1974: 177, 250).

(iii) *Masculine nominative plural*

Continuing a tendency from the nineteenth century, the number of nouns with nominative plural in -á has increased still further. Among the words which Černyšev quotes as taking either -ы or -á in the nominative plural are: дирекtор 'director', инспектор 'inspector', закром 'corn-bin', округ 'region', провод 'wire', профессор 'professor', сорт 'sort', том 'volume' (1915: 63).[1] Ožegov (1972) gives only: директора, инспектора, закрома, округа, провода, профессора, сорта, тома.

Some of the -á plurals already known to Černyšev, however, such as офицера 'officers', консула 'consuls', лектора 'lecturers', are still not accepted in standard Russian. On the other hand, certain forms not even mentioned by him are now approved: бухгалтера 'book-keepers' (colloquial still, but *prostorečno* in the 1930s), лагеря 'camps' (semantically distinguished from лагери 'camps' in the ideological sense). Many further plurals in -á have appeared but remained non-standard: выбора 'elections', инженера 'engineers', etc.

As in the nineteenth century, plurals in -á are particularly characteristic of professional varieties (Ivanova 1967: 64). Professional plurals include: торта 'cakes' (used by confectioners),[2] плана 'plans' (used by draughtsmen), супа 'soups' (used in the catering trade) (Čukovskij 1963: 14). The nautical terms боцмана 'boatswains', лоцмана 'pilots', штурмана 'navigation officers', etc., are non-standard in non-nautical use, but in the Soviet Navy are officially codified (Ivanova 1967: 65; Suleržickie 1967: 69). Further evidence of the professional specialization of the -á type is provided by the RJaSO survey, which shows that while the greatest over-all tendency to use these forms is exhibited by industrial workers, it is the white-collar workers who most favour бухгалтера 'book-keepers' and инспектора 'inspectors'. Most significant of all, perhaps, is the fact that journalists and writers, though over all less likely than any other social category to use these forms as a whole, are more likely than any other category to use the form редактора 'editors' (Krysin 1974: 186, 251).

Despite the efforts of these same editors to regulate the nominative plural in -á, it continues to expand at the expense

[1] Černyšev already regarded these -ы forms as archaic and advocated their replacement.

[2] A group of confectionary workers from various parts of the U.S.S.R. who visited Nottingham in September 1968 referred to themselves as кондитера (non-standard). (Personal observation by G. Stone.)

of the -ы type. Two examples of rapid change are the twentieth-century loanwords трактор 'tractor' and бункер 'bunker', whose plurals in the 1930s were still тракторы and бункеры (Ušakov 1935–40). Ožegov (1972) gives both трактора and тракторы, but only бункера. The RJaSO survey shows that the younger the speakers the more likely they are to prefer трактора (Krysin 1974: 251). However, this word is not typical of the survey as a whole, which shows varying tendencies. Though the general statement holds good that the number of words with nominative plural in -á is growing, some of the words surveyed (инспектор, кондуктор 'conductor', прожектор 'searchlight', редактор, сектор 'sector', слесарь 'locksmith', токарь 'turner') show a decreasing propensity to take -á in each succeeding age-group.

(iv) *Genitive plural*

A number of masculine nouns which in the nineteenth century formed their genitive plural in -ов, now take the zero ending. The following semantic categories are affected:

(*a*) Fruit and vegetables, e.g. помидор 'tomato', апельсин 'orange'.
(*b*) Units of measurement, e.g. грамм 'gram', вольт 'volt'.
(*c*) Members of human groups, including nationalities (e.g. грузин 'Georgian') and military units (e.g. драгун 'dragoon').
(*d*) Objects occurring mostly in pairs, e.g. носок 'sock', сапог 'boot'.

Černyšev gives a list of twenty-seven words which in his time took the zero ending, and eleven more for which he considered zero archaic. They include no fruit or vegetables. However, observations carried out in Russian shops in 1962–3 showed that the zero forms predominated overwhelmingly in the case of абрикос 'apricot', апельсин 'orange', баклажан 'aubergine', гранат 'pomegranate', мандарин 'tangerine', помидор 'tomato'. Not a single instance of апельсинов or баклажанов was recorded. Only in the case of банан 'banana' was the balance different: 33 instances were recorded of бананов, 11 of банан. Answers to the RJaSO questionnaire on апельсин, баклажан, мандарин, and помидор confirm a general preference, but with smaller majorities, for the zero ending (Panov 1968, 3: 82–3).

Some units of measurement, especially electrical units such

as вольт 'volt', ампер 'ampere', ватт 'watt', and ом 'ohm', had already acquired stable genitive plurals with zero ending by the first decade of the twentieth century (Graudina 1964*b*: 217). A few, however, are still unstable. It seems that граммов and килограммов never occur in speech, but owing to the insistence of normative works they are commonly used in writing (Panov 1968, 3: 80–1). The treatment of гектар 'hectare' is similar.

The movement towards the zero ending among names of members of human groups is extremely slow and irregular. Although грузинов, for example, is not acknowledged by Ušakov (1935–40) or Ožegov (1972), the RJaSO survey conducted in the 1960s showed that over 20 per cent of subjects born in the 1940s still preferred it. Башкиров, though admitted by Ušakov (1935–40) and preferred by nearly 38 per cent of subjects born in the 1940s, is rejected by Ožegov (1972) and Gorbačevič (1973). Партизанов, which was still accepted by Ušakov (1935–40), is described as 'archaic' by Gorbačevič (1973). The other military terms are nearly all historicisms.[1] A statistical analysis of 65 ethnonyms in written sources from the 1890s to the 1950s—mostly of very low frequency and therefore low stability—shows a small over-all increase (6·2 per cent) of zero forms (Panov 1968, 3: 73–9; Graudina 1964*a*: 199–206).

The paired objects сапоги 'boots', валенки 'felt boots', носки 'socks', чулки 'stockings' also exhibit a gradual movement towards the zero ending. In the nineteenth century they could all take their genitive plural in -ов, though the zero form also occurred. The -ов forms survived into the Soviet period and, for a time, they were still recognized as standard. But at the present time only носков survives. The RJaSO survey shows a growing preference for genitive plural носок among the younger informants. The recent (post-1930s) loanwords кеды 'plimsolls' and гольфы 'long socks' tend to follow the same pattern (Panov 1968, 3: 81–2).

Change in the genitive plural of feminine nouns has been restricted to those of the first declension whose stems end in soft or palatal consonants, some of which can take the ending -ей.

---

[1] Кадет had ø in the meaning 'cadet' but (usually) -ов in the meaning 'Constitutional-Democrat'. The military and political meanings were sometimes confused, however (Jakobson 1921: 30; Karcevskij 1923: 21).

The general tendency is for -ей to be replaced by a zero ending. Some of the -ей forms, such as пустыней, бурей, каплей (genitive plural of пустыня 'desert', буря 'storm', капля 'drop'), though used in the nineteenth century, were already archaic by the early twentieth century (Černyšev 1915: 97). Among the nouns for which -ей was still acceptable then but is now archaic are: петля 'loop', сплетня 'gossip'. On the other hand, the zero genitive of свеча 'candle', having been approved by normative works until the 1950s, has now been replaced by свечей (Gorbačevič 1971: 193–5).

Until the time of the First World War the neuter плечо 'shoulder' also took either -ей or zero in the genitive plural, but in the Soviet period плечей soon became archaic. Among certain neuters with nominative singular in -ье such as кушанье 'food, dish', поместье 'estate', платье 'dress', угодье 'fertile land', устье 'mouth' (of river), there was vacillation between -ьев and -ий in the genitive plural until the early twentieth century. In the case of all the words quoted, Černyšev regarded both variants as acceptable, but by the 1930s кушаний, поместий, угодий, on the one hand, and платьев, устьев, on the other, were established as the only correct forms. The masculine подмастерье 'apprentice' showed similar instability before 1917, but since then the variant подмастерьев has ousted подмастерий.

(v) *Instrumental plural*

Certain instrumental plurals in -ьми which early in the present century were still acceptable (Černyšev 1915: 79–80, 95) are now archaic or defunct, viz. зверьми (зверь 'animal'), плетьми (плеть 'lash'), сетьми (сеть 'net'), свечьми (свеча 'candle'). Only дети 'children', люди 'people'. дверь 'door', дочь 'daughter', and лошадь 'horse' may now take instrumental plural in -ьми (Vinogradov *et al.* 1960, 1: 170; Švedova 1970: 385). In addition, дверями, дочерями, лошадями are permissible according to the Academy Grammar (Švedova 1970: 385), though the latter two are described as *prostorečno* by Gorbačevič (1973). There are minor areas of disagreement between the normative authorities in their evaluation of -ьми forms, but all are agreed that людями and детями are as yet non-standard (Jazovickij 1969: 24).

(vi) *Vocative*

Nouns, particularly names, ending in unstressed -a/-я have developed a special form with zero ending used in address, especially to attract the hearer's attention. Instead of Нина, Коля, мама, etc. the forms Нин! Коль! мам!, etc., are used. Composite address forms such as дядь Петь! (from дядя Петя), Никит Петрович! (from Никита Петрович) are equally affected, and there is at least one plural: ребят! (from ребята 'lads'). Especially common is the duplicated type Коль, а Коль! Such forms are used by speakers of standard Russian, but they are colloquial (Bolla *et al.* 1970: 558; Zemskaja 1973: 157; Superanskaja 1973: 230). They were in existence before 1917 (Vinogradov *et al.* 1960, 2, 2: 125), but it seems likely that their use has increased in the last half century.

Adjectives

(i) *Hard or soft*

A few adjectives which in the nineteenth century could have either hard or soft stems (e.g. давный/давний 'of long ago', дальный/дальний 'distant')[1] now belong exclusively to the soft type. Generally speaking, the hard variants were already defunct by the early twentieth century (Černyšev 1915: 163–6), but a few cases of instability survived into the Soviet era, e.g. бескрайный/-ий 'boundless', междугородный/-ий 'intertown', искренный/-ий 'sincere'. Since the 1930s искренний and бескрайний on the one hand, and междугородный on the other, have tended to predominate. Related to this is the tendency for the soft adverbs внутренне and искренне to replace внутренно and искренно (Gorbačevič 1971: 199–201).

(ii) *Indeclinable adjectives*

Since before the Revolution Russian has had indeclinable adjectives, such as бордо 'claret, deep red', but only in Soviet times have they become numerically important enough to be treated as a grammatical category (Šmeleva 1966: 27; Panov 1968, 3: 105 ff.). Even so the Academy Grammars have given

---

[1] The variant дальный belonged to the OM pronunciation (Timofeev 1963: 212).

them scant attention. We now have such noun phrases as часы пик 'rush hour', платье беж 'beige dress', стиль модерн 'modern style', коми язык 'Komi language', in which only the noun is inflected according to case and number. The view is also held that units such as гор- 'town', гос- 'state', парт- 'party', used in stump-compounds, e.g. горсовет 'town council', партбилет 'party card', are really invariable adjectives (Panov 1968, 3: 120).

(iii) *Possessive adjectives*

Possessive adjectives ending in -ов/-ев and -ин may, according to prescriptive grammars, take short or long case endings in the genitive and dative masculine and neuter singular. For example, старухин 'old woman's', may decline as старухина or старухиного in the genitive, and as старухину or старухиному in the dative. Such adjectives, which may be derived from animates only (principally persons), are in any case stylistically restricted and of low frequency in the written standard.

Even in the nineteenth century the long forms were already in use in literature, and Černyšev, although he considered them incorrect, quoted a number of examples from well-known writers (1915: 183). Since then the short forms have become ever rarer, until today only the long forms can be regarded as normal (Gorbačevič 1971: 202).

Numerals

Černyšev was aware of a general tendency for cardinal numerals not always to decline as required by the normative rules (1915: 196), a fact which appears to have disturbed him very little. The tendency not to decline numerals, which is known to some Russian dialects, increased during the Second World War, fostered to some extent, apparently, by officialdom (Mirtov 1953: 105). Non-declension is especially common among mathematicians (Panov 1968, 3: 88–9). In general, normative works still insist on declension, except in the case of compound numerals, which colloquially may be declined only partially. Usually the last element only is declined in colloquial Russian, e.g. с шестьсот семьдесят двумя иллюстрациями 'with six hundred and seventy-two illustrations', but in more formal styles the whole numeral is declined (Vinogradov *et al.* 1960, 1: 369; Rozental' and Telenkova 1972: 210). (See also pp. 107–8.)

Verbs

(i) *Present stem*

Certain first conjugation verbs of the non-productive type which contains the vowel -a in the infinitive but loses it in the present tense (such as писать 'to write', пишу, пишешь, etc.) have acquired variant present tenses formed by analogy with the productive type which retains the vowel (e.g. знать 'to know', знаю, знаешь, etc.). They include the following:

алкать	'crave'	мурлыкать	'purr'
брызгать	'splash'	мыкать	'live miserably'
двигать	'move'	плескать	'splash'
капать	'drip'	полоскать(ся)	'rinse'
колыхать(ся)	'sway'	прыскать(ся)	'sprinkle'
крапать	'drip'	рыскать	'roam'
кудахтать	'cackle'	тыкать(ся)	'poke'
махать	'wave'	хлестать	'lash'
жаждать	'thirst'	хныкать	'whimper'
метать(ся)	'throw'	щипать(ся)	'pinch'
(reflexive: 'rush about')			

An investigation carried out in 1948 led to the conclusion that there was preference for the unproductive variants, even where the dictionaries indicated a movement towards the new type (Istrina 1948: 8–11). Long before this, however, Černyšev had indicated that for a number of these verbs he regarded both types as equally acceptable, including the following: капать, колыхать, кудахтать, махать, мурлыкать, мыкать, мяукать 'mew', плескать, полоскать, прыскать, стонать 'moan' (1915: 294–8). Since then certain variants have ceased to be acceptable, and this can be seen from the discriminations made in Soviet dictionaries. Ožegov (1972), for example, describes каплю, мычу, стонаю as archaic; махаю, мурлыкаю, плескаю, полоскаю as colloquial; and does not even acknowledge the existence of колыхаю, кудахтаю, мяучу, прыщу.

The RJaSO survey in the 1960s included questions on колыхаться, махать, брызгать, капать, and showed a growing

preference for the productive type in each succeeding generation. But (except for капает, which was supported by a majority
in all age-groups) only a minority favoured the new type, even
in the youngest age-group (Krysin 1974: 203).

(ii) *Past stem*

A number of verbs with infinitives in -нуть have two possible
forms in the past tense and past participle, e.g. умолкнуть 'fall
silent' can have умолк or умолкнул, and умолкший or умолк-
нувший. Other verbs of this type are: избегнуть 'avoid',
прибегнуть 'resort (to)', сохнуть 'dry', меркнуть 'fade',
глохнуть 'die away', достигнуть 'reach', хрипнуть 'become
hoarse', гибнуть 'perish', вторгнуться 'invade', виснуть 'hang'.
The recommendations of dictionaries are inconsistent, but there
appears to be a tendency to describe as archaic several -ну-
variants which in reality are still in use. For example, сохнул,
умолкнул, and померкнул are given as archaic in Ušakov
(1935–40), but quoted without comment in Ožegov (1972).
Some of the variants in -ну- approved by Černyšev (1915:
244–7) are now quite definitely obsolete, such as исчезнул
'disappeared', зябнул 'shivered', but quite a number are still
in use, albeit rarely in some cases.

(iii) *Biaspectual verbs*

The majority of biaspectual verbs are either borrowings or
have been derived from borrowed elements, e.g. атаковать
'attack', организовать 'organize'. Because problems of communication arise (мы атакуем, for example, may mean 'we
shall attack' or 'we are attacking'), there has been a tendency
to treat the simple verb as imperfective only and create a new
perfective by means of a prefix, e.g. заатаковать. Alternatively,
the simple verb may be treated as only perfective, in which
case a secondary imperfective is produced by suffixation, e.g.
атаковывать. The problem existed before the Revolution
(Černyšev 1915: 226 ff.), and the high degree of instability
which now exists is reflected in the disagreement between
various normative works in their classification of such verbs.
As a rule, the secondary formations are not easily accepted as
standard (e.g. заатаковать, использовывать 'make use of'
are non-standard), but there are several recent formations

which have been given approval (e.g. отредактировать 'edit', сорганизовать) (Mučnik 1961; Gorbačevič 1971: 218–23).

Word formation

(i) *Productivity of suffixes*

The deverbative suffixes -льщик and -щик (-чик), which in the nineteenth century could form only nouns meaning persons, now show a tendency to form nouns meaning things too, e.g. зондировщик (1957) 'aeroplane for probing the atmosphere'. (This is to be distinguished from the process of resemanticization producing, for example, счетчик 'meter' from счетчик 'teller'.) Also -тель, formerly used to form nouns referring to either persons or things, shows an increasing ability to form those meaning things (Panov 1968, 2: 170–90).

From the time of the Revolution onwards the suffix -ка has been extremely productive, forming nouns from both verbs and adjectives, e.g. буденовка 'Red Army helmet', семилетка 'seven-year school', пятилетка 'five-year plan', обезличка 'lack of personal responsibility', уравниловка 'wage-levelling', неувязка 'lack of co-ordination'. Though it had been in use long before the Revolution, this suffix appears to have been at its most active in non-standard varieties, especially the speech of students (Seliščev 1928: 175). Its extended representation in the standard language stems from the general readjustment of social and functional varieties resulting from changes in the structure of social control. Many -ка formations now recorded in dictionaries are still qualified as 'colloquial' or *prostorečno* (Rojzenzon 1966: 110–11; Gornfel'd 1922: 56–7; Natanson 1966: 182; Panov 1968, 1: 67–9; Lopatin 1973: 46–7).

During the first years of Soviet power there was a remarkable burst of activity by the previously unproductive suffix -ия to designate various social groups and areas—regional, political, or professional. In 1918 the area held by the Bolsheviks was called Совдепия by their opponents, but later this name was used by the Bolsheviks themselves (Pavlovskaja 1967: 16). At about the same time Скоропадия (from the name of Hetman Skoropadskij) and Красновия (after General Krasnov) came into existence (Seliščev 1928: 184). The Soviet state or system was called коммуния. To the Komsomol and Pioneers the names комсомолия and пионерия were given. Worker, peasant, and military correspondents (as groups) were referred to as рабкория, селькория, рабселькория, военкория. So quickly did most of these words fall out of use, however, that they were never recorded in dictionaries. The only exceptions are комсомолия, пионерия, инженерия 'engineers', which continue in rare use to the present day but with a very specific literary stylistic colouring. The suffix is now once again unproductive (Mis'kevič 1967; Rojzenzon and Agafonova 1972; Protčenko 1975: 125).

(ii) *Acronyms and stump-compounds*

We know of no totally new word-formation model originating in the Soviet period, though the productivity and functions of certain word-forming elements have varied. However, the method of producing words like ГЭС, загс, колхоз, нарком, etc. from initials or segments of other words is usually thought of as a specifically Soviet procedure. Certainly, a very large number of Soviet neologisms have been formed by this process, but it actually originated before 1917. Even before the First World War a few such words were in existence, some connected with politics, like эсер (с.-р., социалист-революционер) 'Socialist-Revolutionary', кадет (конституционалист-демократ) 'Constitutional-Democrat', others with commerce, such as Лензото (Ленское золотопромышленное товарищество) 'Lena gold-industry company', and Монотоп (Монополия топлива) 'Fuel monopoly', and they were then already in colloquial use (Jakobson 1921: 10). At that time, however, this procedure was merely peripheral to the established word-formation system. During the War its convenience for use in telegrams became apparent to the military and certain conventions were set up for use in communications: Военмин (Военное министерство) 'Ministry of War', командарм (Командующий армией) 'army commander', etc.

During 1917, even before October, a number of new political terms were formed by this method: совдеп (совет депутатов) 'soviet of deputies', армком (комиссар при армии) 'army commissar', исполком (исполнительный комитет) 'executive committee', Викжель (Всероссийский исполнительный комитет союза железнодорожников) 'All-Russian Executive

Committee of the Union of Railwaymen'. After October it was an ideal way of forming the many new words needed to make manageable the titles of many new institutions which came into existence during the first years of the new regime.

Compounds of this type are known by the Russian terms аббревиатура and сложносокращенное слово. In English they are called 'stump-compounds' (Ward 1965: 156 ff.), but we prefer to restrict this term to those actually made of stumps, and refer to the others (made of initials) as 'acronyms'. The following types may be distinguished:

1. Stump-compounds proper, i.e. those in which segments of words—or stumps—are used. The latter are usually, but not always, syllables. E.g. колхоз (коллективное хозяйство).

2. Acronyms, i.e. those in which initials are used, subdivided into:

   (*a*) Those consisting of the names of the letters,
   e.g. КПСС [kapee'ses]
   (*b*) Those consisting of the sounds of the letters,
   e.g. загс [zaks]

Immediately after the Revolution there were a few cases of the names of letters being spelt out, e.g. чека, цека, цеика, but these are exceptional.

Stumps may also occur independently, e.g. зав (заведующий) 'chief', зам (заместитель) 'deputy', спец (специалист) 'specialist', but they are not very numerous and are always colloquial. The production of new words by this method is also mainly a post-1917 phenomenon, but it too originated before the War with the appearance of экс (экспроприация) 'expropriation' (Karcevskij 1923: 47).

In the first few years of Soviet power certain easily recognizable stumps were especially productive, e.g. парт- 'party', полит- 'political', культ- 'culture', гос- 'state', etc. The stump ком- can stand for a number of full words: Коминтерн (Комунистический интернационал), комбед (комитет бедноты), нарком (народный комиссар), краском (красный командир). But homonymy is kept within bounds by certain positional restraints (Jakobson 1921: 14).

From 1917 to the end of the 1920s the stump-compound proper predominated over the acronym as a means of creating words. The fact that pre-Revolutionary phrases could be given a Revolutionary air by abbreviation was convenient, e.g. сберегательная касса 'savings bank' had existed before the Revolution, but сберкасса was new. In the same way the old Донецкий бассейн 'Donets Basin' became the new Донбасс.[1] However, so many new words were being created that objections were voiced, particularly in the press, where the ironic and humorous possibilities of this model were not overlooked (Jakobson 1921: 12). More and more incomprehensible words were added to the vocabulary until the mid 1920s, when a certain moderation in their use can be observed (Seliščev 1928: 168), and from 1930 onwards there was a distinct reduction in both their use and production (Panov 1968, 2: 92). There ensued a period of stabilization, during which a number of stump-compounds fell out of use, e.g. домзак (дом заключения) 'prison', шкраб (школьный работник) 'teacher', дензнак (денежный знак) 'bank-note', стенгаз (стенная газета) 'wall newspaper' (replaced by стенгазета). In the 1930s and 1940s the proportion of new acronyms to new stump-compounds increased (Panov 1968, 2: 94), and this tendency continues.

Both stump-compounds and acronyms (especially the latter) tend to be structurally irregular. They may, for example, contain combinations of sounds not occurring in other words. Consequently, in the 1960s and 1970s, there have been attempts to create forms which are structurally conventional, e.g. лавсан (a synthetic fibre named from the initials of Лаборатория высокомолекулярных соединений Академии наук СССР), БАМ (Байкало-Амурская магистраль), and even to make them coincide with existing words: БУЗА (боевой устав зенитной артиллерии) 'anti-aircraft artillery field manual' (cf. буза 'row'), СУП (строевой устав пехоты) 'infantry drill manual' (cf. суп 'soup'), etc. (Ickovič 1971, 1972).

---

[1] It is significant that the Whites, having rejected the new orthography and the reform of the calendar, could not quite resist the stump-compound: note their добрармия (добровольная армия) 'voluntary army' (Jakobson 1921: 13, 30).

4

SYNTAX

THE subject-matter of this chapter may be divided into two main parts: syntactic variation and syntactic stylistics. The first is similar to the subject-matter of most of the rest of the book, in that it deals with syntactic variants—different syntactic means of expressing the same meaning—where the choice between the variants impinges on the question of which syntactic forms are admissible in the current standard. Except for a few detailed points, there are no surveys of educated syntactic usage comparable to those for pronunciation, stress, or morphology (e.g. the RJaSO survey): the material on syntactic variation is thus rather less comprehensive than on these other components of the language, although much material has been gathered on change in standard written usage, and on deviations from the codified standard in speech and writing.

Verbal government

In a large number of instances, the case or preposition required after a particular verb is arbitrary, not following from the meaning of that verb; in many instances, one even finds synonymous or nearly synonymous verbs requiring different constructions, e.g. предупредить о 'warn about', but предостеречь от, or платить за and оплачивать + accusative 'pay for'. In many such instances where the particular case or preposition governed by a verb is arbitrary, there have been shifts in standard usage between nineteenth-century and current practice, while in other cases one finds variation in practice even where this variation lies outside the current standard.

(i) *Accusative objects, oblique objects, and objects with prepositions*

In Russian, there are three possible forms for the object of a verb: in the accusative case, in one of the other cases (oblique case, i.e. genitive, dative, or instrumental), or with a preposition. Among verbs whose object case is not determined semantically, there has been some tendency over the recent history of the language for oblique objects to be replaced by accusative objects or objects with prepositions. For instance, the verb благодарить 'thank' is often found with the dative case in nineteenth-century literature; in current usage only the accusative is standard (Gorbačevič 1973). A number of verbs which took the genitive in nineteenth-century usage now require a preposition, e.g. бежать от 'avoid', скучать по 'long for', трепетать перед 'tremble before', надеяться на 'rely on, hope for' (Gorbačevič 1971: 229–30). In general, these changes in standard usage were completed during the nineteenth century.

This tendency has even been extended to a number of reflexive verbs, which according to the traditional standard can never occur with a direct object, but which in current usage, especially colloquial usage, often do occur with an accusative object. Traditionally, слушаться 'obey' takes the genitive, but the accusative is common in colloquial speech, and Butorin (1966) cites a number of examples with an accusative object from literature, commenting that this usage can no longer be considered a gross violation of the norm.[1] Butorin cites similar examples for some other reflexive verbs, including бояться 'fear' (though only colloquially, for instance in direct speech in literature), and дождаться 'wait for' (only with animate objects).

Several verbs take an object in either the accusative or the genitive, with subtle semantic differences between the two. With such verbs there is again a tendency in current usage for the accusative to oust the genitive. In the nineteenth century, the verb ждать 'wait' regularly took the genitive case, while nowadays both accusative and genitive are found, even in literature, with concrete nouns (in particular names of means of transport, e.g. ждать поезд/поезда 'wait for a train', and

[1] This calls into question the claim often made, e.g. by Ickovič (1968: 28), that new forms violating general models of the language cannot, in principle, be accepted as standard, since the pattern reflexive verb plus direct object is a clear violation of a general model in the traditional standard. Butorin (1966) also discusses the increasing acceptability in the standard language of the accusative as object of the category of state, e.g. слышно музыку 'music is audible'.

names referring to people, e.g. ждать сестру/сестры 'wait for one's sister'); with abstract nouns, however, the genitive is still preferred by most normative handbooks, though examples with the accusative are found, e.g. ждать покорно беду—нет, это, извините, не в моем характере 'to wait submissively for misfortune—no, forgive me, that's not my character' (Polozov, *Хождение за три моря*, quoted by Gorbačevič (1971: 234)). A similar change has occurred with искать 'look for', though here the earlier standard is for the accusative case when referring to specific individual objects, and the genitive when referring to abstracts, although the current tendency is to allow both the accusative and the genitive with more general and abstract nouns, the accusative being used particularly when reference is to a specific instance of the abstract concept.

Related to the general tendency for oblique objects to be replaced by other kinds of object is the tendency towards lower frequency of the partitive genitive,[1] and the genitive direct object of a negated verb.[2]

Although the general trend has been from oblique objects towards accusative or preposition objects, there are a few verbs that have undergone the reverse change. In many instances this has been determined semantically, e.g. with руководить 'lead, be in charge of', дирижировать 'conduct (orchestra)', which used to take the accusative in the nineteenth century, but now require the instrumental, like other verbs with the general meaning of 'control', e.g. управлять 'control'.[3] In the nineteenth century the verb писать 'write' could take an indirect object with the preposition к, as in Lermontov's *Валерик* (1840): Я к вам пишу случайно;... 'I write to you by

---

[1] One use of the partitive genitive, the 'genitive of temporary use', is impossible in current usage, though still found in nineteenth-century literature, e.g. одолжить карандаша 'lend a pencil' (sc. for a while) (Ickovič 1968: 57–8).

[2] e.g. я не встретил сестру 'I didn't meet my sister' for traditional я не встретил сестры. On the other hand, Ickovič (1968: 63–5) claims that the genitive of the direct object of an infinitive dependent on a negated verb, as in он не хотел читать этой книги 'he did not want to read this book', is on the increase, though without quoting the statistical basis of this claim.

[3] But дирижировать still occurs with the accusative in musicians' jargon (Zolotova 1974a: 150).

chance . . .'. In current usage this indirect object, like other indirect objects (e.g. after дать 'give') takes a simple dative: я вам пишу.[1] Some other instances are more clearly just exceptional: льстить 'flatter' takes the dative in current usage rather than the accusative of the nineteenth century, although the earlier construction remains in the expression льстить себя надеждой 'flatter oneself with hope'. Касаться 'touch, concern' takes a simple genitive in current standard usage, although in the nineteenth century it also occurred with the preposition до (and less commonly with к, or with a prepositionless dative) (Gorbačevič 1971: 230–1), and the construction with до is still common in current non-standard usage (Gorbačevič 1973). One verb, следить 'track, keep an eye on' has shifted from taking an accusative object to taking за with the instrumental, though the older construction survives in the literal sense of 'track' in hunters' jargon (Gorbačevič 1971: 229–30).

The trend away from verbs taking prepositionless objects in an oblique case is one that has operated, slowly, throughout the history of Russian and other Slavonic languages.[2] The over-all tendency is towards a situation like that of Bulgarian, or English, where there is only a two-way distinction among object types: those with prepositions and those without; this may therefore be compared with the general trend towards analyticity.

(ii) *Analogy and object cases*

Where the case of the object of a verb (or adjective or noun, especially deverbative noun) is arbitrary, then there is likely to be pressure for a change in this case from semantically similar verbs that take a different case. Thus we have already noted verbs like руководить 'be in charge' and дирижировать 'conduct' which have shifted to take an instrumental object, parallel to other verbs with the general meaning of 'control'. Most of these analogical changes have their origin in the spoken language, and many of them remain outside the bounds of

---

[1] The noun письмо 'letter' still allows both constructions: письмо (к) другу 'letter to a friend'.

[2] See Sjöberg (1964) for Old Church Slavonic, and Bobran (1974) for Polish (in comparison with Russian).

standard usage.[1] Thus, under the influence of платить за 'pay for' one finds оплачивать за instead of оплачивать with the accusative; under the influence of приговорить к 'sentence to' one finds осудить к instead of осудить на; under the influence of the large number of verbs expressing informational content which take the preposition о 'about', one finds указать о instead of указать + accusative 'indicate'.

In some cases, however, the frequency of the newer form, and its use by writers, suggests that there may be reasons for accepting that a change in the standard has taken place. Thus the traditional government of the verb поразиться 'be astounded' is with the instrumental, and this certainly remains as a possible construction. However, many other verbs expressing surprise take the dative case, e.g. удивиться 'be surprised', изумиться 'be astounded', and under their influence поразиться is also found with the dative, even in literature. In many recent normative handbooks, the dative case is cited as a possibility after поразиться: thus Ožegov (1972) cites both поразиться известию 'be astounded at some news' and поразиться красотой героини 'be astounded at the beauty of the heroine' without comment; Gorbačevič (1973) recommends the instrumental, but cites the dative as 'permissible'. The noun прогноз 'forecast', especially 'weather forecast', traditionally requires the genitive, although by analogy with other nouns expressing informational content it is also found with the preposition о 'about', and also with относительно 'relative to'; Gorbačevič (1973) recommends the genitive, but cites as 'permissible' the variants with о and относительно.[2] In the nineteenth century, контроль 'control' occurred only with the preposition над; in current usage it is also found with за + instrumental (cf. наблюдение за 'observation', надзор за (also над) 'supervision'), and with the genitive (cf. проверка + genitive 'check'). All three variants are listed, without comment, in Gorbačevič (1973). Gorbačevič (1971: 239–40) again permits all three variants, but suggests semantic and stylistic differences among them: both над and за are used with deverbal nouns indicating a process, while над is

---

[1] For a full discussion, with numerous examples, see Švedova (1966).

[2] This work also cites another variant, прогноз на + accusative, presumably under the influence of указание на 'indication'; this variant is qualified as incorrect.

preferred with other nouns (thus контроль над/за работой '. . . work', but контроль над финансами '. . . finances', контроль над поставщиками '. . . suppliers'), and the genitive is used primarily in official and technical language.

The extent to which native speakers can be uncertain in practice of standard usage in some of these instances is well illustrated by L. Čukovskaja's *В лаборатории редактора* (M., 1963), quoted and criticized by Švedova (1966). Čukovskaja condemns such contaminations as контроль за/+ genitive, катастрофа самолета (cf. гибель самолета 'the wreck of the plane' and катастрофа с самолетом 'the plane disaster'), смириться с 'resign oneself to' (cf. смириться перед 'resign oneself to' and примириться с 'reconcile oneself with'), but then uses in her own text constructions that violate against the traditional standard in just this way: испуг перед разнообразием естественных интонаций 'fear of the variety of natural intonations' (for испуг + genitive, cf. боязнь перед 'fear of'), чутье к языку 'feel for the language' (for чутье языка, cf. чувствительный к языку 'sensitive to language').

Preposition government

(i) по

In current usage по followed by a numeral with distributive meaning takes either the dative or the accusative of most numerals, e.g. по пяти or по пять 'five each'; exceptions are the numeral 'one', which is always in the dative, and the numerals 'two', 'three', 'four', 'two hundred', 'three hundred', 'four hundred', which are always in the accusative. For the other numerals, the traditional standard required the dative case (i.e. по пяти), a requirement that remained virtually unchallenged until the early twentieth century. For the numeral 'hundred', the old dative сту was used (по сту), rather than the dative form ста used in other constructions;[1] for the indefinite numerals such as много 'much, many', несколько 'some', сколько 'how many', again a special dative form in -у was used (по многу 'many each'). During the twentieth century,

---

[1] Ušakov (1935–40) does, however, recommend по́ста (which would be identical in pronunciation with по́сто); he considers по сту *prostorečno*, and does not mention по сто.

there has been a tendency for these dative forms to be replaced by accusative forms.[1] Ušakov (1935–40) still considered the newer forms like по пять to be *prostorečno*, but most current dictionaries admit both forms, though qualifying the citation form as colloquial. An exception is 'hundred', where only the newer form, по сто, corresponds to the current standard (Avanesov and Ožegov 1959).

The survey reported in Panov (1968, 3: 93–4) tends to confirm this picture. Only 3 per cent of those asked preferred по сту to по сто. Only 5 per cent preferred по сорока to по сорок; сто and сорок tend to behave alike morphologically, although Avanesov and Ožegov (1959) and Gorbačevič (1973) still recommend по сорока, qualifying по сорок as 'colloquial'. For numerals declined like пять, the percentage of informants preferring the dative varied from 8 per cent to 25 per cent. For the indefinite numerals there were more informants preferring the dative forms: 26 per cent for по нескольку, 29 per cent for по скольку, and 56 per cent for по многу, the last being the only example where the majority favoured the dative. We may conclude by referring the reader to a note in the September–October 1974 issue of the *Association of Teachers of Russian Newsletter*, discussing linguistic aspects of the Russian commentary on a Davis Cup tennis match between the U.S.S.R. and Czechoslovakia, in which both umpire and commentator used по пятнадцать and по пятнадцати 'fifteen all', по тридцать and по тридцати 'thirty all' indiscrimately in calling the score.

There have been some other minor changes in the use of cases after по between nineteenth- and twentieth-century usage.[2] For instance, in its basic meaning of motion across a surface, по regularly took the prepositional case of personal pronouns in the nineteenth century, whereas in current usage pronouns, like nouns, stand in the dative (по нему 'across it', rather than по нем); the prepositional here was still required by Ušakov (1935–40), but is qualified as *prostorečno* by Gorbačevič (1973). After verbs of grieving like тосковать по 'yearn for', current

---

[1] Perhaps more accurately, citation forms, since nominative and accusative of these numerals are alike, and the use of the citation form can be seen as part of the general trend towards analyticity. For further details of the changes, with examples from literature, see Butorin (1964).

[2] For details, see Astaf'eva (1974: 20–5), Gorbačevič (1973).

usage has the dative of nouns, but preferably the prepositional of pronouns (and only the prepositional of first- and second-person pronouns); the use of the prepositional case of nouns is not uncommon in the nineteenth century.

(ii) *Other prepositions*

The case required after a number of other prepositions has also changed during the recent history of the Russian language. Thus навстречу 'towards, to meet' and вопреки 'despite' took the genitive case in the nineteenth century, whereas now they require the dative.[1] Благодаря 'thanks to' could take the accusative, whereas nowadays only the dative is possible; as noted above (p. 103), of the variants found earlier with the verb благодарить it is the accusative that has triumphed. Gorbačevič (1973) considers благодаря + accusative to be archaic. One preposition whose usage is not completely stabilized is между 'between', at least in the sense 'between like objects'. In current prose fiction and scientific writing preference is clearly for the instrumental, except in a few set phrases (читать между строк 'read between the lines', между двух стульев 'between the devil and the deep blue sea'), although the genitive, common in earlier periods of the language, is still to be found in recent fiction; Gorbačevič (1973) quotes the following sentence from G. Markov's *Соль земли*: на земле между стволов было тихо 'on the ground among the tree-stumps it was quiet'. In fact, the only normative recommendation made in Gorbačevič (1973) is that with the instrumental one usually finds между, and with the genitive usually меж; this seems to be too non-partisan an assessment, since the preference in current non-stylized prose is clearly for между and the instrumental.

Such variation in prepositional government can also lead to the appearance of variation where previously there was none. Thus, in both nineteenth-century and current standard usage согласно 'according to' requires the dative. Gorbačevič (1973) condemns the use of согласно + genitive as incorrect. Mazon (1920: 54) refers to 'the adoption by the language of administration and official prose of the incorrect construction of согласно with the genitive'. In addition to the dative and

[1] Gorbačevič (1973) also allows к + dative after навстречу, as a rarer form.

archaic accusative, благодаря is also found with the genitive in non-standard usage.

Agreement

(i) *Conflict between semantic and grammatical agreement*

There are several instances in Russian where the semantic and grammatical gender or number of a noun phrase are at variance, for instance in the use of the masculine noun врач 'doctor' in referring to a woman doctor, or the use of the grammatically singular words много 'many', большинство 'majority' in referring to a plurality of entities. In Russian, as in many other languages (including English), there is some variation within normative usage in such cases, over whether agreement with such nouns should be on a semantic or a grammatical basis; the traditional standard in the nineteenth century was with grammatical agreement, but at the present time there is much more variation. Conflict between semantic and grammatical agreement for gender is dealt with in Chapter 6, and the present section is concerned with number agreement.

Conflict between semantic and grammatical number agreement occurs in Russian where the subject of the sentence has plural reference, but is either a numeral expression (e.g. пять солдат 'five soldiers'), including an indefinite numeral expression with the neuter singular form of the indefinite numeral (e.g. много солдат 'many soldiers'), or a collective noun with quantitative meaning (e.g. большинство солдат 'the majority of the soldiers').[1] The traditional standard in such constructions is for the predicate to stand in the singular, i.e. to agree grammatically with the subject, and this is by and large adhered to in nineteenth-century literature, though there are occasional examples that go counter to the general principle, such as the following from Lermontov, quoted in Rozental' (1971: 217): несколько дам скорыми шагами ходили взад и вперед по площадке 'several ladies were walking back and forth across

---

[1] In Russian, unlike (British) English, grammatical agreement prevails with collective nouns that do not have quantitative meaning, e.g. молодежь 'youth', армия 'army', правительство 'government', although occasional deviations can be attested (Mullen 1967: 48–9). Semantic number agreement with such collective nouns is found in Old Russian and in regional dialects (Borkovskij and Kuznecov 1965: 352–8).

the landing with rapid steps.' During the course of the late nineteenth and twentieth centuries there has been a tendency for semantic agreement to become more widespread, so that in current usage both singular and plural predicate forms are in principle possible with all such numeral and collective–quantitative subjects. However, recent detailed studies of contemporary usage[1] suggest that, while there are no inviolable rules prescribing when the singular is to be used and when the plural is to be used, there are certain tendencies which determine preference for one or the other form (for instance, the plural is more likely with verbs of action, or where the various individuals subsumed under the subject noun phrase act independently).

(ii) *Adjective case after numerals*

The numerals два 'two', три 'three', четыре 'four' require a following noun to be in the genitive singular, irrespective of gender. However, an adjective agreeing with such a noun does not stand in the genitive singular, but in either the nominative (–accusative) or the genitive plural, e.g. два новые/новых дома 'two new houses', две новые/новых книги 'two new books'. In discussing the relative frequency of nominative and genitive adjectives, it is necessary to treat separately on the one hand masculine and neuter nouns, and on the other feminine nouns.

With masculine and neuter nouns the overwhelming preference in current usage is for the genitive. In a statistical survey of contemporary literature, Suprun (1957: 73) found that over 80 per cent of the relevant examples contained the adjective in the genitive case. In nineteenth-century literature, the nominative was quite usual in such constructions, e.g. только две звездочки, как два спасительные маяка сверкали на темно-синем своде 'only two stars, like two safety beacons, sparkled on the dark-blue vault' (Lermontov, *Герой нашего времени* (1838–41), *Тамань*). The genitive is given as the only admissible form by Rozental' (1971: 230).

The situation is much more complex with feminine nouns, and there has even been disagreement as to the direction of the recent trend: Bulaxovskij (1952: 315) and Suprun (1957: 75,

---

[1] Mullen (1967), Skoblikova (1959); a detailed set of normative guidelines, based on tendencies of the type noted in these two works, is given by Rozental' (1971: 213–19).

79) claim that the nominative is becoming more common, whereas Vinogradov *et al.* (1960, 1 : 373–4) say that the nominative is the older form. Certainly the nominative is very frequent in nineteenth-century literature, e.g. три скользкие, мокрые ступени вели к ее двери 'three slippery, wet steps led to her door' (Lermontov, *Герой нашего времени* (1838–41), *Бэла*), and it is the nominative rather than the genitive that is recommended as the preferred form by most normative handbooks; thus Vinogradov *et al.* (1960, 1 : 372–3) say that such adjectives usually stand in the nominative, but that this can no longer be considered the sole norm.[1] Gorbačevič (1973), in the articles две and четыре, simply describes the genitive plural as less usual; the article три makes no gender distinction, qualifying the nominative–accusative plural as 'rarer' in general. As a striking instance of the inconsistency that can be found in current usage, even written usage, we may note that in an article in *Вопросы языкознания* (1974, no. 1), we find on page 20 the phrase две исходные конструкции 'two initial constructions', and in the next sentence, two lines below, две производных конструкции 'two derived constructions'.

Analyticity and apposition

Different aspects of the trend towards analyticity in the Russian language are discussed in various parts of this book; in particular, indeclinable words, i.e. words which are inherently indeclinable, irrespective of their syntactic role in the sentence, are treated in Chapter 3 on morphology. The present section will look at syntactic aspects of analyticity: certain words are inherently declinable, i.e. in general they can and do decline, but in certain syntactic constructions they are, or may be, indeclinable. The constructions in question are where the declinable word occurs in apposition to, or as an attribute to, some word which is declined (or is itself indeclinable).

Even in traditional usage there are many examples of this kind, in particular where the title of a literary, musical, or other work stands in apposition to the noun describing the

---

[1] In two instances, however, the genitive plural is recommended: after the prepositions на and по, and where the noun in question distinguishes genitive singular and nominative plural by stress alone.

genre to which it belongs, or where the proper name of some organization stands in apposition to the generic name for organizations of that kind; the title or proper name is usually written in guillemets, e.g. роман «Евгений Онегин» 'the novel *Evgenij Onegin*', опера «Пиковая Дама» 'the opera *The Queen of Spades*', газета «Правда» 'the newspaper *Pravda*', кино «Волга» 'the Volga cinema'. With the preposition в 'in', these appear as: в романе «Евгений Онегин», в опере «Пиковая дама», в газете «Правда», в кино «Волга». Where the generic term is omitted, then declension of the title or proper name is usual: в «Евгении Онегине», в «Пиковой даме», в «Правде», в «Волге». One of the functions of the use of the generic term in such expressions can be seen in a desire to retain unaltered the citation form of the work or institution referred to.

With many other kinds of apposition, however, there is an increasing trend away from a traditional standard which requires declension towards indeclinability. This can be seen particularly clearly with geographical names in apposition to generic terms, such as город Москва 'the city Moscow', река Волга 'the river Volga', остров Мальта 'the island Malta', планета Венера 'the planet Venus'. The question that arises concerning standard usage is whether one should say, for instance, with the prepositions в 'in', на 'on': в городе Москве or в городе Москва, на реке Волге/Волга, на острове Мальте/Мальта, на планете Венере/Венера. The traditional, nineteenth-century standard was for declension of the proper name in such constructions. Most current normative handbooks recommend declension in certain instances, indeclinability in others, and occasionally allow either declension or indeclinability indifferently.[1] While the recommendations of these handbooks do not always correspond to current educated usage, in particular in that both variants are often found in educated usage where only one is recommended by the handbooks, yet still the tendencies noted there are essentially the same as those observed in practice. For instance, the handbooks recommend declension of names in apposition to город 'town', and in practice в городе Москве is still commoner than в городе Москва. Rozental' (1971: 236) allows (and seems even to

[1] See, for instance, Superanskaja (1965*b*: 137–43), Rozental' (1971: 236–7); apart from a few points of detail, their recommendations coincide.

recommend) indeclinability of little-known town-names, citing the example в городе Мина 'in the town Mina', where the Saudi Arabian town of Mina is unlikely to be known to the Russian reader, and в городе Мине would leave it unclear whether the town was called Mina or Min; Superanskaja (1965*b*: 137–8) criticizes this practice. Rozental' also recommends the distinction between в городе Кирово 'in the town Kirovo' and в городе Кирове 'in the town Kirov'.[1] The indeclinable forms here and elsewhere have undoubtedly been fostered by the practice in military communiqués, and also to a lesser extent in other administrative documents, of leaving place-names in their citation form and accompanying them by a declined generic term. At the other extreme, names of islands (especially if not well known) in apposition to остров, and names of planets in apposition to планета, are usually indeclinable, and this is the recommendation of both handbooks cited. Janko-Trinickaja (1964: 303–4) cites examples of the names of planets in apposition to планета, and indeclinable, but notes also the following example where Венера declines: на далекой звезде Венере солнце пламенней и золотистей 'on the far-away star Venus the sun is more fiery and golden' (N. Gumilev). With many other generic terms both declension and non-declension are found, indeclinability tending to be preferred where the proper name is unfamiliar, where it is composed of an adjective plus noun, and where it differs in gender from the generic term. Janko-Trinickaja (1964: 304) notes that in all these cases, nineteenth-century and early twentieth-century usage preferred declension, the only widespread exceptions being a few generic geographical terms (e.g. станция 'station') in technical or administrative works relating specifically to rail and water transport.

In the examples considered so far there has been a single proper name corresponding to the generic name, but often there is a series of proper names corresponding to a single generic name, as in совместный полет «Союз–Аполлон» '"Sojuz–Apollo" joint flight'.[2] Here both 'Sojuz' and 'Apollo'

---

[1] He does not discuss в Кирово; see pp. 87 f.

[2] The use of indeclinables in such constructions has been studied in detail by Janko-Trinickaja (1966*a*), from which many of the examples below are taken.

are essential to the concept of the joint flight. Particularly frequent examples of this construction in current usage are with a series of geographical names indicating an itinerary (e.g. магистраль Абакан—Тайшет 'the main Abakan–Tajšet line, line from A. to T.'), a series of personal names indicating a meeting (e.g. встреча Брежнев–Форд 'the meeting (between) Brežnev (and) Ford', матч Ботвинник–Таль 'the Botvinnik–Tal' match'), and a series of numbers indicating a relation, for instance a score (e.g. со счетом 4:5 'with a score of 4:5'). Such examples are characteristic of current usage, but were rare in the nineteenth and early twentieth centuries. Thus even in the *Вестник Министерства путей сообщения* (*Bulletin of the Ministry of Communications*) at the end of the nineteenth century it was common to find explicit expressions of the type прямое беспосадочное сообщение Варшавы с Москвой 'direct communication without change of Warsaw with Moscow', Витебско-Орловское шоссе 'the Vitebsk–Orel highway', even though it is precisely in official documents of the Ministry of Communications that indeclinable geographical names in apposition to generic names are most frequent in the nineteenth century (Janko-Trinickaja 1966*a*: 177).

A further instance of the spread of analyticity in appositional constructions concerns numerals in apposition, but here the distinction is not simply between declined and indeclinable form, but between the ordinal form (which must then agree with its noun) and the cardinal form (which is then invariable, in the citation form), e.g. номер третий and номер три 'number/room three'. In the written language such constructions usually appear with the numeral written in figures, in which case the written form номер (abbreviated N°) 3 is ambiguous as to whether it should be read as ordinal третий or cardinal три. It is not certain, for instance, how Čexov himself read the title of his short story *Палата № 6* 'Ward 6'. In a number of instances from the late nineteenth and early twentieth centuries, however, we do have the numeral written out in full, or explicit indication of the ordinal form by means of the orthographic device 3-й for третий. Thus in a letter from Korolenko to Čexov we find explicit reference to Палата N° 6-й (Janko-Trinickaja 1964: 305).[1] The ordinal was the usual

¹ Where the expression номер plus numeral occurs in apposition to

form until the twenties of the present century, when usage began to fluctuate, leading to the present situation where the cardinal form predominates. Janko-Trinickaja (1964: 305) quotes examples from the twenties where both cardinal and ordinal forms are found in the same work, with apparently no difference between them. Panov (1968, 3: 90–1) notes a small majority in a survey of 100 informants for the cardinal in палата N° 3 'ward 3' (54: 46), and a large majority for the cardinal in из дома N° 1 'from house no. 1' (90: 10).

The inclusion of the word номер is by no means a necessary feature of such constructions, so that in addition to в квартире номер двадцать семь 'flat no. 27' one can have simply в квартире двадцать семь/в квартире двадцать седьмой; with such examples, Panov (1968, 3: 91) notes a preference for the ordinal (with this particular example, 59: 41). Product names with numerals without номер are common with products that have appeared in several different versions, e.g. aeroplanes, such as ТУ-154, ИЛ-62, satellites and space-ships, such as Салют-4, which are usually read with cardinal numerals, although Janko-Trinickaja (1964: 307–8) observes that in the professional jargon of pilots, etc., ordinal forms are used. With such product names the overwhelming majority of informants in the survey discussed in Panov (1968, 3: 90–1) preferred the cardinal numeral (92: 8 for самолетом ТУ-104).

Although current usage tends toward the cardinal forms, this is not to say that the ordinal forms are not found, indeed one often finds both almost side by side: thus Maršak's poem *Мистер Твистер* has on the one hand номер девятый 'room nine' and номер десятый 'room 10', and on the other номер сто девяносто 'room 190'. In such examples, the numeral in question may be a conditioning factor, the cardinal being particularly preferred if the numeral is high or complex. It is doubtful whether anyone would read паспорт N° 379205 with an ordinal numeral, rather than a series of cardinal numerals. The use of fractional house numbers is another factor militating against the ordinal, since it is simply impossible to form an

another noun, номер itself is always indeclinable, and the point at issue is whether or not the numeral agrees with the preceding noun (whether or not this is номер), i.e. whether it is cardinal or ordinal. The fullest treatment of this problem is Janko-Trinickaja (1964).

ordinal from a fraction, e.g. Волхонка, дом 18/2 (read: дом восемнадцать дробь два), which happens to be the address of the Russian Language Institute of the Soviet Academy of Sciences.

With these examples one may compare the frequent current use of an expression of measure in the citation form in apposition to the expression of the parameter of which it is a measure, e.g. двигатель мощностью 35 (тридцать пять) лошадиных сил 'motor of power 35 h.p.', глубина 300 (триста) метров 'depth of 300 metres', ров глубиной 3 метра 'ditch 3 metres deep' (Zolotova 1974*a*: 161–75). The more traditional form is with the preposition в, i.e. мощность в 35 лошадиных сил, глубина в 300 метров/в 3 метра, although the forms without в are frequent in current writing and speech. Gorbačevič (1973), in the article высота 'height', lists the following, without any further comment, though in this order: дом высотою в двадцать метров, дом высотою двадцать метров 'house twenty metres high'.

Predicate cases

In Russian, predicate nouns can stand in either the nominative or the instrumental, while predicative adjectives stand in either the short form, the nominative long form, or the instrumental long form. Over the whole history of Russian, there has been a tendency for the instrumental to encroach upon the nominative, and for the long form to encroach upon the short form; this process is by no means complete, and normative and pedagogical handbooks still have to list the criteria that require or favour one or other of these forms,[1] but in the recent history of the Russian language we can see some reflections of this general change away from nominative and short forms, in particular in constructions where nineteenth-century usage allowed the nominative or the short form (as an alternative), but where current usage does not. We shall be concerned here only with instances where there has been a shift in usage, and

---

[1] In dialect and colloquial speech the use of the short and long adjectives, in particular, is markedly different from their use in the written language, with much more use of long forms; cf. Zemskaja (1973: 196–214), and references cited there.

not with the general problem of the choice among the predicate variants.

(i) *Predicate nouns after* быть *in the past tense*

Most normative handbooks, including Vinogradov *et al.* (1960, 2, 1: 421–2, 428–9), say that the difference between the nominative and the instrumental of a noun predicate here is that between permanent and temporary characteristic, e.g. Пушкин был великий поэт 'Puškin was a great poet', but в то время я был студентом 'at that time I was a student'. Vinogradov *et al.* (1960, 2, 1: 422) note, moreover, that in nineteenth-century literature the nominative was also possible for a temporary characteristic, e.g. конечно, мы были приятели 'of course, we were friends' (Lermontov, *Герой нашего времени* (1838–41), *Максим Максимыч*), i.e. note a shift of usage in favour of the instrumental. In a detailed study of the use of the nominative and instrumental in recent literature, including political and other non-fictional literature, Křížková (1968: 213–14) finds no strong confirmation for the alleged semantic distinction between permanent and temporary characteristics, but rather a stylistic distinction: in more colloquial texts the nominative is more frequent than in non-fictional texts, in particular political texts.[1] Thus while over all the nominative case was used on average in 12·8 per cent of relevant instances, it did not occur once in *Материалы XXII съезда КПСС* (*Materials of the XXII Congress of the CPSU*), occurred in 2·1 per cent of instances in *Из жизни древней Москвы* (*From the Life of Ancient Moscow*), in 4·1 per cent of instances in *Pravda*, in 31·1 per cent of instances in Leonov's novel *Русский лес* (1950–3), and in 61·5 per cent of instances in Kataev's novel *Белеет парус одинокий* (1936). Thus, while there may have been some shift between nineteenth-century and current usage, the variation within current usage, dependent largely upon style, is itself immense.

[1] The trend in the current written language to replace the predicative nominative by the instrumental is more advanced than in the colloquial language; whereas the trend to replace short adjectives by long adjectives is more advanced in the colloquial language. For a statistical account restricted to fiction, see Røed (1966).

(ii) *Predicate nouns after* быть *in the future tense, conditional, and imperative*

In current usage the instrumental is virtually obligatory after the future tense, conditional, and imperative of быть, although the use of the nominative here is not uncommon in the nineteenth century, e.g. он решил, что женитьба на Элен была бы несчастье (L. Tolstoj, *Война и мир* (1863–9), quoted in Vinogradov *et al.* (1960, 2, 1: 425)). As an illustration of the variation found in the nineteenth century, we may note the use of the instrumental and nominative in successive lines of Lermontov's *К**** (*Мы случайно сведены судьбою*) (1832):

> Будь, о будь моими небесами,
> Будь товарищ грозных бурь моих…

'Be, oh be my heavens,
Be the companion of my fearful storms . . .'

(iii) *Predicate nouns after other copular verbs in the present and past tenses*

With other copular verbs, with the general meaning of being (e.g. являться 'be'), seeming (e.g. казаться 'seem'), or becoming (e.g. стать 'become'), current usage has the instrumental of a noun predicate. In nineteenth-century literature, the nominative is also found, e.g. я грубиян считаюсь 'I am considered a boor' (Ostrovskij, *Гроза* I. i. (1859)).

(iv) *Predicate adjectives after verbs other than* быть

The morphological possibilities for adjectives as predicate to быть are essentially the same in current usage as in the nineteenth century, although again there are widespread divergences depending on style in current writing.[1] After other verbs, however, whether they are copular (like стать 'become') or not (e.g. verbs of motion and position like вернуться 'return', стоять 'stand'), current usage allows only the long form of the adjective (nominative or instrumental), whereas the short form is not infrequent in nineteenth-century literature, e.g. я стал раздражителен, вспыльчив, резок, мелочен 'I have become irritable, irascible, abrupt, petty' (Čexov, *Иванов* I. iii. (1887–9)). In addition, there seems to be a current trend

---

[1] Cf. the statistics in Křížková (1968: 219).

towards the instrumental. The author of this chapter has witnessed a generation fight within a Moscow family over the acceptability of автобусы идут переполненными 'buses travel crowded', with mother rejecting this variant and son accepting it; both accepted the nominative, автобусы идут переполненные.

Prepositional usage

(i) В *and* на

Although the difference between the prepositions в 'in' and на 'on' in general corresponds to that between position in an enclosed space and position in an unenclosed space, more specifically on the surface of an unenclosed space, there are several instances where the choice of one or other of these two prepositions is essentially arbitrary; such differences between в 'in' and на 'on' with the prepositional are paralleled by similar differences between в 'into' and на 'onto' with the accusative, and из 'out of' and с 'off' with the genitive. Such arbitrary uses of the distinction can give rise to doubts and arguments about standard usage, and there have been some shifts in standard usage since the nineteenth century, most typically in the encroachment of на upon в. More widespread use of на is characteristic of non-standard speech, and of the professional jargon of certain occupations: thus sailors usually say на флоте for standard во флоте 'in the navy', cinematographers на киностудии for standard в киностудии 'in the film studio'.[1]

With names of theatrical performances and other entertainments, meetings, etc., current usage prefers the preposition на, e.g. на концерте 'at the concert'. However, в концерте is found throughout the nineteenth century, and Gorbačevič (1973) considers it obsolescent, rather than archaic, citing both ходить на концерты 'go to concerts' and был в концерте 'was at a concert' from Žuxovickij's *Я сын твой, Москва*.

---

[1] An additional factor is that in many dialects the difference between из and с is lost, giving rise to с or з in both meanings, thus reducing the degree of differentiation between the two series. Another common confusion in non-standard usage is between от and с in time expressions, e.g. магазин работает от 11 до 19, instead of ...с 11 до 19 'the shop is open from 11 to 19'.

Names of streets in current usage require the preposition на, e.g. на улице Горького 'on/in Gor'kij Street', на Невском проспекте 'on Nevskij Prospekt'. In the nineteenth century, both в and на are found. In fact, there was a difference between streets in Moscow and those in St. Petersburg: Moscow streets invariably took в, while in St. Petersburg some took в while others took на (Astaf'eva 1974: 30, referring to observations by N. Greč in 1840). With the word переулок 'alley' there is variation in current usage between в/на переулке, and similarly with proper names of alleys containing переулок; the traditional form is в переулке, reflecting the fact that a narrow alley is more of an enclosed space than a broad street, but Gorbačevič (1973: 320) cites на переулке as a permissible alternative to the recommended form в переулке, and the same work on p. 50 gives both forms, in the order в, на переулке, without comment.

Another example where there is variation at present is в/на кухне 'in the kitchen'. The traditional form is again в, with на as the newer form, at least in the standard language. Gorbačevič (1971: 253) notes that in current speech and writing на is much more frequent, and was preferred by the majority in a survey he conducted; Gorbačevič (1973) cites both variants, and lists на first. The author of this chapter has been corrected by Russians for saying в кухне.

In at least one case the existence of competing norms has led to a semantic differentiation in the standard language, namely with двор 'courtyard', where во дворе means literally 'in the courtyard', e.g. машины стояли во дворе 'the cars were standing in the courtyard', and на дворе 'outside, out of doors', e.g. дети играли на дворе 'the children were playing outside'. In the latter sense, на дворе seems in any case to have been largely replaced in current urban usage by на улице, literally 'on the street'.

A number of examples where на, and even more so с, are heard in current usage are, however, clearly outside the current standard, e.g. на клубе 'in the club', с клуба 'from the club'; the latter occurs, presumably with deliberate stylistic effect, in *Krokodil* of June 1975, in the caption to a cartoon showing a rickety bridge supported by two rather tasteless neo-classical statues: Молодцы! И излишества с клуба убрали и мост подремонтировали! 'Clever chaps! They've both got rid of the left-overs from the club and mended the bridge!'

In some instances the development has been the reverse of this, на being replaced by в. For instance, with the names of towns we find examples in the nineteenth century like: царь вернулся на Москву 'the tsar has returned to Moscow', where nowadays only в Москву would be possible. Expressions like поезд на Ленинград are still possible, but differ somewhat in meaning from поезд в Ленинград 'the Leningrad train, the train to Leningrad'. Поезд на Ленинград simply states that the train is going in the Leningrad direction, not necessarily the whole way to Leningrad, and the speaker's attention is probably focused on the fact that it stops at various intermediate points even if it does terminate in Leningrad. Gorbačevič (1973) characterizes на деревне 'in the village' as incorrect, for current standard в деревне, while noting that на деревне was possible in the nineteenth century, and is still occasionally found as a stylistically marked form.

The tendency for в to be replaced by на particularly in colloquial speech has led to a certain extent to a rear-guard action being fought against на in certain constructions, as a hyper-correction. For instance, the use of на with enclosed means of transport (e.g. на автобусе 'by bus') is quite acceptable according to the traditional standard when emphasis is on the means of transport rather than on position in the particular vehicle (when в автобусе is required); in the former case, на автобусе is synonymous with автобусом 'by bus'. However, many native speakers of Russian, under the influence of normative pronouncements against на in other constructions where both в and на may be heard, maintain that на автобусе is impossible in this sense, but can only mean literally 'on (top of) the bus'. Although the origin of this stricture is a misunderstanding of normative pronouncements, it will be interesting to observe if the belief in the unacceptability of на автобусе 'by bus' will be sufficient to effect a change in usage, more especially standard usage, with time.

(ii) По

Russian has a number of traditional constructions for expressing a relation of purpose, or simply some general, unspecified relation, between one noun and another, such as a noun followed by a genitive (программа литературы 'literature syllabus'), a noun followed by a prepositional phrase (автомат для продажи сигарет 'cigarette-vending machine'), a noun preceded by an adjective (футбольная встреча 'football match'), or a compound noun (мастер-технолог 'foreman-technician'). One of the relevant prepositional phrases is with the preposition по and the dative, as in товарищ по школе 'school-friend'. In present-day Russian, this preposition is tending to take over from the other means outlined above, so that one often comes across expressions like: программа по литературе, автомат по продаже сигарет, встреча по футболу, мастер по технологии.[1] The preposition по has the great advantage, in such constructions, that it has no lexical meaning of its own, but can serve simply to express the most general kind of relation between the two nouns.[2] In a number of instances this construction is a useful addition to the complement of relational constructions in the language, but in many other instances this is not so, and it is in such cases that normative grammarians have tended to inveigh against the innovation.

In some constructions the inclusion of the по phrase is simply redundant, e.g. магазин по продаже уцененных товаров 'shop for the sale of reduced-price goods' (shops can be expected to sell things, so one needs only магазин уцененных товаров 'reduced-price goods shop', with the traditional genitive construction), работа по продаже газированной воды 'work in selling mineral water' (here работа 'work' is redundant, and продажа газированной воды on its own suffices).

In some instances, however, there is no real alternative to по, and here normative grammarians seem agreed that the spread of this construction should be evaluated positively. For instance,

---

[1] The standard discussion, with numerous examples from the Soviet press, is Švedova (1966: 40–52); see also Gorbačevič (1971: 247–50). Švedova, incidentally, says little about the normativity of such constructions, apart from criticizing obvious instances of redundancy.

[2] Popova (1974: 184) suggests that for this reason the use of the preposition по should be encouraged by normative grammarians, although she is looking specifically at a more restricted range of uses of по, namely where it relates a specific kind of work activity to a more general description of that kind of work, e.g. помощь по переборке кукурузы 'help in sorting maize'.

although инженер по технике 'technology engineer' is redundant, this is not so if one needs to specify what kind of technology
or techniques are involved, as in инженер по технике безопасности 'engineer concerned with safety techniques'. It is not
possible to form a compound noun of the type мастер-технолог
if one of the components is an adjective plus noun rather than
just a noun on its own, and there is no other compact construction to express this general relationship. Since the noun лифт
'lift, elevator' has no derived adjective, there is again no real
alternative to механик по лифтам 'lift mechanic'. Although
Россия 'Russia' has the derived adjective российский 'Russian'
(relating to the Russian state) and the related русский 'Russian',
the expression специалисты по России 'Russia specialists' is not
synonymous with российские/русские специалисты. Other
such examples quoted by Švedova (1966: 41–2) include
эксперт по борьбе с колорадским жуком 'expert in the fight
against the Colorado beetle', почтальон по доставке телеграмм
'postman who delivers telegrams'.

   In addition to occurring with nouns, по also occurs frequently
after verbs, particularly in order to give a more specific description of a verb describing some work activity more generally,
e.g. принять меры по сохранению молодняка 'take measures
for the preservation of saplings', работать по истории боев в
нашем крае 'work on the history of the battles in our area'.
Popova (1974: 183–4) takes a positive attitude towards the
spread of по in such constructions, though many other normative grammarians are particularly opposed to the spread of по
to constructions where there is already a different established
standard (in these cases, принять меры для, работать над).
With this one might compare Gorbačevič's criticism (1971:
248) of the book-title *Футбол. Указания судьям и игрокам по
правилам игры* (*Football: Instructions to Referees and Players
Concerning the Rules of the Game*), where the traditional standard
clearly requires указания на правила. Compare the discussion
of changes in government of verbs, pp. 105–7.

Syntactic stylistics

   Syntactic stylistics is one of the most important areas in
which to study the relations among the various styles in the

process of the 'democratizing' of the Russian language in the Soviet period, whereby constructions that had previously been inadmissible in the written language come to be acceptable (often via journalistic practice), and on the other hand constructions that had previously been considered literary, high-style, filter down into the lower styles. As an initial example, we may note the history of the conjunctions раз 'if, once' and поскольку 'in so far as'. Раз was originally colloquial but, though still predominating in colloquial style, is now to be found in stylistically neutral writing. Поскольку originated, in this meaning, as a bureaucratic form, but is now much more widely acceptable in the written language, in addition to being common in speech (Rogožnikova 1966).

Many of the examples to be discussed, especially those spread by journalism and popular science, are of deviations from what had hitherto been standard syntactic practice in the direction of a more expressive language. Although many of these expressive devices can be found occasionally in pre-Revolutionary journalistic writing, it is only during the Soviet period that they have become at all widespread—initially as stylistically marked devices, though increasingly, with greater use, losing their stylistic markedness and becoming ordinary features of journalistic style.[1] As illustrative material, we have cited examples from *Izvestija* of late July and early August 1975.

(i) *Question and answer sequences*

One of the most salient differences between colloquial speech and the written language, particularly in such variants as the language of scientific writing, is the high frequency of question and answer sequences in the former. Thus the inclusion of question and answer sequences in the written language is an obvious way of making it more expressive, closer to the spoken language. There is, of course, a certain artificiality in this stylistic device, since in a newspaper article or piece of popular scientific writing, the writer both asks the question and gives

[1] For further treatment of the problems discussed below, and examples from newspapers, mainly of the fifties and sixties, see Popov (1964), Ivan-čikova (1966), Popov (1966), Prokopovič (1966), Švedova (1966), Uxanov (1966), Panov (1968, 3: 233-366).

the answer (indeed, he usually assumes that his addressee does not know the answer—this is a device for presenting information, rather than for eliciting it), but none the less it can serve to create a closer rapport between writer and audience. In the issues of *Izvestija* examined this device occurs so frequently that it seems almost to have lost any stylistic markedness, having become one of the usual ways of presenting information in all but the most formal pronouncements. In an article on the Moscow Film Festival in the issue of 24 July 1975 we find: Чем дорог нам Московский фестиваль? Прежде всего тем, что на его экранах в течение двух недель можно увидеть как бы весь мировой кинопроцесс... 'Why is the Moscow festival so dear to us? Above all because on its screens we can see in the course of two weeks the whole world cinematographic process . . .' An article in the issue of 27 July 1975, discussing the relation between superior and subordinate, bears a question as title: Как стать любимым? 'How can one become loved?', to which the whole article is an answer. The article contains a number of more specific questions and answers such as: А какая же здесь сухость и строгость? Здесь налицо отеческая мудрость и прямо-таки материнская нежность. 'And what dryness and strictness is there here? Here we are faced with fatherly wisdom and veritable motherly tenderness.' The issue of 3 August 1975 contains an article on tourism and ecology: Кто палит леса? Вытаптывает травы? Распугивает зверье? Люди. 'Who sets fire to forests? Tramples grass? Frightens the animals? People.' The issue of 5 August 1975 has an article about the effect of industrial waste on a forest: Какого цвета хвоя может быть у сосны? Мы тоже думали: зеленая... А она в здешнем лесу — белая. 'What colour can the needles of a pine-tree be? We also thought: green . . . But in the local forest they are white.'

(ii) *Parcellation*

In colloquial speech, whether in Russian or English, the normal syntactic structure of a sentence is often dislocated in such a way that certain elements of the sentence are added to the end of the rest of the sentence and separated from it by a pause, i.e. added as an afterthought, e.g. *He's already gone. To see his grandmother.* Such dislocation is perfectly normal in speech, where the speaker may not plan the whole of his sentence in advance, and has no chance to correct what he has already said by erasing it and constructing the sentence again from the beginning. These constraints are not present in writing, and the use of such dislocations can therefore serve as a stylistic device. In current Russian linguistic work they are referred to as парцелляция 'parcellation' (the separate, dislocated parts being парцелляты), or присоединительные конструкции 'connective constructions'. Such constructions are rare in nineteenth-century writing, at least outside of the reported speech of characters (Ivančikova 1966: 12), but are very characteristic of current journalism, in particular. The article already quoted above on the effect of industrial waste on a forest bristles with such examples: Гражданка Д. сделала несколько неверных шагов. С дворовой дорожки за ограду, где росла небольшая ель. 'Citizen D. took a few unsteady steps. From the courtyard path through the fence, where a small fir-tree grew'; ...о том, что нужно беречь природу, она знала из самых различных источников. В том числе из фельетона «Злоумышленники»... '. . . she knew from the most varied sources that one should protect nature. Including from the article "The Ill-intentioned" . . .'; Оглянемся назад. Всего на восемнадцать лет. 'Let us look back. A mere eighteen years'; Он намерен сделать здесь пожарный водоем. В нескольких километрах от Волги. Для охраны лесов, которые целеустремленно уничтожает подведомственный ему завод. 'He intends to make a fire-brigade reservoir here. A few kilometres from the Volga. To protect the forests which the factory under his supervision is purposefully destroying.' This last example contains two dislocations.

(iii) *Thematic nominative*

In colloquial speech, another kind of dislocation frequently found is that whereby the noun phrase expressing the topic of conversation, irrespective of its syntactic function in the sentence, is presented at the beginning of the sentence, separated from it, in its citation form (i.e. nominative case); in the most typical instances, the topicalized (thematic) noun is then repeated, in the appropriate syntactic form, in the body of the sentence, usually as a pronoun, as in English: *Children. You never know what they'll be up to next.*[1] Such examples have become very frequent in contemporary journalistic and popular scientific styles, as in the article on cups for sporting events in *Izvestija* of 12 August 1975: Кубки, кубки! Сколько ныне их в футболе. 'Cups, cups! How many of them there are nowadays in football.' Sometimes, instead of the thematic noun phrase being repeated in full or as a pronoun, its semantic content is repeated by the inclusion of some semantically related expression in the main sentence, as in this example from the same article: Кубки, кубки. Приятно видеть, сколько наших команд ныне включились в спор на этих популярных европейских турнирах. 'Cups, cups. It is pleasant to see how many of our teams have now entered the fray at these popular European tournaments', where the idea of the cup or prize is subsumed in на этих турнирах 'at these tournaments'. Another straightforward example is to be found in *Izvestija* of 5 August 1975, in an article on Bhutan: Традиции. Они сильны в Бутане, где власть... верховного ламы почти равносильна власти монарха. 'Traditions. They are strong in Bhutan, where the power . . . of the head lama is almost equal to the power of the monarch.' According to Švec (1971: 50), thematization of this kind became particularly common in the fifties and sixties.

(iv) *Nominative sentences*

Most of the stylistic devices discussed so far in this section have been characteristic of colloquial speech, although some of them can also be found, though less frequently, in expressive writing of the nineteenth century, for instance in rhetorical poetry. The next stylistic device to be discussed is one that is essentially foreign to the spoken language, but is found traditionally in higher styles of the written language (especially poetry; Popov (1966: 83–4)), namely the frequent use of nominative sentences (номинативные предложения). These are sentences consisting solely of a noun phrase in the nominative

---

[1] In addition to this kind of topicalization (thematization), colloquial Russian has a number of other devices which are not found in the written language, at least not outside dialogue, such as the thematic nominative not taken up in the body of the sentence, which then lacks an expected syntactic constituent, e.g. Толстой я прочла 'Tolstoj I've read'. See Zemskaja (1973: 241–64).

case, and used to set the scene for some action or series of actions. An example is to be found in *Izvestija* of 12 August 1975, where a football match is introduced by the paragraph: 9 августа 1975 года. Москва. Центральный стадион имени В. И. Ленина. 70.000 зрителей. '9 August 1975. Moscow. The V. I. Lenin Central Stadium. 70,000 spectators.' With this form of scene-setting there is no specification of tense (i.e. not: было 9 августа... 'it was 9 August . . .'). In earlier periods this technique was largely restricted to the stage instructions at the beginning of a scene in a drama. As noted by Popov (1966: 89–92), it is not uncommon in current prose writing to find long chains of such nominative sentences, each of which may consist of a long noun phrase with various attributes. He suggests moreover that one possible influence on the spread of nominative constructions is their use in film scenarios (Popov 1966: 79–81). In current usage they are frequent with some (by no means all) writers (Popov 1966: 83), still rare in the spoken language, and common in newspaper reporting.

(v) *Verbal nouns*

In many constructions in Russian, it is possible to use either some form of a verb, or the abstract noun derived from that verb (verbal noun), e.g. я привык наблюдать такие явления 'I have grown accustomed to observing such phenomena', and я привык к наблюдению таких явлений 'I have grown accustomed to the observation of such phenomena'. In most instances where both verbal and nominal construction are possible, there is a stylistic difference between them: the nominal construction is more characteristic of scientific, political, and bureaucratic language, whereas the verbal construction is more usual in other styles, especially in speech. The spread of nominal constructions in the former styles is very marked in the recent history of Russian, as of many other European languages. Meromskij (1930: 52–3) notes that 'rural speech is characterized by the primacy of the verb, where the townsman would tend towards use of the noun', i.e. this stylistic change was more widespread in urban than rural usage, the former being generally more susceptible to the influence of scientific, political, and bureaucratic language. Meromskij quotes a statistical analysis by M. Gus, Ju. Zagorjanskij, and N. Kaganovič, showing that out of 648 phrases in *Рабочая газета*, an urban newspaper, where both noun and verb would be possible, the noun is used in 38·5 per cent of them; in the rural newspaper *Беднота* the corresponding figure is only 4·4 per cent.

Ickovič (1974: 44–60) notes that in current non-standard usage there is a tendency for verbal nouns governed by a verb or noun to be replaced by infinitives, contrary to standard usage, e.g. препятствует вести наблюдения for препятствует ведению наблюдений 'prevents the carrying out of observations'. In his corpus there are some 200 examples of violation of the standard in this direction, and only two examples of violation in the other direction, e.g. умение выбора формы for умение выбрать форму 'ability to choose the form' (Ickovič 1974: 45–6). He concludes that the verbal noun tends to win out in scientific and administrative language, partly also in journalistic language, whereas the infinitive is tending to become more widespread in other styles, perhaps as a reaction against the proliferation of verbal nouns, which is often criticized in normative handbooks.

5

VOCABULARY

Motivation of change

THE reflection in language of extra-linguistic reality is easier
to demonstrate on the lexical level than on any other, and the
social motivation of linguistic change is consequently most
easily demonstrated by change in vocabulary. The appearance
of new things, concepts, qualities, activities, etc., is always
accompanied or quickly followed (and sometimes even preceded) by changes in the lexical system. New words appear
and old words change their meaning. But, as we have mentioned
already, language varies not only along the scale of time,
but along social, functional, and regional scales, too. Lexical
innovation can therefore operate in many different ways,
including the transfer of words and meanings from one variety
to another.

Many of the new Russian words which have come into being
since 1917 closely reflect, and owe their existence to, the new
social and political structures of the Soviet Union. Words such
as загс 'registry office', колхоз 'collective farm', нарком
'people's commissar', made their first appearance in the Soviet
period and as a result of the new political system. On the other
hand, there are many new words that have arrived on the scene
since 1917 whose arrival can scarcely be attributed to the
Soviet system. This type includes, for example, вертолет
'helicopter', грейпфрут 'grapefruit', майка 'vest'.

Social distribution

There is, in addition, a third type: those words which existed
in Russian before 1917 but which are nevertheless regarded as
particularly characteristic of the Soviet epoch. Many of them
before the October Revolution were severely restricted both
territorially (being mainly urban), and, above all, socially.

The use of most of the philosophical, political, and economic vocabulary of the revolutionary movements of the nineteenth and early twentieth centuries was restricted to participants in those movements and to certain social spheres either connected with or interested in such movements. The users of such words lived mainly in towns, but in addition, of course, many revolutionaries spent years in emigration. There are thus many words of this kind which were attested before 1917 (in some cases many years earlier) but which only came into widespread popular use after that year. Such words as агитация 'agitation, propaganda', альянс 'alliance', демократия 'democracy', демонстрация 'demonstration', депутат 'deputy', коллегия 'board', коммуна 'commune', ликвидация 'elimination', лозунг 'slogan', ленинизм 'Leninism', резолюция 'resolution', штрейк-брехер 'strike-breaker', for example, penetrated the vocabulary of the working class and peasantry only after the October Revolution, though they had existed before that in the language of certain social groups. Similarly the pre-eminently Soviet words большевик 'Bolshevik' and меньшевик 'Menshevik' came into existence soon after the Second Congress of the Russian Social-Democratic Workers' Party, held in London in 1903, when the split occurred between the supporters of Lenin (the majority—большинство) and the rest (the minority—меньшинство), but it was not until after 1917 that they came into use among the whole population. Several contemporary observers of the linguistic events following the Revolution noted the growing use of foreign words by ever widening spheres of users after (and only after) 1917 (Barannikov 1919: 77; Karcevskij 1923: 22–3; Seliščev 1928: 30–5). Even in the press (which was one of those restricted areas where the number and frequency of loan-words was already comparatively high) their frequency in political articles appears to have shown a slight but significant increase (Krysin 1965).

The fact that much of the characteristic vocabulary of the early Soviet period is first attested before 1917 and only subsequently entered the personal vocabularies of the vast majority of the users of Russian underlines one of the weaknesses of historical lexicology: the fact that the attestation of words in texts often reveals nothing of their actual use. Some words of the kind referred to above are attested even as early as the seventeenth (e.g. демократия, депутат) and eighteenth (e.g. альянс, демонстрация) centuries. If we could map their social distribution in the same way as regional isoglosses can be shown on dialect maps, we should find that throughout their two centuries or so of use in Russian they occupied a very small area indeed. Strictly speaking we cannot describe such words as Soviet neologisms, yet to the greater part of the Russian language community that is precisely what they were (Černyx 1929: 50).

The social spread of many of these words began with the Revolution of 1905, but it was only in 1917 that the flood-gates were opened wide. Such words were originally restricted to those who may be described as politically unorthodox and constituted a distinctive attribute of their language separating them from other users of Russian. The nineteenth-century novelists provide evidence of this. Leskov in his novel *Некуда*, for example, parodies the characteristic speech of young nihilists in the 1860s (Šor 1929: 52). But still more useful is the picture given by L. N. Tolstoj in *Воскресение* of the revolutionary Vera Efremova (Černyx 1929: 52):

Речь ее была пересыпана иностранными словами о пропагандировании, о дезорганизации, о группах, и секциях, и подсекциях...   (*Воскресение*, Part 1, Chapter 55)

Her speech was interspersed with foreign words about propagandizing and disorganization, about groups and sections and subsections . . .

An important factor in the borrowing of West European words was the fact that revolutionaries had long-standing links with the West. Many of them had been in exile abroad, sometimes for many years. The theoretical works on which their ideologies were based were written in and had been translated from West European languages. It is thus not possible to say how far the Western words borrowed in the seventeenth, eighteenth, and nineteenth centuries had a continuous independent existence within the Russian speech community, and to what extent they were renewed and reinforced by renewed Western contacts. Emigration was undoubtedly an important factor. André Mazon, who was in Russia during the whole of 1918 and the first weeks of 1919, was in no doubt as to its effect on the Bolshevik leaders (Mazon 1920: i–ii). On the other hand, it is known that Western words abounded in the speech of even those revolutionaries who had not been abroad, a fact which led Černyx to conclude that the role of emigration in this process had been greatly exaggerated (1929: 52). It is certainly true that some of the political words which came to the fore in 1905–17 had a history in Russian going back to the time of the French Revolution. Some, in fact, were particularly associated with the French Revolution and for that very reason were revived by Russian revolutionaries (Seliščev 1928: 21–2; Černyx 1929: 54).

Lexical change, 1905–17

The slow spread of existing loanwords to new social spheres was accelerated by the Revolution of 1905. Among the examples given by Seliščev of words known for their increasing popularity at this time are: аграрный 'agrarian', аграрник 'one condemned for participation in agrarian disturbances', баррикады 'barricades', бастовать 'strike', бойкот 'boycott', фракция 'faction' (1928: 28). Newspapers and political speeches were responsible for extending the vocabularies of their audiences; but when assessing the role of newspapers we should not forget the low literacy rate at this time and the fact that it was not destined to rise significantly until the 1920s. But even for the few who could read, the increase in new vocabulary (mostly of foreign origin) was already a problem. Words were being introduced to the press faster than the reading population could digest them. Symptomatic of this state of affairs is the unusually large number of small dictionaries and vocabularies published during the first two decades of the twentieth century, explaining words of foreign origin, related principally to political and economic matters (Krysin 1968: 62). Konduruškin's dictionary (1917), for example, is actually sub-titled 'an aid to reading the newspapers'.

The war years 1914–18 saw a drop in the rate of borrowing. Those foreign words that were borrowed at this time were mostly connected with the war (Karcevskij 1923: 39; Krysin 1968: 63). There were also manifestations of a nationalistic purism: attempts were made to reject certain existing loanwords of German origin. These efforts, which were inspired by the anti-German feelings aroused by the war, had little lasting effect. The projected replacement of бутерброд 'slice of bread and butter' by хлеб с маслом and of плацкарт(а)[1] 'place in sleeping-car' by спальное место came to nothing (Barannikov 1919: 74). Здравница 'health resort, sanatorium', which originated during the war, reportedly on the initiative of Nikolaj II to replace the loanword санаторий 'sanatorium', has survived (Karcevskij 1923: 61), but the two words only overlap semantically. Demands that the German loanword фельдшер 'medical assistant' be replaced by лекарский помощник were at least temporarily successful, though the motivation in this case was not simply nationalistic but also based on class considerations (cf. p. 155). The renaming of certain towns, e.g. Санктпетербург 'St. Petersburg' as Петроград 'Petrograd',[2] was another aspect of this puristic tendency.

Borrowings, 1917–27

Strangely enough, even the Revolutions of 1917 did not accelerate the rate of borrowing. It remained low during the first decade of Soviet power and the number of loanwords first attested in this period is surprisingly small. They include: дансинг (1923) 'dance-hall' (Fr. *dancing*), докер (1925) 'docker' (Eng. docker), конферансье 'master of ceremonies' (Fr. *conférencier*), такси (1926) 'taxi' (Fr. *taxi*), фокстрот (1923) 'foxtrot' (Eng. foxtrot), шезлонг 'deck-chair' (Fr. *chaise longue*). (For further examples, see Krysin 1968: 70–1.) Not only the small number but also the areas of human activity covered by these words come as something of a surprise. How are we to explain the fact that in a time of political events unique in the history of mankind the Russian language was borrowing words like конферансье, фокстрот, шезлонг? The answer is to be found in the fact that the vocabulary was simultaneously enlarging itself from another source—from

[1] According to Krysin (1968: 63 n.) this word was masculine at that time, but Barannikov (1919: 74) has плацкарта.

[2] Since the change was made by imperial decree and reflected tsarist chauvinism, the old name was partially revived in the left-wing press after the Revolution (Jakobson 1921: 9).

native elements using new word-formation models (Krysin 1968: 72). Loanwords originating in this period are simply so few in number that they are not in any way typical. At the same time, it is important to remember that this was a period when loanwords from the preceding years were being digested by the masses (Karcevskij 1923: 39; Krysin 1968: 63–4). New words were not being borrowed by Russian from non-Russian sources, but within the Russian speech community existing loan-words were being borrowed from one social variety to another.

Russian linguists working in the 1920s were aware of the necessity of observing social variation in the vocabulary. Their attention was drawn not so much to the moment of birth of some new formation as to its spread (Černyx 1929: 62). The fact that certain loanwords were known to some social strata and not to others is attested in a number of ways. First, there are recorded instances of their inaccurate use, some even in writing. In 1928 *Krokodil* (no. 15) published the following example from a notice displayed in a chemist's shop:

В виду острого дефекта хинина в СССР отпуск товаров прекращен.   (Quoted by Černyx 1929: 50)

In view of an acute defect of quinine in the U.S.S.R. the issue of goods is discontinued.

(This demonstrates confusion between дефект 'defect' and дефицит 'shortage'.)

Folk-etymology

Secondly, the fact that many words were new to their users is shown by folk-etymological interpretations. The term folk-etymology is applied to the creation of new forms or meanings, often resulting from language contact, when users of a given variety begin to use words from another variety without understanding their meaning. The new word may acquire a new form (to make it appear to have some kind of etymological motivation), or it may acquire a new meaning (to link it semantically with existing words of similar form). The emergence of such words is characteristic of situations of cultural transfer, when not only the word but also the referent is unfamiliar to the receiving group. This was the situation in early revolutionary Russia, when many words relating to new concepts were taken into use by new users (Šor 1926: 94, 127). Many of the folk-etymological innovations of the early Soviet period were recorded by contemporary observers and they testify to the social and linguistic upheaval at that time. The following were noted during the first ten years or so of Soviet rule: бубличное место for публичное место 'public place' (being linked to the familiar бублик 'kind of bread-roll' instead of unfamiliar публика 'public'); космомолец for комсомолец 'member of Komsomol' (linked to косо 'askew' and молиться 'pray'); купиратив for кооператив 'co-operative' (linked to купить 'buy') (Šor 1926: 94); перелетарий for пролетарий 'proletarian' (linked to перелетать 'fly over'), пример-министр for премьер-министр 'prime minister' (linked to пример 'example'), леворуция for революция 'revolution' (linked to лево 'left'), ликтричество, ликстриство for электричество 'electricity' (linked to лик 'image' (religious)), скупилянт, скупиляция for спекулянт 'speculator', спекуляция 'speculation' (linked to скупить 'buy up') (Barannikov 1919: 79); скопулянт for спекулянт (linked to скопить 'amass') (Jakobson 1921: 9); элементы 'elements' for алименты 'alimony', дистанция 'distance' for инстанция 'instance' (legal) (Seliščev 1939: 76). In some country districts пробольшевики 'pro-Bolsheviks' was understood as meaning противобольшевики 'anti-Bolsheviks' (Karcevskij 1923: 63). Šor quotes the interesting case of куманист for коммунист 'communist', occurring in a North Russian tale, where it is derived from the dialect word куманика 'cloudberry' (1926: 94).

Problems of understanding

In certain other changes of meaning there is no apparent similarity between the two forms involved, and the motivation of change is consequently obscure. It was recorded, for example, that in parts of the countryside персонально 'personally' was understood as редко 'rarely' (Šor 1926: 127) and серьезный 'serious' as хороший 'good' (Šafir 1927: 131).

One can only speculate on the precise origins of these new meanings, but the way in which a shift from a particular to a general meaning could produce the opposite of the intended message in a given utterance is demonstrated by the story of an argument between Maksim Gor'kij and another man as to whether the common people could understand the slogan Религия — опиум для народа 'Religion is the opium of the people'. They decided to ask a Red Army man on guard: Что такое опиум? 'What is opium?' The reply was: Знаю... это лекарство 'I know . . . it is medicine.' It is not known whether it was merely coincidence that дурман 'dope' was later used in this slogan instead of опиум (Šklovskij 1925: 29–31).

Some contemporary observers, such as Seliščev (1928, 1939), aimed simply to record the linguistic facts they heard and saw before them. Others, however, were concerned with practical problems. Šafir (1924, 1927), for example, was concerned with the press and the task of writing in words which would be understood by workers and peasants, both those who, in the 1920s, were beginning to read for themselves, and those who still relied on others to read the newspapers aloud to them. In 1923 he carried out surveys and experiments to discover whether peasants could understand the words being used in the press, and discovered that in many cases they could not. His survey of sixty-four Red Army men (who, presumably, reflected the general make-up of the population and were thus mainly peasants) showed a high degree of ignorance of certain words. Among the words with which Šafir's informants showed a particularly low degree of acquaintance are the following (1927: 131–2): система 'system', ультиматум 'ultimatum', регулярно 'regularly', элемент 'element', авторитет 'authority', инициатива 'initiative', реклама 'advertisement', меморандум 'memorandum', репарации 'reparations', официально 'officially'. His survey also covered industrial workers in Voronež, however, and their knowledge of words used in the newspapers was much greater.

In order to assist correspondents to make their language more accessible to the masses Šafir published lists of words often not understood and accompanied them by better-known Russian equivalents. His point was that the language of the press should be closer 'to the colloquial language' (1927: 130).

The amount of difficulty experienced by the newly literate in understanding the newspapers was a constant topic of public debate in the 1920s and it engaged the attention of leading political figures (Špil'rejn *et al.* 1927: 8). This was not a new problem: both before and after the October Revolution politicians and correspondents had used synonyms or explanations to make political terminology comprehensible. The following examples of this method are taken from the 1920s (Seliščev 1928: 29–30):

Эта модификация, это изменение тактики...
(*Pravda*, 29 May 1924)
Стимул (побуждение) к борьбе...
(*Izvestija*, No. 295, 1924)
Сбалансировка (уравновешивание) бюджета...
(*Pravda*, No. 65, 1926)

We have no way of telling precisely at what rate and in which directions vocabulary formerly restricted to privileged groups spread to other sections of the population, but things were undoubtedly moving fast in the late 1920s and 1930s. It is characteristic of this volatile period that only three years after Šafir was expressing dismay at the extent to which words were still not known among the peasantry, another observer (Meromskij 1930) was registering his admiration for the skill with which the village correspondents (селькоры) of the central *Крестьянская газета* were using loanwords which 'formerly would have sounded very unusual in the mouth of a peasant' (1930: 99–100). To Meromskij it was evident that a flood of words which before the Revolution had had what he calls a 'restricted learned and urban sphere of dissemination' had in the last few years poured into the everyday speech of the village, 'Europeanizing' it (1930: 100–1). He describes the surprise of the members of an agitation and progaganda expedition to the village of Nenaševo (Paxomovo *rajon*, Tula *gubernija*) in 1928 on discovering that all the children there knew the word компот 'stewed fruit', which had until recently been known only in the central parts of towns (1930: 108).

An important agency for spreading literacy and education in the early years of Soviet power was the Red Army, and the tests of passive vocabulary carried out among men of the Moscow garrison in 1924–5 (Špil'rejn *et al.* 1928) showed that knowledge, especially of socio-political vocabulary, increased rapidly during the time spent in the army (1928: 112–13).

Derivation, 1917–1927

The number of borrowings dating from the early Soviet period may be small, but between the February Revolution and the beginning of the first Five-Year Plan (1917–28) the vocabulary was growing fast by forming new words from elements already present in Russian. The method of forming new words from initial letters or from stumps is especially characteristic of this period. Although it had been used before 1917 the number of words produced in this way was small. From 1917 onwards the productivity of this type increased out of all proportion to what had gone before. (See also Chapter 3, p. 101.) A good part of these innovations had a relatively short lifespan, however, and it has been estimated that most of those created in the 1920s (a particularly productive period) have since fallen out of use (Ward 1965: 157). The following examples of this type originating in the first decade of Soviet power constitute only a tiny fraction of the total number:

(i) Using initials: вуз (высшее учебное заведение) 'higher educational institution', ГПУ (Главное политическое управление) 'Central Political Administration', НЭП (Новая экономическая политика) 'New Economic Policy', МАПП (Московская ассоциация пролетарских писателей) 'Moscow Association of Proletarian Writers', РСФСР (Российская Советская Федеративная Социалистическая Республика) 'Russian Soviet Federative Socialist Republic', ЦИК (Центральный Исполнительный Комитет) 'Central Executive Committee', чека (ЧК) (Чрезвычайная комиссия по борьбе с контрреволюцией и саботажем) 'Cheka'.

(ii) Using stumps: Госиздат (Государственное издательство) 'State Publishing House', зарплата (заработная плата) 'wages', исполком (исполнительный комитет) 'executive committee', истпарт (комиссия по истории партии) 'Commission on the History of the Party', истмат (история материализма) 'history of materialism',[1] комбед (комитет бедноты) 'Poor Peasants' Committee', Коминтерн (Коммунистический Интернационал) 'Comintern', партбилет (партийный билет) 'Party card', пролеткульт (пролетарская культура) 'proletarian culture', профсоюз (профессиональный союз) 'trade

---

[1] Nowadays исторический материализм (historical materialism).

union', Персимфанс (Первый симфонический ансамбль) 'First Symphonic Ensemble', рабкор (рабочий корреспондент) 'worker correspondent', совхоз (советское хозяйство) 'sov-khoz', совзнак (советский знак) 'Soviet bank-note', шкраб (школьный работник) 'school-teacher'.

At the same time new words were continuing to be coined by conventional methods: by affixation and compounding whole words. The following are first attested in the period 1917–25: аллилуйщик 'one who overpraises', белогвардеец 'white guard', беспризорник 'waif', воскресник 'Sunday of voluntary work', красноармеец 'Red Army man', красногвардеец 'Red Guard', ленинец 'Leninist', керенщина 'Kerenskyism', партиец 'party member', продуктовый 'grocery' (adjective), митинговать 'hold meetings', проработка 'collective discussion, criticism', правозаступник[1] 'lawyer', субботник 'Saturday of voluntary work', советизировать 'sovietize', царизм 'tsarism', чрезвы-чайка 'Cheka'.

The new acronyms and stump-compounds were themselves capable of being used to form further new words by affixation: исполкомствовать, комсомолец, комсомольский, нэпман, нэпач, чекист. (These examples all date from 1917–25.)

There is also the question of semantic change as a means of enlarging the vocabulary. Among the many new meanings which arose in this early part of the Soviet period are: абиту-риент 'university candidate' (formerly 'secondary school leaver'), бригада 'work-team' (formerly only on trains), молодняк 'young people' (formerly 'saplings'), чистка 'purge' (formerly 'clean-up'), чиновник 'bureaucrat' (formerly 'civil-servant' only).

Historicisms

With the overthrow of the old regime and the disappearance of many tsarist institutions the status of the words referring to them changed. While, for example, the words городовой 'policeman', дума 'duma, council', земство 'Zemstvo', столо-начальник 'table-master', жандарм 'gendarme', экзекутор 'seneschal', фрейлина 'maid of honour', did not disappear from the language, new circumstances meant that the frequency of

[1] Replaced адвокат which, owing to its class connotations, was abolished (1918), but later restored (1922) (Karcevskij 1923: 59–60).

such words was bound to fall, providing conditions for their eventual disappearance, at least from the active vocabulary of most speakers. Such words are sometimes called историзмы 'historicisms' by Russian linguists. Further examples of words which fell into this category either immediately in 1917 or in the following decade, are: губернатор 'governor', казначейство 'exchequer', стражник 'constable', полицейский 'policeman', государь 'sovereign', государыня 'sovereign lady', наследный 'hereditary', князь 'prince', камер-юнкер 'gentleman of the chamber', лицей 'lyceum', гувернер 'tutor', гувернантка 'governess', бонна 'nursery-governess', гимназия 'grammar school', посол 'ambassador', посольство 'embassy', аттестат зрелости 'school certificate', градоначальник 'governor of a town', министр 'minister', министерство 'ministry', вос-кресник[1] 'Sunday-school pupil (or teacher)'.

Some of these words were later reinstated (e.g. посол, министр) and some continued to have referents in other countries. Thus the word царь continued to be used to refer to the king of Bulgaria, полицейский to refer to foreign police, губернатор to governors of American states, etc.

Archaisms

To be distinguished from historicisms are true archaisms, i.e. words which virtually have ceased to be used—even to refer to past events. They include: дантист 'dentist' (now зубной врач), лавка 'shop' (now магазин), нервический 'nervous' (now нервный), and the two adjectives сей and оный characteristic of chancellery language before 1917 (Jakobson 1921: 9). However, the vocabulary always seems to acquire new words faster than it discards old ones, and the number of words which have become truly obsolete since 1917 is small. Curiously enough, they include a fair proportion of words created in the 1920s and 1930s, e.g. желдорога (железная дорога) 'railway', лимитрофы 'independent states formerly part of the Russian Empire', правозаступник 'lawyer' (cf. p. 141).

In some cases it is only a certain meaning that has become obsolete, e.g. возразить formerly 'reply', now only 'object'

[1] Cf. Karcevskij (1923: 60). The new воскресник (see p. 141) is too remote in meaning for this to be regarded as semantic change.

(Kalinin 1971: 106), покойный formerly 'quiet' (replaced in this meaning by спокойный), now only 'deceased'.

1928–38

During the First and Second Five-Year Plans (1928–38) the number of loanwords increased notably. They include the following:

аттракцион (1935) 'show, entertainment', комбайн (1933) 'combine', контейнер (1932) 'container', пикап (1937) 'pick-up', стенд (1931) 'stand', танкер (1933) 'tanker', траулер (1933) 'trawler', троллейбус (1933) 'trolley-bus', джаз (1933) 'jazz', скетч (1933) 'sketch', джемпер (1932) 'jumper', авто-страда (1930s) 'motorway', демпинг (1930) 'dumping', кок-тейль (1933) 'cocktail'. (For further examples, see Krysin 1968: 85–126.)

It is worthy of note that by this time the predominant source of borrowings was English. At the same time, of course, the old word-formation processes were also adding to the vocabulary, producing such innovations as: авоська 'string bag', встречный 'counter-plan', глубинка 'remote point', грузовик 'lorry', вертолет 'helicopter', коллективизация 'collectivization', раскулачивать 'dekulakize', стахановец 'Stakhanovite', пяти-летка 'five-year plan', уравниловка 'wage-levelling'.

The number of new acronyms and stump-compounds was drastically reduced by comparison with the preceding decade. Among those that did arrive on the scene at this time were: МТС (1928) (машинно-тракторная станция) 'machine and tractor station', детсад (1932) (детский сад) 'kindergarten', универмаг (*c.* 1930) (универсальный магазин) 'department store'. A few more pre-Revolutionary words lost currency: волость '*volost*'', уезд 'district', губерния '*gubernija*'.

The picture of lexical change at this time begins to be complicated by the revival of some words which had been deliber-ately abandoned in 1917. They include certain items from the old military terminology, such as лейтенант, майор, полковник.

1938–45

In the period from the beginning of the Third Five-Year Plan (1938) to the end of the Second World War (1945) the most easily distinguished group of lexical innovations is composed of words connected with the War. The majority of them were very specifically connected with military matters and short-lived. They include a number of German loanwords, such as: блицкриг 'blitzkrieg' and полицай 'member of the local population (in occupied areas) serving in the Nazi police'. Probably the only German loanword from this period to acquire a general meaning and remain in use after the War is ас 'ace' (Ger. *As*), which first referred to German pilots but later to Soviet aces, too. Eventually, it came to be applied to ace performers of other kinds (Kožin 1961: 196–7; Krysin 1968: 127). The English loanword бульдозер (early 1940s) 'bulldozer' has also survived from the War period.

Native formations relating to the War include катюша 'Katjuša rocket-projector', ГКО (Государственный комитет обороны) 'State Defence Committee', дзот (дерево-земляная огневая точка) 'log pill-box'.

The outstanding characteristic of the War years 1941–5 is the drop in the rate of lexical borrowing by comparison with the preceding period (Krysin 1968: 126), which had seen the appearance of a fair number of loanwords, including the following: диверсант (1939) 'saboteur', велюр (1940) 'velours', грейпфрут (1939) 'grapefruit', гангстер (1941) 'gangster', телетайп (1940) 'teletype', роллер (1939) 'scooter', призер (1939) 'prize-winner', перманент (1939) 'permanent wave', газовать (1939) 'accelerate' (*prostorečno*).

It would seem, in fact, that not only borrowing but lexical innovation of all kinds was restricted during the War. Apart from the single word гангстер there appear to be few, if any, innovations dating from 1941–5 except those motivated by the military events. There were, however, a few revivals, viz. посол 'ambassador', посольство 'embassy', гвардия 'guards', офицер 'officer'.

1946–55

The reluctance to borrow foreign words was even stronger after the War, in the late 1940s and early 1950s. These were the years of the Struggle against Cosmopolitanism, when efforts were made to restrain borrowing and to 'purify' the language by rejecting existing loanwords. When Ožegov's one-volume dictionary *Словарь русского языка* made its first appearance in 1949, it was condemned for including such foreign words as аббревиатура 'abbreviation', бекар 'natural' (musical), диакритический, 'diacritic' диатонический 'diatonic', лозунг 'slogan' (Rodionov 1950). Even французские булки 'French rolls' were renamed городские булки 'town rolls', the sweets called американский орех 'American (Brazil) nuts' became южный орех 'southern nuts', and the name of the Café «Норд» in Leningrad was changed to «Север».

It was proposed that бульдозер and the names of certain other mechanical implements be replaced, and a number of sports terms of English origin actually were changed: половина игры replaced тайм 'half', вратарь replaced голкипер 'goalkeeper',[1] угловой удар replaced корнер 'corner', полузащитник replaced хавбек 'half-back', вне игры replaced офсайд 'off-side' (Krysin 1968: 141).

Despite all efforts, however, a few new borrowings did appear: аллергия (1949) 'allergy', адаптер (1954) 'gramophone pick-up', драндулет (1949) 'jalopy', бойлер (1950) 'boiler', гандбол (1954) 'handball', дзюдо (1954) 'judo', кросс (1949) 'cross-country', офис (1949) 'office', робот (1948) 'robot'.

Neologisms arising from internal word-formation processes in this decade include: болельщицкий (1954) (from болельщик 'fan'), витаминизировать (1951) 'vitaminize', стиляга 'teddy-boy' (Kostomarov 1959*a*).

1956–70

The relaxation in relations with the outside world that came with Stalin's death in 1953 did not have much immediate effect on the vocabulary. Tourism was made possible, cultural and scientific contacts with other countries were established or re-established, and knowledge of their way of life grew. An increase in the rate of borrowing foreign words, however, does not become noticeable until the 1960s. The following borrowings all date from the late 1950s: акваланг (late 1950s) 'aqualung', геофизик (1956) 'geophysicist', круиз (1957) 'cruise', шорты (1959) 'shorts'. From its own resources Russian produced such words as: анонимщик (1959) 'writer of anonymous

[1] Вратарь with this meaning had, however, existed since 1908 (Faktorovič 1966), though it had not previously succeeded in replacing the English loanword.

letter', бескомпромиссность (1957) 'quality of being un-compromising', верхолаз (1957) 'steeple-jack', целинник (1950s) 'worker on virgin lands'.

The rate of borrowing increased in the 1960s and the following appeared: аутсайдер (1963) 'outsider', бадминтон (1963) 'badminton', бармен (1960) 'barman', бикини (1964) 'bikini', битник (1964) 'beatnik', дизайнер (1966) 'designer', секс (1963) 'sex', твист (1961) 'twist', хобби (1964) 'hobby'.

Lexical developments in the post-war years are well documented (Kotelova and Sorokin 1971; Bragina 1973; Kolomijec' 1973), and it is clear that growth in the 1960s exceeded that of the 1940s and 1950s. The launching of the first sputnik in 1960 not only gave a new meaning to спутник (formerly only 'companion' or 'satellite') but initiated a whole new terminology (Bragina 1973: 9–83). However, internal processes also produced several hundred new terrestrial words in the 1960s, including the following: блинная (1964) 'pancake bar', водолазка (1970) 'polo-necked sweater', грудник (1966) 'breast-fed baby', общепит (1963) (общественное питание) 'public feeding organization', окномойка (1966) 'window-cleaning machine', показуха (1960) 'bluff', фарцовка (1965) 'illegal dealings in goods or currency bought from foreigners'.

Objections to the use of foreign words continued to be made occasionally even after the Struggle against Cosmopolitanism had passed into history. The use of шортики 'shorts', найлоны 'nylon stockings', тоуст 'toast', and кар 'car' in the speech of the (then) younger generation, and of оранжад 'orangeade', шорты 'shorts', and тренинг 'training' by translators were condemned by Kostomarov (1959*b*), but шорты and тост are now accepted. A reader's letter to *RR* (1972, 1: 156–7) complained about the loanwords хобби 'hobby' and сервис 'service', but no one, apparently, has taken any notice. Lexical purism has since ceased to be an issue of any significance and apparently plays no part in present-day language planning.

Areas of lexical change

From our broad chronological survey of lexical change we now turn to change in particular thematic areas. The links between social and lexical change are better demonstrated by dealing with particular areas in detail, concentrating the material by taking a higher proportion of all the words under each thematic heading.

(i) *Politics and public administration*

It was especially in the public and political spheres that deliberate steps were taken to replace old words by new ones. New institutions which might be externally similar to old ones, yet, being based on a new philosophy, were internally different from their predecessors, needed new names to symbolize their new content.

The early attempts following the February Revolution to set up a new organization which would maintain public order and protect life and property against crime involved the abolition of many words associated with the old police system: полиция 'police', полицейский 'policeman', городовой 'policeman', полицмейстер (полицеймейстер) 'police chief', пристав 'police-officer', жандарм 'gendarme', жандармерия 'gendarmerie', участок 'police station'. (The last of these, участок, survives with other meanings.) To signify that the new organization was different from the tsarist police (despite external similarities) it was given the new name милиция 'militia', and its members the new name милиционер 'militiaman'. The fact that some people drew an analogy between the new and the old organizations is shown by the hybrid form милицейский (by analogy with полицейский), which Mazon heard in use in 1918–19 (1920: 29; also Jakobson 1921: 8). On the other hand, a definition recorded in the countryside (Jaroslavl' *gubernija*) in 1925 shows that the new word, though not properly understood, was not associated with the tsarist police system (Seliščev 1928: 215). The abolition of стряпчий 'solicitor' and адвокат 'lawyer, barrister' was similarly motivated; only the latter was subsequently reinstated (1922).

The words министр 'minister' and министерство 'ministry', which had been used both by the Provisional Government and in tsarist times, were also abolished as a planned measure to break with the past. The decision was taken at a meeting of the Central Committee in the Smol'nyj Institute during the night 24–5 October 1917, while the outcome of the Revolution was still uncertain. According to Miljutin (who made notes of the discussion) the word министр 'smelt of bureaucratic stuffiness' and the question of replacing it was discussed. Trockij proposed народный комиссар 'people's commissar', which pleased Lenin and was approved by all. The proposal that the new government should be called Совет Народных Комиссаров 'Council of People's Commissars' came from Kamenev, and it was with that name that it was formed on 26 October (Miljutin 1918). The ministries were called народный комиссариат, which in accordance with the current trend soon became наркомат. Народный комиссар became нарком and Совет Народных Комиссаров became Совнарком. The titles of the individual commissars and commissariats were also made into stump-compounds: Наркомпрос (Народный комиссар(иат) по просвещению) 'People's Commissar(iat) of Education', Наркомзем (Народный комиссар(иат) земледелия) 'People's Commissar(iat) of Agriculture', Наркомвнудел (Народный комиссар(иат) внутренних дел) 'People's Commissar(iat) of Internal Affairs', etc. The compounds all refer to either the commissar in question or his commissariat. Other types of abbreviation were also used. Наркомвнудел, for example, came to be better known as НКВД. The words комиссар and комиссариат were not new. Not only had they been used in the eighteenth and nineteenth centuries, but комиссар was also used under the Provisional Government. It is said that the new purposes to which these words were put resulted from an analogy being drawn with similar French terms employed in the Paris Commune of 1871 (Altajskaja 1960: 18). Subsequently, after nearly thirty years of being applied only to ministers and ministries of other countries, министр and министерство were reintroduced to the Soviet Administration (1946), while нарком and наркомат passed into history.

Another deliberate break with the terminology of the old regime was the replacement in 1918 of посол 'ambassador' and посольство 'embassy' by the new compounds полпред (полномочный представитель) and полпредство (полномочное представительство). The new words served to distinguish Soviet diplomatic representation from that of all other states (which continued to be referred to by the old words), but they also resulted in technical difficulties as to protocol, and eventually, for the sake of convenience in international relations посол and посольство were reintroduced by edicts dated 1941 and 1943 (Altajskaja 1960: 18). Полпред has survived, however, not in its original strictly terminological meaning, but with the general sense of 'representative', as shown in the following recent example of its use:

Безымянный комбат стал символом, полпредом наших славных командиров... (*Неделя*, №. 43, 21–7 October 1974: 6)

The nameless battalion commander has become a symbol, a representative of our famous commanders . . .

The fact that the Party itself has changed its name four times has had certain repercussions. РСДРП (Российская социал-демократическая рабочая партия) 'Russian Social-Democratic Workers Party' was changed to РКП(б) (Российская Коммунистическая партия (большевиков)) at the Seventh Party Congress in March 1918, and soon afterwards the form компартия appeared, later being applied to foreign communist parties, too. Thus the word большевик, which had originated following the Second Congress of the RSDRP in London in 1903, was adopted as part of the title. A further change was made in 1925 at the Fourteenth Congress to ВКП(б) (Все-союзная Коммунистическая партия (большевиков)) 'All-Union Communist Party (Bolshevik)' to take account of the fact that it was now the party of the Soviet Union, the U.S.S.R. having come into being in December 1922, with the title Союз Советских Социалистических Республик 'Union of Soviet Socialist Republics', abbreviated as СССР. In 1952 the Nineteenth Congress changed it yet again, this time to Коммунистическая партия Советского Союза 'Communist Party of the Soviet Union', abbreviated as КПСС—the name which it retains to the present day. This latest alteration removed the word большевик and consequently a member came to be called коммунист, -ка 'communist', instead of большевик, -чка 'Bolshevik'. According to Ožegov (1972) коммунист, -ка now has only one meaning, viz. 'member of the Communist Party'. Большевик, -чка now refers to members of the Party before 1952 or, in a general way, to supporters of Bolshevism (Altajskaja 1960: 15–16).

The naming of new organs of government, administration of Justice, and the Party at all levels has involved the creation of many new words, the majority of which are stump-compounds, such as:

(i) Party organs: партком (партийный комитет) 'Party committee', райком (районный комитет) 'district committee', горком (городской комитет) 'town committee', etc.

(ii) Organs of justice: нарсуд (народный суд) 'people's court', облсуд (областной суд) *'oblast'* court', etc.

(iii) Government organs: сельсовет (сельский совет) 'village council', райисполком (районный исполнительный комитет) 'district executive committee' (known in the 1930s as РИК), горсовет (городской совет) 'town council', etc.

Terms relating to the territorial division of the U.S.S.R. into administrative districts was affected by innovations made in the 1920s and completed with the division into *rajony* (райониро-вание) of 1929–30. Thus the words волость, уезд, губерния, disappeared, except in reference to the past, giving way to сельсовет (both a region and a government body), район, область, край. (The last three are old words with a new terminological meaning.) The office of губернатор 'governor' was abolished in 1917. The only function of this word nowadays is to refer to other states and pre-Revolutionary Russia.

Owing to political and administrative change since 1917 several words introduced in the early Soviet period have since fallen out of use. Some we have mentioned already; others are: комъячейка 'communist cell', батрачком 'farm labourers' committee', крестком 'peasants' committee', ревком 'revolutionary committee', реввоенсовет 'revolutionary military council'. The word совнархоз 'national economy council'—which Lenin said foreigners took to be a place-name and checked it in their railway guides (Rybnikova 1925: 115)—first came into existence in 1917. It has subsequently had an eventful career, for совнар-хозы were later abolished, reintroduced in 1957, and later abolished again (Meščerskij 1967*a*: 19).

A number of Soviet political terms are now applied equally to Soviet or foreign institutions. This is so, for example, in the case of исполком, компартия, комсомол.

The РКСМ (Российский Коммунистический Союз Моло-дежи) 'Russian Communist Union of Youth', founded in 1918, was known as the комсомол 'Komsomol' (Коммунистический Союз Молодежи 'Communist Union of Youth'), a title which has not been affected by subsequent changes in the official name, first to РЛКСМ (Российский Ленинский Коммунистический Союз Молодежи) 'Russian Leninist Communist Union of Youth' in 1924 and then to ВЛКСМ (Всесоюзный Ленинский Коммунистический Союз Молодежи) 'All-Union Leninist Communist Union of Youth' in 1926 (Altajskaja 1960: 15). Both комсомол and its derivatives комсомольский, комсомолец, -ка, (but not комсомолия, which is exclusively Soviet) are applied to communist youth organizations in other countries. For example:

Одной из главных задач, стоящих сейчас перед КПВ,[1] Дж. Голлан назвал работу по увеличению численности рядов партии и комсомола. (*Pravda*, 13 November 1974)

As one of the many tasks now facing the Communist Party of Great Britain, J. Gollan named the job of increasing the membership of the Party and the Komsomol.

The Soviet word исполком is also employed in this way:

Здесь состоялось заседание национального исполкома лейбористской партии, где была принята резолюция, критикующая проведение совместных маневров британского и южноафриканского флотов... (*Pravda*, 4 November 1974)

A meeting of the national executive committee of the Labour Party has been held here, at which a resolution was passed criticizing the holding of joint manœuvres by the British and South African fleets . . .

(ii) *Agriculture*

The October Revolution took place in a predominantly agricultural country, and agricultural reorganization and modernization were from the beginning matters of prime importance. The Land Decree passed on 26 October 1917 proclaimed the abolition of private ownership of land, but it was only with the beginning of the First Five-Year Plan (1928) that collectivization was introduced. The word коллективизация, which still has only the specialized meaning 'collectivization of agriculture', came into existence a few years earlier, when the question first came under discussion (Seliščev 1928:

[1] Коммунистическая партия Великобритании 'Communist Party of Great Britain'.

109). It was accompanied by колхоз 'collective farm' (1925), whereas совхоз 'state farm' is older, dating back to at least 1921.

The early Soviet years saw the specialization of бедняк 'poor peasant' and its collective беднота 'poor peasantry', referring to a specific socio-economic category. The words provided the source of others including комбед 'committee of poor peasants', the name given to committees organized throughout the R.S.F.S.R. during 1918 to strengthen Soviet power in the villages (Rybnikova 1925: 114). Collectivization meant dispossessing the kulaks of land and equipment, a process which brought into being the verb раскулачивать (1929) 'dekulakize' (Ovsjannikov 1933: 222). Apart from the бедняк and кулак, the new social category of 'middle peasant', neither exploiting nor exploited, came under discussion, producing the new word середняк (1921) and its derivatives. To refer to those peasants who continued, as long as possible, to work alone without joining an agricultural commune the new noun единоличник 'individual farmer' (early 1920s) was derived from единоличный 'individual' (Šanskij 1963–). In the late 1920s подкулачник came into use, meaning a middle or poor peasant who supported kulaks (Ovsjannikov 1933: 196). Since collectivization кулак, бедняк, середняк, раскулачивать have become historicisms. Also, батрак 'farm labourer', помещик 'landowner', and имение 'estate' have had no referents in Russia since the Civil War, but they are still used with reference to capitalist countries.

Essential to collectivization was mechanization, and state-owned machine and tractor stations serving the collective farms were set up throughout the country during the First and Second Five-Year Plans. This was the origin of the well-known abbreviation МТС 'machine and tractor station' (1928–58).

The use of machinery transformed Russian agriculture: by 1937 there were 450,000 farm tractors and 121,000 combine harvesters in use. The word трактор 'tractor' arrived round about the time of the Revolution: Šanskij (1963–) and Kalinin (1971: 112) consider it an innovation of the Soviet era, but it is difficult to be sure. That many of its derivatives originated after 1917 is beyond dispute, however: тракторист,[1] -ка,

---

[1] In his report to the Eighth Party Congress (1919) Lenin (lacking anything better) could only use the word машинист to refer to tractor drivers (Ovsjannikov 1933: 121).

тракторизация, тракторизм. The English loanword комбайн 'combine harvester' arrived in the late 1920s (Krysin 1968: 96) and, similarly, led to a string of derivatives: комбайнер, -ка, комбайновый.

The training of agricultural experts and the application of their skills brought in: агротехник (агрономический техник) 'agrotechnician', агробаза (агрономическая база) 'agronomical station', and other stump-compounds with агро-. Further neologisms connected with agriculture are: сельмаш (отдел сельскохозяйственных машин) 'agricultural machinery department', посевкампания (посевная кампания) 'sowing campaign', мичуринец 'Michurinite', трудодень 'workingday' (unit by which collective farm's income is calculated).

(iii) *Industry*

Industrialization and urbanization have changed the Russian language not only by changing the social make-up of its users, but also by motivating change in the vocabulary. Modernization, new methods of production, and improved technology have been accompanied by the appearance of new words, many of which are restricted to specialized use. Many others, however, have entered the general vocabulary. In a country where the industrial worker occupies such a prominent position in society it is not surprising that the vocabulary of industry is well known.

New methods in the organization of labour to increase productivity include the system of work-teams or 'brigades', introduced in the 1920s. The word бригада thus acquired a new meaning, for previously, apart from its military meaning, it had been applicable only to a team of workers running a train. Similarly, бригадир (a military rank in the eighteenth century) acquired a new meaning as 'leader of a work-team', and the derivative бригадничество came into existence to describe the brigade system (Ovsjannikov 1933: 38; Klinskaja 1957: 25), though it later gave way to the phrase бригадная система 'brigade system'.

In 1929 workers of a machine-building factory in Leningrad introduced their own amendments, or counter-plan (встречный план), to the management's production plan, thereby increasing productivity. Counter-plans became a regular part of the industrial scene and the nominalized adjective встречный came into everyday use. Changes in industry in the 1920s also brought in: пятидневка 'five-day week', непрерывка 'id.', норма 'norm', нормировка 'establishment of norms', останов 'work stoppage', планировать 'plan', самотек 'drift', обезличка 'lack of personal responsibility', субботник 'Saturday of voluntary work', диспетчер 'dispatcher'.

Words of common knowledge resulting from improvements in industrial technology include the following: грузовик (contracted from грузовой автомобиль) 'lorry', машинизация 'mechanization', моторизация 'motorization', электрификация 'electrification', амортизатор 'shock absorber', автоматизация 'automatization'.

(iv) *The armed forces*

In the armed forces, too, deliberate changes were made in terminology in order to symbolize the break with tsarism. Even the word солдат 'soldier' was rejected by the Red Army together with nearly all the pre-Revolutionary names of ranks. When the Рабоче-крестьянская Красная Армия 'Workers' and Peasants' Red Army' was founded in 1918 the lowest rank was красноармеец. In the navy матрос 'seaman' was replaced by краснофлотец.

Ranks, as such, were abolished and replaced by the names of appointments. The word офицер 'officer' became obsolete and was replaced by командир 'commander' or красный командир 'red commander', abbreviated to краском. The names of ranks ефрейтор 'lance-corporal', бомбардир 'bombardier', сержант 'sergeant', прапорщик 'ensign', лейтенант 'lieutenant', поручик 'id.', капитан 'captain', майор 'major', полковник 'colonel', генерал 'general', fell out of use together with чин 'rank' and звание 'id.'.

Appointments in the new army were named as follows: командир отделения 'section commander', помощник командира взвода 'deputy platoon commander', командир взвода 'platoon commander', старшина роты 'company warrant officer', командир роты 'company commander', командир батальона 'battalion commander', командир полка 'regimental commander', командир дивизии 'divisional commander'. They were often abbreviated as комбат, комдив, etc.

In 1935 the concept of rank and the word звание were revived, together with the words лейтенант, капитан, майор, полковник. In 1940 генерал, сержант, and ефрейтор were reintroduced, followed in 1943 by офицер. After the War, in 1946, солдат made its come-back, and прапорщик returned in 1972 (Protčenko 1973: 13). In the navy адмирал (together with контр-адмирал, etc.) returned in 1940; матрос was reinstated in 1946.

The system of political command in the Red Army produced several new words, including политрук 'political instructor' (1919–42) and замполит 'political deputy'. The latter is still in use.

Since 1917 денщик 'batman' has not been used, though words of similar meaning have had limited functions at times, viz. вестовой, ординарец. During the First World War there were nationalistic attempts to replace the German loanword фельдшер 'medical assistant' with лекарский помощник (Barannikov 1919: 74). It was as part of the rejection of old discriminatory practices in the medical profession that this change actually took place (Meščerskij 1967a: 6), however, and the Red Army regulations retained ветеринарный фельдшер for veterinary assistants but introduced лекарский помощник to refer to medical personnel (*Устав* . . ., 1918: 30–1). The new term was generally abbreviated to лекпом. During the 1940s фельдшер was reinstated and replaced лекпом both in the armed forces and in general use.

Sources of borrowings

Considering the question of foreign influence in Russian around the time of the Revolution, Mazon concluded that the contribution made by English had been minimal (1920: 17). Not very long afterwards, however, English became the largest single identifiable source of loanwords. At the same time, it must be admitted that there are cases of loanwords with possible models in several different European languages and that sometimes it is not possible to identify the source. The adjective превентивный 'preventive', for example, though described by Krysin (1968: 119) as a French or German borrowing, could well have its source in several languages, including English.

Not in every case are we able by some semantic or formal peculiarity of one of the models to identify it as the true source. Many Soviet borrowings can only be classified as Europeanisms. There is room for argument, for example, in the case of кемпинг which Krysin (1968: 158) identifies as an English loanword, though the fact that it means not 'camping' but 'camping site' makes some other language a more likely source, such as French, in which the latter meaning is present. But we are dealing in probabilities only.

Internal borrowings

The vocabulary of the standard language has expanded by borrowing not only from other languages, but also from non-standard varieties of Russian itself. This internal process depends on changes in attitude towards non-standard words, which can consequently be accepted first in the colloquial and possibly later in the written standard.

Some of the words which in the Soviet period have ceased to be non-standard are: балка 'ravine' (Kuznecova 1970), задира 'troublemaker' (Kuznecova 1971), расческа 'comb' (Balaxonova 1967), фарцовщик 'dealer in goods bought illegally from foreigners' (Skvorcov 1972: 52–3), халтура 'hack-work' (Skvorcov 1972: 53–4), шпаргалка 'crib'. (All these, except балка and расческа, are considered colloquial by Ožegov 1972.)

It is remarkable, however, that many non-standard words and meanings (largely from the language of criminals), which in the early 1920s were gaining wide currency among the young, who considered them 'the language of the proletariat' (Seliščev 1928: 80), are still shown in Ožegov (1972) as *prostorečno*: e.g. барахло 'old clothes', буза 'row', липовый 'faked', мура 'nonsense', сволочь 'scum'. There are also several other, more recent words and meanings which Ožegov (1972) records as *prostorečno*, even though they are now sometimes used colloquially by educated speakers: доходяга 'emaciated person', дуриком 'uselessly', загорать 'to hang about', кореш, корешок 'friend', левый 'illegal', левак 'one who earns illegally on the side' (also левачество, левачить), мухлевать 'to fiddle', стукач 'informer', хохма 'joke'. The hypothesis that this is another area of discrepancy between normative recommendation and actual usage (cf. Chapter 1, p. 46, and Chapter 3, p. 87) might be tested by a further survey on the lines of the RJaSO project.

Other languages of the Soviet Union

Although it is not formally proclaimed as the first or official language of the Soviet Union, Russian occupies a unique position, and most users of the non-Russian languages also know and use some Russian. Over the centuries Russian has acquired many loanwords from its immediate neighbours, but in the Soviet period their influence has been but slight if compared with that of Western European languages. On the other hand, the influence of Russian on the other languages of the Soviet Union is very strong.

The degree of interference is greatest at the local level, where many people daily use both Russian and the local language. In these circumstances loanwords occur not only in spoken Russian but also in local newspapers and books, in both original and translated literature. In the Russian-language press of Central Asia, for example, the following local words were observed in use in the 1930s: курултай 'congress', меджлис 'conference', аксакал 'village headman', раис 'chairman', мудир 'director', мактаб 'school', муаллим 'teacher'. The total number of such words recorded by Mirtov (1941) is considerable, but none of them has been adopted in the standard language. Even those words from the other languages of the Soviet Union which have become part of the standard vocabulary refer for the most part to strictly local, non-Russian phenomena. The Kazakh loanword акын for example, borrowed in the 1930s (Šanskij 1963–), refers to a folk-singer or poet only of Kazakhstan or Kirgizia. The Uzbek loanword басмач borrowed during the Civil War (Šanskij 1963–), refers to a member of a counter-revolutionary band in Central Asia at that time. Similarly, the Uzbek or Tadjik loanword дехканин 'peasant, farmer', first registered in 1926 (Šanskij 1963–), relates only to Central Asia. Other Central Asian loanwords said to have been borrowed in the Soviet period (Meščerskij 1967a: 27) and having strictly local functions are: кишлак 'village', кетмень 'type of hoe', паранджа 'garment including face-covering, worn by Moslem women'.

An example of that very rare phenomenon, a word borrowed from one of the non-Russian languages since 1917 which has acquired a general (non-local) meaning, is provided by тамада 'master of ceremonies at a banquet', which comes from Georgian. Its earliest dictionary reference dates from 1937 (Meščerskij 1967*a*: 27).

It should be added, however, that several pre-1917 borrowings which were once extremely exotic and little known have become more widely used in recent years, owing to greater familiarity with the Central Asian ethos resulting from tourism (and travel generally). Russian translations of Central Asian literature have also played a part in this process (Suprun 1963: 155). Among the examples is арык 'irrigation ditch' (first borrowed from the Turkic languages of Central Asia in the nineteenth century).

The question of Ukrainian loanwords in the Soviet period is particularly difficult. Examples quoted by commentators often turn out to have been borrowed before the Revolution; others are of doubtful Ukrainian origin. Самостийность 'nationalistic independence' (Mazon 1920: 19) was borrowed from Ukrainian at about the time of the Revolution and has a firm place in the Russian vocabulary. But although Ožegov (1972) defines it without mentioning the Ukraine, in practice it appears to be applied only to Ukrainian affairs. A Ukrainian loanword which is not restricted to a local meaning is хлебороб 'corn-grower', but it was borrowed and had ceased to be felt specifically Ukrainian before the beginning of the twentieth century. Its frequency seems to have increased in the Soviet period, however, and the morpheme -роб has been used to form the new (1930s) хлопкороб 'cotton-grower' (Krysin 1964).

There seems to be a marked desire among some investigators to prove the influence of other Soviet languages on Russian in the Soviet period (e.g. Beloded 1964: 476–7; Meščerskij 1967*b*: 23) despite the scarcity of examples. The fact that so far little evidence of this influence has been assembled, however, does not mean that it does not exist. The problems of detecting the results of interference between genetically closely related systems are notorious, and it is therefore quite possible that details of the influence of Ukrainian, in particular, have yet to be revealed.

6

SEX, GENDER, AND THE STATUS OF WOMEN

Word-formation[1]

TRADITIONALLY, Russian has distinct masculine and feminine forms for nouns that can refer to both men and women, in much the same way as it has separate masculine and feminine adjectives, the main difference being that with adjectives the distinction is shown by inflection (declension), whereas with nouns it is shown by derivation, the latter being less regular in formation. Thus an Englishman is англичанин, an Englishwoman англичанка, and a Muscovite is either москвич or москвичка. With occupations and professions, however, pre-Revolutionary Russian society did not in general concede that the same profession could be carried out equally by both men and women. A few occupations, mainly of low status, could be carried out equally by both sexes, so that we find differentiated pairs like ткач–ткачиха 'weaver'. There were also a few occupations that were exercised only by women, so that there is no masculine equivalent of сестра милосердия 'sister of mercy', the pre-Revolutionary word for a (medical) nurse. But there was no term, for example, for a woman general, correlating with the fact that there were no women generals. In traditional Russian usage there is a word генеральша, formed from генерал by adding the feminine suffix -ша. However, this does not mean a woman who is a general, but a general's wife. Particularly with such names as this, conferring on the bearer higher social prestige, only men could have such prestige in their own right; the woman's place was in the home, and at best she could enjoy the reflected prestige of her husband's rank.

[1] For other discussions, see Janko-Trinickaja (1966*b*), Protčenko (1964; 1975: 189–213, 273–95), and Panov (1968, 2: 191–213).

During the present century, this social system has changed radically. Even in the late nineteenth century, as a result of industrialization, many more women came to be employed in industry, mainly in unskilled jobs. In 1901, 26 per cent of industrial workers were women, and by 1917 the figure was 40 per cent (quoted in Janko-Trinickaja 1966*b*: 170–1). Part of the increase in the years leading up to the Revolution was due to mobilization: many working men were fighting at the front, and their places were taken by women. A similar situation arose during the last war, when women took on various jobs that had previously been considered unsuitable for them. In some sectors women now far outnumber men, for instance in education and the health service. Thus there has been a radical change in social structure.

Less commonly, typically women's professions have become open to men. The term медицинский брат is used in hospitals for a male nurse, cf. медицинская сестра (abbreviated мед-сестра) 'nurse'. Дояр 'man who milks cows' is a back-formation from доярка 'milk-maid'. Many of the masculine terms in such cases are circumlocutions: Rozental' (1971: 165) notes перепис-чик на машине 'typist' (cf. машинистка; машинист means 'engine-driver'). With many occupations that are felt to be essentially women's, specifically female forms tend to be used without any stylistic connotation, e.g. телефонистка 'switchboard operator', массажистка 'masseuse' (Gorbačevič 1973: 514).

The increase in the number of women taking up jobs previously restricted to men was most noticeable during the early years after the Revolution. During this period, the tendency was for women taking up these jobs to be referred to by specifically feminine-suffixed forms (Janko-Trinickaja 1966*b*: 178). The commonest such suffix is -ка added to the masculine form of occupational, political, and other nouns, e.g. комсомолка 'member of the Komsomol', активистка 'political activist', агентка 'agent', женкорка 'women's correspondent' (cf. женкор, an abbreviation of женский корреспондент; most women's correspondents, if not all, were women). Some of these have since fallen out of use, for instance агентка and женкорка. In current usage, the suffix -ка is productive particularly in forming feminine forms from masculine words in -ист. There are certain difficulties in generalizing the use of -ка, in particular because this suffix has a number of other uses (Mučnik 1971: 222). Thus the word электричка has been pre-empted to refer to a kind of suburban train, and is not used as the feminine of электрик 'electrician';[1] similarly, техничка is a colloquial term for a technical college (cf. техник 'technician'), столярка a colloquial term for a joiner's workshop (cf. столяр 'joiner'). Secondly, it is felt inappropriate to use this suffix with occupations of higher prestige; the form славистка for a woman Slavist is unacceptable, and likely to provoke laughter from Russians; as the feminine of филолог 'philologist', филоложка is quite impossible, while филологичка is only marginally better,[2] and would be evaluated in the same way as славистка.

For masculine nouns ending in -тель, -ник, -чик, and -щик, the suffixes -ница (after -тель, or replacing -ник), -чица, -щица (replacing -чик and -щик) became widespread (Protčenko 1964: 109 ff.). In addition to traditional terms like учительница (cf. учитель 'teacher'), such neologisms arose as истопница (cf. истопник 'stoker'), наждачница (cf. наждачник 'sandpaperer'), никелировщица (cf. никелировщик 'nickeller'). The examples quoted give some idea of the sort of occupations concerned here: mainly highly specialized, but unskilled or semi-skilled, with little or no social prestige attached. There are many such terms in the specialized vocabulary of any industry, and while most of them arose in the late nineteenth and early twentieth centuries, they continue in use to the present day. The simple suffix -ица is rare in words of the class under discussion; an example is фельдшерица (cf. фельдшер 'doctor's assistant').

Below we shall examine in greater detail two more native feminine noun-suffixes: -ша and -иха.

Less commonly foreign suffixes were used, such as -есса in адвокатесса (cf. адвокат 'lawyer'), or -иса in инспектриса (cf.

---

[1] Feminine derivatives ending in -ичка are stressed -и́чка, irrespective of the stress of the masculine form (Švedova 1970: 121); thus there would be no stress difference between электричка 'suburban train' and a feminine derivative of электрик.

[2] Gorbačevič (1973: 514) notes that forms like биологичка 'woman biologist, biology-teacher' (cf. биолог) are characteristic of school-children's slang. Филоложка exists as a colloquial term for филология 'philology', especially as a university subject.

инспектор 'inspector'). These formations are now for the most
part defunct, with one or two exceptions, e.g. актриса 'actress'
(cf. актер 'actor'). It is interesting to ask why актриса in
particular should have been retained as a distinct feminine
form. In general, it does not matter from the point of view of
social function in the Soviet Union whether the holder of a
job is a man or a woman. However, there are exceptions,
equally determined by social convention. One such case is that
of actors and actresses: in most plays there are specifically male
and specifically female roles, and actors or actresses are cast
accordingly. Similarly in sport, there are usually separate men's
and women's competitions, whence separate terms for female
athletes, like волейболистка 'volleyball player', дискоболка
'discus-thrower'.[1] Women's athletics is essentially a post-
Revolutionary phenomenon, so the words are largely post-
Revolutionary creations. M. P. Sokolov, in his book *Конько-
бежный спорт* (Moscow, 1952, quoted by Mučnik 1971: 216)
refers to women skaters before the Revolution as женщины-
конькобежцы (this was then an unusual phenomenon), but
to contemporary women skaters as конькобежки.[2] Nowadays,
the forms with preposed женщина 'woman' are common only
where it is necessary to emphasize the unusualness of a woman
doing something, e.g. женщина-космонавт 'woman cosmo-
naut'. In current Russian usage, женщина-врач tends to be
as condescending and patronizing as 'lady doctor' in English.[3]

Some professional names in Russian are adjectives used as
nouns, and these of course easily form feminine equivalents:
дежурный 'man on duty', дежурная 'woman on duty'; управ-
ляющий домом (домами)–управляющая домом (домами)
'manager of a block of flats' (both usually abbreviated to
управдом). However, even here there is, with higher prestige
professions, a tendency to use only the masculine form. Thus

[1] Soviet sports terminology is discussed by Protčenko (1975: 168–214),
with discussion of the use of masculine or feminine forms with reference to
women (189–213).
[2] More recent examples of the use of женщина-конькобежец, and also
of конькобежец with reference to a woman, are noted by Protčenko (1975:
200), alongside more frequent конькобежка; the examples are from newspapers in the early fifties. Ušakov (1935–40) gives a feminine form конько-
бежица, not known to us from other sources.
[3] Cf. Lakoff (1973: 59–60).

the head of a department in a university is, irrespective of sex, заведующий кафедрой.

Some masculine nouns resolutely refuse to allow derived feminine forms. One such word is товарищ 'comrade'.[1] The current tendency to use the masculine form for both men and women is often attributed partly to the influence of the increased frequency of this word, without gender distinction, in the post-Revolutionary period. This general tendency seems to have arisen first in the speech of the intelligentsia around the turn of the century (Janko-Trinickaja 1966b: 181). During the early post-Revolutionary years the influence of the intelligentsia was less prominent, and large numbers of special feminine forms were created. With the re-emerging importance placed on the standard language, the influence of the intelligentsia became more noticeable again, so that the tendency initiated by them among themselves has become much more widespread, particularly with higher prestige occupations. There is no internal linguistic reason why a woman president should not be президентка, but in fact this form is not used. Although both герой 'hero' and героиня 'heroine' exist, there is only the one form Герой Советского Союза 'Hero of the Soviet Union' or Герой Социалистического Труда 'Hero of Socialist Labour'.[2] While both пионер and пионерка exist, the solemn oath taken by children joining this youth organization is invariably: Я, юный пионер Советского Союза, перед лицом своих товарищей торжественно обещаю... 'I, a young pioneer of the Soviet Union, do solemnly promise before my comrades . . .' (Janko-Trinickaja 1966b: 196). In certain cases, the relevant factor seems to be not so much the prestige attached to the occupation as the expectation, at least from a relatively traditional viewpoint, that the occupation is primarily male. Thus although строитель 'construction-worker' belongs to a class of nouns—agentives in -тель—that readily form feminines in -ница, the word строитель is in fact used for a construction-worker of either sex.

Part of the RJaSO survey tested whether people would normally, in official documents, use the masculine or feminine

---

[1] In the sense 'companion', there is an archaic feminine form товарка.

[2] But note мать-героиня, the title awarded to a woman who has mothered ten children or more, which is specifically female and feminine.

form to refer to women's occupations. In the test, described in
Panov (1968, 2: 204–5), the informants did not know that they
were being questioned specifically on this point. They were
asked to give various pieces of information about themselves
in the preamble to the questionnaire, including their own and
their parents' occupations. The relevant replies were collected
(own occupation for women informants, mother's occupation
for all informants) and analysed. In 1,000 replies the nouns
referring to women that appeared more than ten times are as
follows: учитель(ница) 'teacher', студент(ка) 'student', препо-
даватель(ница) 'teacher', воспитатель(ница) 'tutor', лабо-
рант(ка) 'laboratory assistant', продавец (продавщица) 'shop
assistant', фельдшер(ица) 'doctor's assistant'. Of these, сту-
дентка was used 131 times, студент 23; in general, names of
those undergoing education have distinct forms, and if anything
it is surprising that some 15 per cent of the informants should
have used the masculine form. Even as traditional a form as
учительница was used in only about 60 per cent of the relevant
cases (93 : 63). For all the other words, the masculine form was
used by the majority of those replying to the questionnaire.

In Kalinin, during July 1975, the Hotel Seliger required
trainee-waitresses, and advertised for them in the following
terms:

Ресторан «Селигер» приглашает на работу в ресторан и его
филиалы... учеников официантов (девушек в возрасте до 25 лет
со средним образованием).

The Seliger restaurant invites to employment in the restaurant
and its branches . . . trainee-waiters (girls aged up to 25 with
secondary education).

Here, the parenthesis makes it clear that only female applicants
are sought, so that although the reference is specifically to women,
the author of the notice felt justified in using the masculine form
ученик официант 'trainee-waiter'. The variation in usage in such
cases can be seen from the fact that further along the same street,
the café Russkij čaj was advertising for официанток (accusative
plural) 'waitresses', with the specifically feminine form.

For some of the suffixes that can be used to make feminine
forms, there are additional sociolinguistic factors that have led
to their loss of popularity in forming female occupation names.

One of these suffixes is -иха. This was used, even before the Revolution, to form some names of female occupations, e.g. ткачиха (cf. ткач 'weaver'), повариха (cf. повар 'cook'), портниха (cf. портной 'tailor'). However, it was at least as widespread in its use to indicate the wife of someone holding a certain (usually relatively low) rank or job, e.g. купчиха (cf. купец 'merchant'), полковничиха (cf. полковник 'colonel'); in regional dialects it even forms wives' names from male forenames, e.g. Иваниха 'Ivan's wife' (Švedova 1970: 122). In addition, it is the only productive suffix for forming female animal names, e.g. дельфиниха 'cow-dolphin'. In the twenties it was used quite widely to form female occupation names, without any particular stylistic nuance, e.g. слесариха (cf. слесарь 'locksmith'), шпиониха (cf. шпион 'spy'), even члениха (cf. член 'member') (Janko-Trinickaja 1966*b*: 180–1). In the course of time, however, it went out of use as a productive suffix, no doubt owing to the recollection that it is associated with the socially obnoxious practice of classifying a woman solely in accordance with her husband's position, perhaps also to the fact that the suffix is now associated in particular with female animals' names. The word врачиха, formed from врач 'doctor', is not listed as standard (not even colloquial standard) in current dictionaries, and is usually avoided, unless an insult is deliberately intended. Interestingly, there is one new word where this suffix is used: пловчиха (cf. пловец 'swimmer') (Mučnik 1971: 216; Protčenko 1975: 209–10). As already noted, with names of people engaged in sport there is considerable pressure for having separate masculine and feminine words, and in this case this pressure has overcome the prejudice against -иха. Protčenko (1975: 210) also notes a rarer term гребчиха (cf. гребец 'rower').

The fate of the feminine suffix -ша has been similar, except that in traditional usage this suffix was even more restricted to indicating wives of holders of ranks or professions, e.g. генеральша (cf. генерал 'general'), фабрикантша (cf. фабрикант 'factory-owner').[1] In the early twentieth century it was also

---

[1] Forms in -ша with this meaning are no longer current in educated usage. The form профессорша, which before the Revolution meant 'professor's wife', is now used colloquially for a woman professor (Švedova 1970: 123).

used for women exercising certain professions, e.g. авиаторша (cf. авиатор 'airman'), without any stylistic markedness (Janko-Trinickaja 1966*b*: 173), and such forms became productive particularly in the twenties: агитаторша (cf. агитатор 'agitator'), редакторша (cf. редактор 'editor'). In general, these have since fallen into disuse. Certainly, with the jobs just mentioned, to the extent that the masculine forms are still in use, they are used for both men and women. A few words in -ша do survive in the current standard to indicate women's occupations, but are used mainly in the colloquial standard. Examples are кассирша (cf. кассир 'cashier'), секретарша (cf. секретарь 'secretary'), and less commonly кондукторша (cf. кондуктор 'conductor'). A form like секретарша again reveals the social classification of occupations into high and low prestige: this form would be used only of a secretary in an office, a shorthand-typist; the secretary of, for instance, a Party committee would be секретарь, irrespective of sex. Very few forms in -ша are now used in neutral style: exceptions are a few typically women's occupations (e.g. маникюрша 'manicurist'; маникюр 'manicure' refers to the process); even in sports terminology, such forms as партнерша 'partner', призерша 'prize-winner' are considered colloquial (Protčenko 1975: 208).

In principle, the separate feminine forms are obligatory with nationality and place-of-origin names, like англичанка 'Englishwoman', москвичка 'woman from Moscow'. Occasionally, however, one finds the masculine forms even here, as in the example quoted by Janko-Trinickaja (1966*b*: 208) from a review in *Вечерняя Москва* (27 June 1964): Приятно рекомендовать читателям «Вечерней Москвы» нового автора и старого москвича 'It is a pleasure to recommend to the readers of *Вечерняя Москва* a new author and an old Muscovite.' The author in question is identified as V. Krupennikova.[1] This may be indicative of the next area in which the traditional gender distinction will break down.

In current usage, then, the masculine form is unmarked for sex. Thus if a state farm is advertising for a tractor-driver, the announcement will just say совхозу требуется тракторист,

---

[1] A relevant factor, not noted by Janko-Trinickaja, may be the presence in this example of the masculine noun автор, the usual form even with reference to a woman.

without specifying sex, and it is assumed that both men and women tractor-drivers are eligible. Just as we can use англичане to refer to the English as a whole, so we can use учителя to refer to teachers, men and women, as a whole. While англичане always allowed of this possibility, this has not always been true of учителя (Janko-Trinickaja 1966*b*: 188): in the early twentieth century it was more usual to say учителя и учительницы. Note also the semantic difference between она наилучший учитель в школе and она наилучшая учительница в школе, where the former means that she is the best of all the teachers, the latter that she is the best among the women-teachers, i.e. учительница is specifically feminine, учитель is non-specific.

If we use a personal noun metaphorically to refer to a thing, then traditional usage required the use of the feminine form if the other noun was grammatically feminine, the masculine otherwise, i.e. опыт (знание)—лучший советчик 'experience (knowledge) is the best counsellor', but жизнь—лучшая советчица 'life is the best counsellor'. Nowadays, the masculine form may be used irrespective of the gender of the other noun, i.e. also жизнь—лучший советчик (Janko-Trinickaja 1966*b*: 209).

Syntax[1]

In those cases where the masculine form is also used for women, a further difficulty arises. Russian regularly requires gender agreement, for instance of singular adjectives and past-tense verb forms. When the word врач refers to a woman, should one say врач пришел (masculine) or врач пришла (feminine) 'the doctor arrived', молодой (masculine) врач or молодая (feminine) врач 'young doctor'?[2] There is a conflict felt by many Russians in using a feminine adjective or verb with reference to a masculine noun, and in using a masculine adjective or verb to refer to a woman—in other words, there is here a real conflict between natural gender (sex) and grammatical gender.

---

[1] For other discussions, see Protčenko (1961), Panov (1968, 3: 19–41), Mučnik (1971: 205–44); the last two references are essentially the same (both having been written by Mučnik), but Mučnik (1971) also contains a comprehensive bibliography.

[2] Rothstein (1973) discusses some theoretical implications of the existence of these variants.

It seems not to be true, contrary to the claim sometimes made, that forms like врач пришла are used because it is felt necessary to indicate the sex of the person referred to: if this were so, then we should expect discomfort equally with the present tense врач идет, whereas this is not the case (Janko-Trinickaja 1966*b*: 203–5). Janko-Trinickaja (1966*b*: 175) points out that in the early twentieth century one sometimes finds a masculine word referring to a woman as subject of a present tense verb, and the equivalent feminine form (even if otherwise avoided on stylistic grounds) as subject of a past tense verb, to avoid the conflict, as in this quotation from *Женский вестник* (1908, No. 3): Автор энергично восстает против фарисейства общества… Эпиграфом этой книги авторша взяла изречение… 'The author takes an energetic stand against the hypocrisy of society . . . As the epigraph of this book the author has taken the dictum . . .' In nineteenth-century usage, when grammatical and natural gender conflicted (e.g. with подлец 'scoundrel' applied to a woman), the grammatical gender prevailed. Widespread encroachment of natural gender agreement is a more recent phenomenon.

Informants for the RJaSO survey were asked whether they preferred врач пришел or врач пришла when speaking of a woman. The full results are given in Panov (1968, 3: 19–41) and Mučnik (1971: 228–44). The majority of people asked preferred the variant врач пришла (51·7 per cent) to врач пришел (38·6 per cent), with 9·7 per cent undecided. When the figures were broken down according to social groups, it emerged that within each social group except writers and journalists there was a majority for the feminine form, and even with writers and journalists the majority for the masculine form was small (50·7 per cent). The figures were also broken down according to age: only with the oldest group (born before 1909) was the masculine form preferred to the feminine (49·8 per cent: 42·2 per cent), and preference for the feminine form was clearly greater the younger the informant, except that the very youngest group (born 1940–9) showed slightly less preference than the group born 1930–9. Mučnik (1971: 234) suggests that this may be due to the influence of prescriptive grammar taught in school and still remembered by the younger informants. Since prescriptive grammars still often condemn forms like врач пришла, it will be interesting to observe if their recommendations have any long-term effect. Those who replied to the questionnaire were also invited to air their views more discursively. The majority of views expressed were in favour of the feminine form, though some extreme views were expressed on both sides. Many writers were either outright hostile, or prepared to accept the feminine form only under pressure. Prescriptive grammar is a great area for airing one's prejudices: one worker replied that the masculine form should be used because врач есть врач 'a doctor is a doctor', irrespective of sex; another that the feminine form should be used because женщина есть женщина 'a woman is a woman', irrespective of profession (Mučnik 1971: 233). Perhaps the most intelligent comment came from the linguist V. Kudrjavcev: грамматика вступила в противоречие с жизнью 'grammar has come into conflict with life', although he continues: но пока я на стороне грамматики 'but so far I'm on the side of grammar' (Mučnik 1971: 231).

Where the common noun is accompanied by a proper name, then it is much more usual to have agreement with the natural gender. Thus Vinogradov *et al.* (1960, 2, 1: 510–11) hesitate to admit as grammatical the construction кондуктор дала 'the conductor gave', but recommend оперировала хирург Мария Григорьевна Каменчик 'the surgeon Marija Grigor'evna Kamenčik operated', and go so far as to make the strange recommendation that in such cases one should always insert a proper name. This fails to allow for the possibility that the speaker or writer may not know the name of the person he is discussing.

A second question on the questionnaire asked informants to choose between the variants у нас хороший бухгалтер and у нас хорошая бухгалтер 'we have a good accountant'. Here the overwhelming preference, for all social and age groups, was for the masculine adjective (69·9 per cent, with 25 per cent for the feminine adjective and 5·1 per cent undecided); the highest figure for the feminine adjective was from industrial workers (38·7 per cent), and from the age-group born 1940 and later (28·4 per cent), although there is in fact little variation among those born after 1910. Peškovskij, writing in the twenties, noted that while a Russian might say товарищ вошла 'the comrade entered', he would hardly say уважаемая товарищ 'dear comrade' (quoted in Mučnik 1971: 243). Where such examples occur in literature, it is usually as a stylistic device, or to characterize spoken language, as in Voznesenskij's Танцуй, моя академик! 'Dance, my academician!' (Mučnik 1971: 241–2). There are numerous examples from literature and the press where a past tense verb is in the feminine form, but an attributive adjective is in the masculine form, e.g. избранный организатор пришла ко мне 'the elected organizer came to me' (*Коммунист* 1925, No. 4; quoted by Janko-Trinickaja 1966: 192–4); the reverse is at best very rare, and we know of no actual examples (see Švedova 1970: 555).

Different normative handbooks give different recommendations concerning standard usage in this area. Many normative handbooks try to restrict врач пришла, preferred by a clear majority of informants, to colloquial speech. Švedova (1970: 555), however, says simply that in such cases 'there is no strict rule for the choice of gender'. With хорошая бухгалтер, the situation is different: the overwhelming majority of informants prefer the more traditional form with the masculine attributive adjective. Different attitudes towards уважаемая товарищ Иванова 'dear comrade Ivanova' have provoked a polemic involving Panfilov (1965), condemning this variant, and Janko-Trinickaja (1967), defending it. Švedova (1970: 489) allows this use of the feminine adjective in 'colloquial and relaxed (непринужденный) speech', and does not refer to it as non-standard.

One problem to which some of the informants addressed themselves was whether women were being upgraded or downgraded by the various alternatives. The answers they and others have suggested are sometimes diametrically opposed. Thus the writer V. Bokov suggested that the form врач пришла is an attempt to honour women grammatically (Mučnik 1971: 231). Timofeev (1963: 227–30) says that the existence of separate feminine forms for nouns indicates the equality of women, and that wherever possible the special feminine noun suffixes should be used. A. V. Mirtov, in a remark from a dissertation quoted by Janko-Trinickaja (1966: 194), says that the use of the same form for both men and women indicates the absence of discrimination between the sexes. Those concerned with this problem in English tend towards the latter view (cf. their rejection of such forms as *poetess* and *authoress*), though it should be borne in mind that formal gender distinction, often paralleling sex distinction, is a much more important and integral feature of Russian than of English, and that there is no simple correlation between societies that practise discrimination against women and languages that have grammatical gender.

Over all, in the conflict between derivational and syntactic means of referring to women exercising various professions, etc., the twentieth century has seen a marked increase in the use of syntactic means relative to derivational means, although the results of this process have not always been entirely harmonious (note the conflict surrounding the normative status of врач пришла). Perhaps because of this latter factor, there has been a certain rear-guard action in favour of resuscitating derivation. Thus the writer Natal'ja Il'ina, when replying to the RJaSO questionnaire, said that she rejects outright the forms врач пришла and хорошая бухгалтер, and would herself use врачиха and бухгалтерша (Mučnik 1971: 239). The latter is classed as colloquial by most dictionaries, while the former is nonstandard. Over all, such rear-guard actions in favour of the feminine derivational suffixes are directly contrary to the prevailing tendency in the language, and seem unlikely to have any long-term effect.

7

MODES OF ADDRESS AND
SPEECH ETIQUETTE

Pronouns

RUSSIAN, like nearly all other European languages, has a system of address entailing a choice between pronouns (including other parts of speech agreeing with them), depending on social factors. In Russian the pronominal system involves a choice between ты (hereafter abbreviated as T) and вы (abbreviated as V). The abbreviations T and V are also used here to refer to grammatical forms implying the potential existence of the pronoun itself; for example, понимаешь and понял are T, while понимаете and поняли are V. The social relationships corresponding to the patterns of choice between T and V are many and various, but the choice is basically indicative of social distance, i.e. its presence or absence to a greater or lesser degree.

Since V is grammatically obligatory in addressing groups of more than one person, the choice between T and V is restricted to situations in which only one person is addressed. The system is therefore fully operative only in relationships between two interlocutors.

Brown and Gilman (1972) compare choices of the T/V type in a number of European languages (not including Russian), showing the operation of three dyadic types in the dimensions of power and solidarity. The dyads in question are the symmetrical V (in which V is given and received by both speakers), the asymmetrical relationship (in which one speaker gives T and the other gives V), and the symmetrical T (in which T is given and received). The operation of these dyads in nineteenth-century Russian literature has been described by Friedrich (1966, 1972). Brown and Gilman also trace the history of this kind of address in European languages (without Russian), but since the rules for the choice between T and V when addressing one person are undoubtedly different in Russian from other European languages, it may be as well to begin with an acccount and explanation of their emergence in Russia.

An important contribution to the history of this question was made by Černyx (1948), in which he refers to A. P. Sumarokov's discussion of the problem in the eighteenth century. Sumarokov (1718–77) attributed the growth of the use of V in addressing one person to the influence of French and thought it a new phenomenon. Černyx (1948: 91–8) was able to show, however, that in fact it is found very much earlier. Isolated instances occur as early as the sixteenth century in diplomatic correspondence. Although by the eighteenth century there is ample evidence of the use of V, there is also evidence of confusion; for example, a letter from Fonvizin to Ja. I. Bulgakov dated 25 January 1778 begins with V and ends with T (Černyx 1948: 99). Clearly, by the nineteenth century there was considerable social differentiation in pronominal address (Friedrich 1972: 278). Among the peasants V was little known and used, whereas it was in wide use among the nobility, so wide in fact that some nobles hardly ever used T, even to subordinates. On the other extreme, many peasants were totally ignorant of V and even addressed nobles with T. In Puškin's *Капитанская дочка* we find such forms as 'Думал ли ты, ваше благородие, что...', though only in the speech of uneducated characters (Černyx, 1948: 95 n.). There were also, however, a number of people in positions of (probably moderate) power, who carefully distinguished T from V and attached great importance to the distinction; see, for instance, Čexov's story *Ты и вы* (1886). (It would be interesting to discover the social make-up of these people.) In the nineteenth century there were a number of official spheres where the distinction was institutionalized. It was laid down that witnesses in court should be addressed as V—a procedure which could lead to misunderstanding when the witness was totally unfamiliar with the system and interpreted V as plural. It was also laid down that prisoners were to be addressed as T, even if they were from the privileged classes (Černyx, 1948: 103 n.).

The asymmetrical relationship reflected by the use of T to subordinates and V to those in power was institutionalized in the army and, by convention at least, in industry. And these were two areas where revolutionaries made attempts to change the rules of pronominal address. One of the demands made by the Lena strikers in 1912 was that the management should address the workers not as T but as V. In the army the regulations before 1917 actually named the ranks (officers down to sub-ensign (подпрапорщик)) which were to be addressed V, and added: 'To all lower ranks not named in the above list T will be used.' (Černyx 1948: 107.)

The rules of address in the army were changed by the February Revolution: *Prikaz* No. 1 of 1 March 1917, issued by the Petrograd Soviet of Workers' and Soldiers' Deputies, included under its seventh point the following:

Offensive treatment of soldiers of all military ranks and in particular addressing them with T is forbidden, and any infringement of this, as well as any misunderstandings between officers and soldiers, must be reported by the latter to their company committees.

(Quoted by Černyx 1948: 108)

A decree of the Provisional Government (No. 114) dated 5 March 1917 contained similar provisions. On the pronominal question it said: 'I command . . . (3) That in addressing all soldiers, both on and off duty, V will be used' (*Сборник указов...*, 1917: 318). Subsequent regulations made under the Bolsheviks confirmed the new practice.[1] The 1918 *Устав внутренней службы* stated: 'All military personnel when addressing each other, both on and off duty, use V.' (*Устав...*, 1918: 10.)

But it is not easy to change modes of address by decree, and T continued in use despite all efforts, mainly because a large proportion of the new commanders in the Red Army came from the ranks and from that social level at which T was unmarked, but also because they used it to express solidarity rather than power, and partly because some of the Red commanders had been officers in the old army and could not rid themselves of old habits (Černyx 1948: 108). The latest *Устав внутренней службы* (approved in 1960) continues to insist on V: 'On questions of duty military personnel must address one another with V.' (*Общевоинские уставы . . .*, 1971: 14–15.) But

[1] There is no evidence to support Friedrich's assertion that 'the Red Army reintroduced *ty*, eventually extending it to all subordinates' (1972: 282).

breaches of this rule have been, and perhaps still are, not un-common; e.g. see Kantorovič (1966: 31, 41, 66).[1]

Only in the armed forces and in certain organizations such as factories and other places of work are there codified rules governing the choice of pronoun. It is evidently not considered a linguistic matter and is therefore ignored by the Academy Grammars. It is nevertheless a matter of interest to Russians as part of the general question of correct social behaviour, and is consequently dealt with in books on etiquette. Among these is Aasamaa (1974),[2] which considers the asymmetric form of discourse acceptable between the young (giving V, receiving T) and old (giving T, receiving V), and suggests that a young man may ask his elders to call him T while he continues to address them as V (Aasamaa 1974: 39). Another book dealing with etiquette from a prescriptive standpoint (including forms of address) is Pažin (1969), which on some points disagrees with Aasamaa. Pažin strongly emphasizes the fact that the use of V is a sign of good manners and condemns the use of T expressing power. He makes concessions to its use in certain circumstances, however: 'In small businesses with old-established traditions, where there is a considerable difference in the age of the workers and the managers, address with T on the part of the latter is recognized, particularly if their authority is indis-putable'. (Pažin 1969: 21–2.)

A third source of recommendations on pronominal usage is Xodakov (1972), which mentions a number of points not in-cluded by the other two. Most significant of these is the fact that there are also situational factors involved and that to ignore them may offend against etiquette. This may involve switching from symmetrical T in private to symmetrical V in public.[3]

---

[1] Two useful contributions to the subject of pronominal address in Russia have appeared since the present work was completed and delivered to the publishers, viz. Corbett (1976) and Nakhimovsky (1976). The latter refers partly to current usage in the Soviet Army.

[2] The fact that this book has been translated from the Estonian raises doubts as to its value as a source on Russian etiquette. A number of changes have been introduced in the Russian version, however, especially in the section on forms of address.

[3] Kantorovič mentions a case of switching from reciprocal T in private to asymmetric usage in public in order to bolster the authority of the receiver of V (1966: 40–2).

Xodakov (in agreement with Pažin) condemns the T of power used by people in authority and refers to what he calls 'a certain inflation of the word T' (Xodakov 1972: 39), by which he apparently means that T is used more often than etiquette would allow. The leader of the campaign against the asymmetric usage of power is the writer V. Ja. Kantorovič, who in literary journals and in his book «*Ты» и «вы»* has again and again advocated its abandonment (Kantorovič 1966: *passim*).

In his study of nineteenth-century usage Friedrich enumerates ten components determining the choice between T and V, viz.:

(1) Topic of discourse
(2) Context of the speech event
(3) Age
(4) Generation
(5) Sex
(6) Kinship
(7) Dialect (i.e. regional or social varieties)
(8) Group membership
(9) Relative authority
(10) Emotional solidarity
(Friedrich 1972: 276–8)

Most, if not all, of these components are included in the books on etiquette mentioned, though they are of course not enumerated in Friedrich's manner. But while the components are the same, the twentieth-century system of pronominal address is different from that of the nineteenth century, just as twentieth-century society is different.

Before the Revolution asymmetric usage often occurred within the family; it was particularly common among the peasantry and merchants but not characteristic of the intelligentsia (Kantorovič 1966: 41). Parents gave T and received V from even adult children; a husband gave T and received V from his wife. (The same usage operated also between some other kinship degrees.) In a pre-Revolutionary guide to etiquette in correspondence the examples of letters to parents all use V, whereas those to sisters, brothers, and friends use T (Nikolaev and Petrov 1903: 415–66). During the Soviet period asymmetric usage in the family has become increasingly rare and is now restricted to rural areas, mainly in South Russia (Jachnow

1974: 351). Xodakov mentions its survival with nostalgic approval (1972: 35). Ervin-Tripp's assertion that this is the only respect in which the old pronominal address system has changed[1] is mistaken, however, for the asymmetric usage in power relationships of all kinds has to a very large extent given way to reciprocal usage. The prevailing ethic condemns the use of T to subordinates as offending the spirit of Soviet society. In Soviet fiction, for example, the non-reciprocal T has been portrayed as a sign of boorishness and ignorance (Kantorovič 1966: 29–32).[2] In the 1960s the question was widely aired in the press and, following public discussion, the workers in some factories succeeded in persuading the management to use V. Subsequent proposals for the inclusion in local work regulations (правила внутреннего распорядка) of instructions for workers to be addressed with V (Kantorovič 1966: 38, 45) have now been generally implemented (e.g. see Kačalovskij 1975). A particular quarter from which non-reciprocal T may still be heard is the militia; but here too its use evidently contravenes instructions. A proposal that militiamen should be formally empowered to address citizens with T was not only rejected but condemned (*Izvestija* 29 January 1963, quoted by Kostomarov 1965: 41 n.).

In pre-Revolutionary Russia the use of plural forms to express deference was not restricted to the second person. There was also a system of third-person reference in which either the pronoun они replaced он or она, even though referring to one person (with plural agreement), or other parts of speech occurred in the plural, even though the subject was grammatically (and really) singular. This peculiarity of Russian was noted by Maurice Baring and mentioned in his account of experiences in Russia at the time of the Russo-Japanese War:

'I want to speak to his honour,' the soldier said; 'he is washing his face in the washing-room . . .'

[1] 'The current system is identical to the old with one exception: Within the family, asymmetry has given way to reciprocal T' (Ervin-Tripp 1972: 227).

[2] Among Kantorovič's evidence is a quotation from N. Pogodin's *Янтарное ожерелье*, in which a character who is corrupt and hated uses the T of power to a subordinate. Ervin-Tripp (1972: 227) misinterprets Kantorovič by taking this as evidence not of the condemnation but of the general survival of asymmetric T.

'Why don't you go and knock at the door?' we asked.

'They are' (to speak of a person in the third person plural is respectful in Russian, and is always done by inferiors of their superiors)—'they are "drink taken" (*oni wypimshi*)', he replied . . .

(Baring n.d.: 190)

It would appear that this usage was restricted to certain social groups, low in the scale of power, especially personal servants, minor officials, etc. The claim that it was 'always considered as not corresponding to the norms of the literary language and of good form («хороший тон»)' (Šmelev 1961: 55–6) requires qualification. To support his point Šmelev quotes the following exchange from Dostoevskij's *Подросток* (Part 1, Chapter 6):

— Я их месяца три знала, — прибавила Лиза. — Это ты про Васина говоришь *их*, Лиза? Надо сказать *его*, а не *их*. Извини, сестра, что я поправляю, но мне горько, что воспитанием твоим, кажется, совсем пренебрегли.

'I knew them for about three months', added Liza.

'Are you saying "them" of Vasin, Liza? You should say "him" and not "them". Forgive me, sister, for correcting you, but it distresses me that your education appears to have been quite neglected.'

The objection to Liza's use of the plural here is not that it was regarded as incorrect absolutely, however, but only in-appropriate to her social position. This plural usage in pre-Revolutionary Russian deserves further, detailed study; it raises the interesting question whether the rules for assessing forms as standard or non-standard can also handle social variation. Whatever the former status of the third-person plural of de-ference, however, it has become increasingly rare in the Soviet period, and there can be no doubt that nowadays such sentences as Мария Ивановна работают учительницей (Derjagin 1968: 139) belong exclusively to non-standard varieties, except when used as deliberate archaisms for ironic, comic, or some other special effect. In the following exchange from Bulgakov's *Мастер и Маргарита* (written 1929–40) it is used by one of the assistants to the magician Voland (who is really the Devil in disguise) adding to the alien (non-Soviet) aura surrounding the latter (reinforced by the titles господин and мосье):

— Артиста Воланда можно попросить? — сладко спросил Варенуха.

— Они заняты, — ответила трубка дребезжащим голосом, — а кто спрашивает? (*Мастер и Маргарита*, Chapter 10)

'May I speak to the artist Voland?' Varenuxa asked sweetly.

'They are busy,' answered the telephone receiver in a jarring voice, 'and who is asking?'

Its survival as an unmarked polite form to the present day is noted by Isačenko (1960: 414), however, who in August 1956 in Saratov observed the sentence (referring to a third person): Пусть они тебе скажут, они-то должны знать! Isačenko says it is a polite form used to refer to a third person *present at the conversation*. According to Jazovickij (1969: 38–9), however, it is also used (in fact, particularly used) of respected persons *in their absence*. From a normative point of view, of course, it is condemned. Jazovickij favours the use of он or она to refer to the respected person in their absence and forename+patronymic in their presence. (See also Kantorovič (1966: 66).)

Names

Every Russian has three names, viz. forename (имя), patronymic (отчество), and surname (фамилия). Various combinations of these three units are used in address, the list of determinants being the same as for the choice of pronoun (T or V). Names are inevitably used in conjunction with pronouns and thus various combinations correspond to various points on the scales of power and solidarity. Names and titles, together with pronouns, operate in a complex system of address which still awaits description. Names and titles differ from T and V, however, since they operate not only in a system of address but also in a system of third- and first-person (self-naming) reference. The realization in certain situations of types of first-, second-, and third-person reference by names and titles among Russian intellectuals aged 30–60 at the present day has been described in Nikolaeva (1972).

It is useful to divide forenames into (1) those which have a short form (имя сокращенное) and (2) those which do not. (This is a separate question from that of diminutives, which will be dealt with later separately.) The following is a list of some of the common forenames belonging to Type 1, showing both full and short forms:

Full form (имя полное)	Short form (имя сокращенное)
Александр	Саша, Шура, Саня
Александра	Саша, Шура, Саня
Алексей	Алеша
Борис	Боря
Валентин	Валя
Валентина	Валя
Виктор	Витя
Владимир	Володя
Евгений	Женя
Евгения	Женя
Екатерина	Катя
Иван	Ваня
Марья, Мария	Маша
Николай	Коля
Петр	Петя
Татьяна	Таня
Юрий	Юра

The over-all number of names belonging to the other type is probably smaller. Examples of Type 2 are: Андрей, Вера, Денис, Зоя, Илья, Игорь, Иосиф, Максим, Марина, Никита, Нина, Олег, Осип, Потап, Роза, Федот, Юлий.

In certain relationships and situations the appropriate mode of address is by forename alone, co-occurring with either T or V. If the forename in question belongs to Type 2, then the full (and only) form will be used; there is no other possibility. In the case of Type 1, however, there is a choice. In stylistically neutral address only the short form is appropriate, as the full form has an expressive function which varies according to the determinants of the situation and relationship between interlocutors. Type 2 lacks this function.

In a different set of relationships and circumstances, the appropriate mode of address is by forename and patronymic together (usually, but not always, co-occurring with V). In this case the full form of Type 1 is used (corresponding to the only form of Type 2). The total possible range of combinations of forename, patronymic, and surname is as follows:

(1) Full forename alone (Type 1), e.g. Владимир
(2) Full forename alone (Type 2), e.g. Андрей
(3) Short forename alone (Type 1), e.g. Володя
(4) Full forename (Type 1 or 2) + patronymic, e.g. Татьяна Петровна
(5) Full forename (Type 1 or 2) + surname, e.g. Татьяна Иванова
(6) Full forename (Type 1 or 2) + patronymic + surname, e.g. Татьяна Петровна Иванова
(7) Short forename (Type 1) + surname, e.g. Таня Иванова
(8) Patronymic alone, e.g. Петровна
(9) Surname alone, e.g. Иванов
(10) Diminutive or nickname alone.

In official documents the order is often surname + full forename + patronymic, e.g. Петров Владимир Андреевич and rarely this order may also occur in speech, in which case it expresses an official attitude or possibly disapproval (Nikolaeva 1972: 138–40). Combinations other than the above (such as *Таня Ивановна, *Владимирович Петров) are ungrammatical, at least in standard varieties. All the combinations given may occur as modes of address, though some are much rarer than others in this function.

In the absence of proper accounts of the social and functional determination of Russian address by name and title both before and after the Revolution, only tentative assessments of change in the system can be made. Most obvious are the changes in the functions of combinations 1 and 8 above.

The system for the use of forename alone has changed in one significant respect since the nineteenth century: the respective functions of the full and short forms of Type 1 are different from what they were. Nowadays the short form is stylistically neutral, while the full form is expressive.[1] In the nineteenth century the converse held: the long form was neutral and the short form expressive. Exactly when and how this change came about is a matter that has yet to be investigated, but it is well attested,

---

[1] However, the precise stylistic distinction between long and short forms is not identical in all cases.

especially by the usage portrayed in narrative fiction. In Čexov's *Дама с собачкой* (1899) Dimitrij Gurov is addressed by his wife as follows: — Тебе, Димитрий, совсем не идет роль фата. — 'The role of a fop doesn't suit you at all, Dimitrij.' Gurov himself says to his beloved mistress: — Но поймите, Анна, поймите... — 'But understand, Anna, understand . . . In neither case is there reason to think any expressive meaning was intended by the author.

A significant observation on the use of a short form is made by the author in Čexov's *Дом с мезонином* (1896), where one of the heroines is introduced as follows:

Когда она уехала, Петр Петрович стал рассказывать. Эта девушка, по его словам, была из хорошей семьи, и звали ее Лидией Волчаниновой...

When she left, Petr Petrovič began his story. This girl, he said, was from a good family, and her name was Lidija Volčaninova...

Soon afterwards the author's words continue:

Лидия, или, как ее звали дома, Лида, говорила больше с Белокуровым, чем со мной.

Lidija, or Lida as she was called at home, spoke more with Belokurov than with me.

The significant point is that Čexov felt an explanation necessary. Лида was then a marked form appropriate to domestic use. Nowadays (assuming address by forename alone) she would be called Лида everywhere, not only at home.

In present-day usage full forms (Type 1) function in several different ways, expressing either a positive or a negative attitude to the person addressed. The expressive information they convey depends on the situation and on who the interlocutors are. As Superanskaja (1969: 127–8) points out, the appropriate address form in a given set of circumstances depends on a number of determinants including age, social position, the subject of discourse, the situation, etc., and it is therefore not possible to divide particular forms into marked and unmarked. Nevertheless, as in the case of T/V, it is possible in the presence of a known set of determinants to say which forms of other parts of the address system are neutral and which are marked. In the case of the full forms of Type 1 forenames, however, there is no set of determinants in whose presence their use would be neutral. We therefore find ourselves unable to agree with Superanskaja's statement (1969: 134): 'For Russians the short form (сокращенное имя) is not the real forename. The real forename is recorded in a person's passport, and by that name he is addressed on official occasions.' In official situations it is most unlikely that anyone but a child would be addressed by his forename alone, and the full forename alone used to a child expresses a particular attitude on the part of the speaker. What is perhaps meant (but not stated) here is that on official occasions the full forename together with patronymic is used.

A position similar to Superanskaja's is taken in Bondaletov and Danilina (1970), where it is claimed that neither long nor short forms are neutral, but that each is connected with specific situations. Although certain situations are cited, there is no example of the use of the full form alone. In an earlier article Danilina (1969) argued that the short forms could be either affectionate or neutral, but that in most situations they were affectionate and occupied a special intermediate position. She here (1969: 159) stated bluntly that the full forms were stylistically neutral, but gave no relevant examples. It is doubtful whether any are possible.

The forms and functions of forenames, as of names and elements of address generally, have yet to be described adequately. Particularly needed is a scheme for distinguishing between full, short, and diminutive forms with a means of assessing the emotional information they convey. Superanskaja (1969: 132) puts forward a tentative framework as follows:

(1) The short forename (without 'emotionally loaded' suffixes), e.g. Юра
(2) Forms with suffixes of 'subjective assessment':

    (*a*) Caressing (ласкательный), e.g. Юрочка
    (*b*) Diminutive (уменьшительный), e.g. Юрик
    (*c*) Familiar/vulgar (фамилиарный/вульгарный), e.g. Юрка
    (*d*) Teasing (поддразнивающий), e.g. Юрище
    (*e*) Scornful (пренебрежительный), e.g. Юрашка
    (*f*) Pejorative (уничижительный), e.g. Юришка
    (*g*) Contemptuous (презрительный), e.g. Юрчище, etc.

Further suffixes, and further shades of emotion, are possible. The full form is significantly absent from this scheme.

It is important not to lose sight of the fact that the threefold system of forename, patronymic, and surname was not always in operation in Russia. There are records of nobles with fore-name, patronymic, and surname dating from the fifteenth century onwards, but the word фамилия and official interest in recording surnames date only from Peter the Great's time.

Although nineteenth-century literature provides examples of patronymics and surnames in use among peasants, the claim that before the beginning of the twentieth century they were only exceptionally used in the everyday speech of the common people (Superanskaja 1969: 65–6) is, on the whole, probably sound. Even to the present day there are regions of Russia where anthroponymical systems differing from the official one survive, though the latter is of course used for official purposes everywhere (Superanskaja 1969: 64–7; Simina 1969; Čuma-kova 1970).

Unlike the Russian language itself, Russian modes of address have not been standardized, except in so far as the three-fold system of personal names has been canonized by the state administration and certain handbooks on etiquette recommend certain usage. (To this we might add those cases where a particular usage has been institutionalized, as in the army, the courts, schools, etc.) Nor has there been a high degree of normalization: even at the present time norms of address vary both regionally and from one social group to another. Even among speakers of the standard language there are variations. The main territorial distinction is between the towns and the countryside. The main social distinction is between workers and intellectuals. It is therefore not possible to distinguish unconditionally between standard and non-standard address forms. Nevertheless, the system of reference by names and titles in use among middle-aged intellectuals (Nikolaeva 1972), even though not to be treated as standard, might well at least be taken as a model for foreigners learning Russian.

The use of the patronymic alone is nowadays mainly restricted to the countryside, and is said to be the appropriate form when both respect and familiarity are present in the relationship (Bolla *et al.* 1970: 272–3). It is particularly suitable for addressing old people (Kantorovič 1966: 121; 1974: 49). Among the nineteenth-century functions of the patronymic alone was one as a form of address between spouses.[1] This is now almost obsolete.

Spellings of the kind Иваныч found in nineteenth-century sources indicate that the normal allegro pronunciation of patronymics known to present-day Russian was already in existence then. Syncope now produces realizations of the type Иванч with the result that the type Никитич (with the ending for masculine a-stems) is no longer automatically felt to be distinct from other patronymics (the type Иванович). This leads to hyper-correct spellings, such as Никитович, which, however, are still regarded as incorrect (Ickovič 1961).

In the nineteenth century, in addition to the present-day type ending in -ович/-овна, -ич/-инична, patronymics in -ов(а), -ин(а), were still in use. Many surnames, such as Иванов, Еремин, are by origin patronymics of the short type. In the country systems other than the official threefold one have long been established, and in a twofold system it is often not possible to identify the second element in official terms, since patronymics and surnames are often identical. The following extract from a work of literature by a writer renowned for his knowledge of the Russian countryside demonstrates this problem:

На межрайонном совещании председателей колхозов и директоров совхозов Николай Алексеевич Аксенов, председатель колхоза «Пламя коммунизма», — Аксеныч, как его попросту называли, — выдал такую огневую речь, что сам потом удивился. (Vasilij Šukšin, *Правда*, in *Сельские жители*, Moscow, 1963: 176)

At the inter-district conference of collective-farm chairmen and state-farm managers Nikolaj Alekseevič Aksenov, chairman of the 'Flame of Communism' collective farm—Aksenyč, as he was simply called—made such a fiery speech, that afterwards he was surprised himself.

Seliščev mentions the practice in the 1920s of using patronymics alone to refer to popular political figures (1928: 81). The most famous example is Lenin's patronymic Ильич, by which he was both addressed and referred to, originally by the

---

[1] Attested, for example, in Puškin's *Дубровский*.

peasants (Bolla *et al.* 1970: 273) and later by all sections of the population.[1] Seliščev's other example, Калиныч is derived from the surname Калинин (itself by form and origin a patronymic).

Address by patronymic alone (and by pseudo-patronymics like Аксеныч) still occurs in the Russian countryside, but in the towns it is rarer. In particular, it is not used by intellectuals, who regard it as characteristic of the speech of workers and peasants, especially the latter. The kind of exchange in which it is thought to be appropriate may be seen from two recent cartoons in *Krokodil*. In one the conversation is between a woman, who is apparently a shop assistant helping herself illegally to some of the stock, and a man, who appears to be a manager or supervisor:

— Ты почему так много выносишь?
— Так я же, Петрович, вчера не брала!
(*Krokodil*, 1974, 2: 11)

'Why are you taking so much?'
'Well, you see, Petrovič, I didn't take any yesterday.'

In the other, two watchmen are keeping guard over various items of imported equipment, and one says to the other:

— Слышь, Петрович, говорят, скоро нам и зонтики импортные выдадут...   (*Krokodil*, 1973, 31: 10)

'Have you heard, Petrovič, it's said that soon we shall be issued with imported umbrellas too . . .'

Of course, address in the country differs from urban address in many respects. Even without social and regional variation, the realizations of an otherwise uniform system would clearly vary functionally owing to the variation between urban and rural situations and relationships. In the intimacy of a small village the social distance corresponding to the use of V or forename + patronymic is rarer than in a town. It may be absent altogether. Investigation of the modes of address in the village of Akčim, Perm *oblast'*, for example, produced a very small number of instances of forename + patronymic, almost all of which were used in addressing newcomers or visitors. Address by patronymic alone is also very rare here, but appears to have

---

[1] Examples of rural influence on urban speech are very rare.

a separate function, albeit very restricted. The most common form of address by name in Akčim is the long or short form of the forname (Gruzberg 1974: 51–4). In the village of Osipovka, Gor′kij *oblast′*, where a Central Russian dialect is spoken, address is realized almost exclusively in forms of the forename. Patronymics do not occur at all (Čumakova 1970).

Forenames

In pre-Revolutionary Russia everyone had an officially noted religion. (Nationality, on the other hand, was not officially recorded.) All Orthodox children had to be christened and their names had to be chosen from the Orthodox Church's list (known as the *svjatcy*) containing the names of saints (Superanskaja 1970: 184). Other names were not permitted, but in any case only a fraction of the two thousand or so names in the list were ever used. It was the custom to choose the name of one of the saints whose festival fell on the eighth day after the birth or on one of the first eight days of the child's life. This was not compulsory, at least in theory, but in practice the child was often given a name by the priest regardless of, or even contrary to, the wishes of the parents. The custom was in fact very closely observed, as has been shown by an analysis of the names given in an area spread over part of the Tambov and Penza *gubernii* in 1884. Here, for example, 91 per cent of all Tat′janas were born in January and 92 per cent of all Agrippinas in June (Nikonov 1974: 144).

The Church maintained records of those it had christened, but birth certificates were issued not by the Church but by secular authorities. The Church recorded the form of the name given in the Church calendar, but the secular authorities recorded secular forms, including even local forms. The result was inconsistency (Superanskaja 1970). This system came to an end when the Church was deprived of its power following the October Revolution. The duty of recording names was taken over by the загс (отдел записи актов гражданского состояния), and the Church's list ceased to have any legal significance. The end of restrictions had spectacular results. A mass of new names came into use in the 1920s, some of which were to acquire permanent popularity, but most of which were to disappear

before long. The number of new names coming into use at this
time was large, but the number of children being given them
was fairly small, and in the country it was very small. A survey
of girls' names given to babies born in 1930 in Kostroma and
Penza has produced the following figures:

	Number of names			% of new names	
	Total	Old	New	% of all names	% of children
Kostroma	139	41	98	70	29
Penza	88	41	47	53	12

Figures for rural areas in the same part of Russia in the same
year show greater conservatism. In the Čuxloma *rajon* of
Kostroma *oblast'*, for example, less than one in six of the names
given were new and only one baby girl in a hundred was given
a new name (Nikonov 1974: 66–7).

The new names were of various kinds. In the first place there
were foreign names such as Ада, Альберт, Альбина, Артур,
Жанна, Роберт, Эдуард, Эмма, etc., which had been known
from literature before the Revolution. Secondly, there were Old
Russian names which had not been included in the Church's
list; e.g. Злата, Лада, Рогнеда, Роксана, Руслан, Руслана,
Рюрик, Святослав, Славомир. Here we may mention Светлана,
which originated in Žukovskij's ballad of that name (1812) and
is attested in neither the Church calendar nor Old Russian
sources. It has become very popular in the Soviet period. A
third source was provided by words which previously had some
other function as appellatives; e.g. Авангард, Альянс, Барри-
када, Герой, Идея, Лира, Трактор, Электрификация. There
were also former surnames: Веллингтон, Жорес, Марат,
Маркс, Энгельс. Finally, there were new forenames derived
from existing elements, including several stump-compounds.
Among those which have survived is Майя, but even this is
very rare nowadays. Others, which are now never, or hardly
ever, given to children are: Владлен (from Владимир Ленин),
Ревмир and Ревмира (from революция мировая 'world revolution'), Ким (from Коммунистический интернационал молодежи 'Communist Youth International'), Октябрина (from
октябрь 'October').

The principal reason for giving names different from those
in the Church calendar was to break with the past. Another

reason was the rejection of the Church and its rules. It has been pointed out also that some of the strangest names may have arisen from sheer ignorance (Nikonov 1974: 69–70). Even such oddities as Винигрет 'vegetable salad', Эмбрион 'embryo', and Комментария 'commentary' have been noted, and it is easy to see a parallel with the kind of misunderstanding which led, for example, to substitution of элементы for алименты and of дистанция for инстанция (see p. 137). These names were simply fine-sounding exotic words to their users, who may not have known their meaning.

Yet another type of innovation was that of naming children with short forms, i.e. of recording names such as Ася, Ира, Оля, Петя, Слава on birth certificates. In the first twenty years or so of the Soviet period such cases, like other abnormalities, were at least as likely to be the result of low literacy as of deliberate intent.[1] These forms subsequently caused difficulties when the necessity arose of deriving patronymics from them (Superanskaja 1969: 134).

The sudden appearance of large numbers of new names and the growth of the list of names being given to new-born children was an exceptional, temporary, and mainly urban phenomenon. A survey of the names given to babies in the towns of Kursk, Kaluga, Kostroma, Vladimir, Tambov, Penza, and Ul'janovsk, and in the surrounding country areas, shows that the list of names shrank considerably between 1930 and 1961. In the towns it was more than halved (Nikonov 1974: 76).

Before the Revolution Russian forenames were distributed socially along class lines. Certain names were common among workers and peasants, others among the nobility and intelligentsia. Some names were even virtually taboo in one class or the other. Nikonov claims, for example, that 'it is impossible to imagine at the beginning of the present century either a Countess Matrena or Fekla, or a peasant Tamara' (1974: 15). There were, of course, changes in fashion, but usually, as a name became rarer among the lower class, so it became more common in the upper class, and vice versa. It is significant that this should be so despite the constraints of the Church calendar. The

---

[1] This also explains many unusual spellings, such as Ерина (for Ирина), Владимер (for Владимир), Андилина (for Ангелина), Лианора (for Элеонора) (Nikonov 1974: 68, 255).

peasantry, no doubt, even when not actually coerced by priests, were more likely to follow the Calendar, while the upper class was more likely to disregard custom (when they saw fit) and exercise choice, though they too were restricted to the names in the *svjatcy*.

The social dynamics of change in giving names is demonstrated by the example of Мария which at the beginning of the nineteenth century was extremely popular among the nobility. It was also gaining popularity among the peasants, however, and from 1860 onwards, having become well-known as a typical peasant's name, it declined rapidly among the nobility (Nikonov 1974: 15–16).

The social differentiation of forenames went further than a simple division into nobility and peasantry: there were also typical merchants' names (Савва, Фома, Гордей) and priests' names (Никон, Мисаил, Варлаам) (Bondaletov 1970: 18–19). Typical peasants' names in the decade preceding the October Revolution were: Авдотья, Анна, Василий, Екатерина, Иван, Мария. At that time Александр and Николай were typical of the nobility (Nikonov 1974: 16).

Changes in the relative popularity of forenames following the Revolution mainly affected the old names given in the *svjatcy*, for none of the new exotic names permitted by the abolition of Church control were anywhere near the top of the popularity scale. By 1930 Анна, Василий, Екатерина, Иван, Мария were, in the towns at least, being rarely given to new-born children, having been replaced as the most popular names by Валентина, Владимир, Галина, Нина, Тамара, Юрий. Developments in the countryside followed the same pattern but more slowly.

By 1961 further changes in fashion had occurred; the names being most frequently given were Александр, Андрей, Владимир, Галина, Елена, Игорь, Ирина, Марина, Наталья, Ольга, Светлана, Сергей, Татьяна, Юрий. The countryside continued, more or less, to follow, but lag behind the towns while the towns themselves were (and are) led by Moscow. Many peasant names in common use before the Revolution had by 1961, or even earlier, fallen into obscurity: names such as Агафья, Аксен, Анисья, Архип, Афанасий, Гавриил, Матрена, Прасковья, Фекла (Barannikova *et al.* 1970: 178–9). Of the post-1917 innovations Светлана has enjoyed the greatest success, but in 1961 Алла, Валерий, Виктория, Эдуард were still being given to a fair number of children (Nikonov 1974: 79).

The details of the popularity of names given here (quoted for the most part from Ščetinin 1968 and Nikonov 1974) are not based on surveys of the whole U.S.S.R. or even the whole Russian Republic, but it is unlikely that a project of such dimensions would produce significantly different results from the surveys of representative samples already made. One conclusion common to them all is that the over-all number of forenames in use is decreasing, and has decreased particularly rapidly in the Soviet period. Study of the names given to new-born children in the Rostov *oblast'* (the results of which are probably not untypical) shows that the number of masculine names in active use (i.e. being given to over 0·6 per cent of new-born babies), fell from 310 in the seventeenth century to 165 in the first decade of the twentieth century. In the Soviet period, however, the number fell spectacularly to 49 in the first half of the 1960s. The number of female names in use at that time was only 21 (Ščetinin 1970: 249).

In terms of the kind mentioned above, the question of social distinction of names along class lines no longer arises: there is no nobility and no merchant class. On priests' names we have no current information. There are still differences between town and country, it is true, but they are less marked than they used to be and can now be seen simply as the results of the time-lag in fashion. There is also a certain amount of regional variation, though this too has decreased since the Revolution and is still decreasing. The question of social variation on other lines has also been researched, and the results, while they do not justify the claim that 'the children of fitters, managers, manual labourers, and professors have the same names' (Nikonov 1974: 80), show that standard of education and profession are much less clearly reflected in choice of names than they used to be (Barannikova *et al.* 1970: 178–80) and in some districts are not reflected at all (Belyk 1970: 23). The influence of the Church Calendar can still be seen in some rural areas: a count made in several *rajony* of the Brjansk *oblast'* reveals that the annual popularity peaks for certain names were as clear in 1966 as they had been in 1926 (Kondratenko 1970; Nikonov 1974: 145). On the other hand, a similar count in Sverdlovsk—

probably typical of towns—shows total obliteration of traditional patterns (Korotkova 1970).

Legal requirements

After the Revolution the law restricting the choice of forename to those in the *svjatcy* was abolished, but the Soviet Union has its own laws dealing with names. The position today is that parents registering their child's birth at the *zags* have the right to give him or her any name they like, though the officials may draw their attention to the undesirability of odd names. The only circumstances in which the officials may refuse a name (according to a spokesman for the Ministry of Justice) are if it 'offends human dignity or is not compatible with Soviet morality' (Belyk 1974). If the parents are married the child's patronymic must be derived from the father's forename, but an unmarried mother may choose any patronymic. The surname is the same as that of the parents, unless they have different surnames, in which case they make a choice between the two. In this, as in other matters, the *zags* officials may make a decision when the parents cannot agree. If the mother is unmarried, the child is given her surname, unless the father and mother make a joint application or there is a paternity order in existence.

On marriage both partners jointly choose between three possibilities:

(1) Both surnames stay the same as before marriage.
(2) The wife takes her husband's surname.
(3) The husband takes his wife's surname.

The further possibility of a hyphenated form made up of both husband's and wife's surnames is allowed in the Azerbaidzhan, Belorussian, Georgian, Moldavian, Tadjik, and Ukrainian Republics, but not in the Russian Republic.

It is perhaps worth noting in passing that before 1917 surnames too, owing to the different conditions governing their evolution in various sections of the population, were differentiated along class lines (Superanskaja 1973: 235; Nikonov 1974: 216; Avanesov 1975: 151). The high degree of social mobility in the Soviet Union must surely have confused former patterns.

Titles

Tsarist Russia preserved to the end its elaborate system of address by title, based on Peter the Great's Table of Ranks. Holders of ranks in the Table were addressed as follows:

Rank	Form of Address
1st and 2nd Classes	ваше высокопревосходительство
3rd and 4th Classes	ваше превосходительство
5th Class	ваше высокородие
6th, 7th, and 8th Classes	ваше высокоблагородие
8th to 14th Classes	ваше благородие

In addition, the Tsar and Tsaritsa were addressed as ваше (императорское) величество, other members of the royal family as ваше (императорское) высочество, and princes and counts as ваше сиятельство or ваша светлость. Among equals in rank князь and граф were also used in address. Merchants were ваше степенство (a form without official recognition), bishops ваше преосвященство, and monks ваше преподобие or ваше высокопреподобие. The names of holders of ranks and members of the nobility were prefixed by their titles: e.g. князь Волконский, коллежский асессор Ковалев, etc. (Nikolaev and Petrov 1903: 188, 407, 415–66). To the names of other members of privileged social strata the titles господин and госпожа were prefixed. While it may not be easy to define exactly who might reasonably expect to be called господин or госпожа, it is at least obvious that before the Revolution the vast majority of the population was not, and did not expect to be, addressed and referred to in this way. It was thus, in social terms, far from being the equivalent of Mr., Mrs., and Miss, or similar titles in other European languages (Kantorovič 1966: 113). Those to whose names господин and госпожа were prefixed could be addressed as милостивый государь and милостивая государыня, or сударь and сударыня, or мосье, мадам and мадемуазель, or барин, барыня, and барышня, or ваша милость, the choice hingeing mainly on the relative or absolute social status of the interlocutors, but partly on situational factors.

The bulk of the system just described officially ceased to operate with the publication of the Bolshevik decree abolishing civil ranks (Декрет об уничтожении сословий и гражданских чинов) (*Систематический сборник*..., 1919: 13). The titles господин and госпожа with their related forms of address were not affected by this decree, but being alien to the working class and, especially, to the peasants, they soon fell out of use (Suprun 1969: 42; Trofimenko 1973: 15). Сударь and сударыня also disappeared.

The address form товарищ originated long before 1917, but its use at the beginning of the century was mainly restricted to student and political groups (Seliščev 1928: 193).[1] In the plural, however, its sphere of use was wider, as we can see from the address Ко всем рабочим России от депутатов-рабочих государственной думы published in the newspaper *Народный вестник* for 19 May 1906, which contains sentences such as the following: Итак, товарищи, между государственной думой и самодержавным правительством возникло столкновение.... Although it is used here to address *all* workers, the fact remains that the addressees are a finite social group. Since 1906 the functions of товарищи have been so extended that it is now used to address almost any audience (with certain well-known exceptions, such as convicted and unconvicted prisoners, and foreigners from capitalist countries). It has become the most common form of plural address.

In the first post-Revolutionary period товарищ (both plural and singular) retained its exclusivity. It is characteristic that in *Izvestija* dated 27 October 1917 the statement Ко всем рабочим Петрограда 'To all workers of Petrograd' began Товарищи! whereas that addressed to the population at large (К населению Петрограда) began Граждане!

Гражданин was given legal status both by the decree abolishing civil ranks (see above) and by the decree О приобретении прав российского гражданства 'On gaining the rights of Russian citizenship' of 1918 (Uluxanov 1968: 177). It has been asserted that the neutral form of address to any citizen until the 1930s was гражданин/гражданка, and that only from the late thirties did товарищ tend to replace it as a general form applicable to almost any Soviet citizen (Suprun 1969: 42–3). According to Jakobson (1921: 19), however, товарищ had

[1] When the Bolsheviks gained power, certain students expressed opposition by abandoning товарищ and adopting коллега (Jakobson 1921: 19).

even by 1920 to a large extent lost its socialist character and was becoming similar in function to Czech *pane*, except in the countryside where it was still so new that peasants would address delegates from Moscow as господин товарищ. As товарищ became more common, so гражданин became rarer, tending to be restricted to official or even unfriendly address (Uluxanov 1968: 177). Nowadays гражданин is commonly used by the militia to members of the public, but the fact that even in this official usage it conveys expressive information may be deduced from the following statement made by a senior militiaman when questioned on the need for its use: 'We often say товарищ. And the less it is necessary to replace the friendly товарищ with the official гражданин the easier for us' (*Литературная газета*, 12 May 1964, quoted by Kostomarov 1965: 40 n.)

In the armed forces the use of titles and the corresponding address forms was abolished by *Prikaz* No. 1 of the Petrograd Soviet, and this was confirmed by an order of the Provisional Government on 5 March 1917 (*Сборник указов...*, 1917: 318; Černyx 1948: 107–8). The new rules of address using господин генерал, господин полковник, господин унтер-офицер, etc., were in force for only a few months, for after October, in the new Workers' and Peasants' Red Army ranks were abolished (see also p. 154). The notion of superior and subordinate remained, however, and in exchanges between superior and subordinate the form товарищ + name of appointment was instituted; e.g. товарищ красноармеец, товарищ командир роты, товарищ командир полка, товарищ врач, (*Устав...*, 1918: 13–14). Even with the subsequent reintroduction of ranks the system of address with товарищ has remained in operation to the present day; e.g. товарищ рядовой, товарищ сержант, товарищ ефрейтор, товарищ старшина, товарищ генерал, etc. The forms Рядовой Петров, Сержант Кольцов, etc., are used by superiors addressing subordinates (*Общевоинские уставы...*, 1971: 12–15).

Even before the Revolution товарищ could be prefixed to nouns denoting jobs and also to surnames, though these uses were then common only in political circles. They now occur more widely. The combinations товарищ + forename alone (whether in address or reference) and товарищ + a professional noun (in reference), which occurred both before and after the

Revolution for a time, are now obsolete. The following press extracts demonstrate these now archaic combinations:

Смерть вырвала из наших рядов товарища Веру, стойкого борца за дело социализма...   (*Izvestija* 2 November 1917)

Death has torn from our ranks товарищ Vera, a staunch fighter for the cause of Socialism...

На общем собрании товар. солдаты кричали: «Да здравствует Троцкий!» «Да здравствует Ленин!»
(*Izvestija* 4 November 1917)

At the general meeting the товарищи soldiers cried: 'Long live Trockij! Long live Lenin!'

As late as 5 November 1917 we find a letter to the editor of *Izvestija* from a regimental committee addressing him as Господин Редактор, but well before this it is clear that in certain circles господин in both address and reference has acquired an ironic, contemptuous component:

Верноподданные г-на Ленина обязуются верить ему на слово.
(*Дела народа*[1] 28 October 1917)

The loyal subjects of gospodin Lenin pledge themselves to take him at his word.

The Bolsheviks in particular applied господин to their enemies[2] and they continue to do so. Nevertheless, together with certain other pre-Revolutionary titles it has continued to have a neutral function in addressing foreigners from capitalist countries. It is especially common in diplomatic usage, where titles such as ваше высочество and ваше превосходительство also occur. In diplomatic exchanges even Soviet leaders may be given the titles господин and ваше превосходительство.

Unlike барин and барыня, which were identified with the old regime and quickly dropped, барышня survived for a time in both address and reference to young women, especially in certain professions (Seliščev 1928: 156; Karcevskij 1923: 14; Obermann 1969: 173–4). It was in use until the end of the 1920s, but Obermann's assumption (1969: 198) that it was

---

[1] Organ of the Socialist-Revolutionary Party. Its readers were addressed as товарищи.

[2] For examples of Lenin's use of this word, see Mizin (1975).

still current in the 1960s is wrong. It is said that even in the 1960s and 1970s мадам might still occasionally be heard from old people (Suprun 1969: 42; Trofimenko 1973: 15). The problem of how to address strangers has not been solved by the introduction of молодой человек, девушка, and гражданочка. There are occasions when neither they nor товарищ can be appropriately used, and this has led to proposals for the revival of сударь and сударыня (Solouxin 1964).

An element in address which is well known from nineteenth-century literature is the particle -c (known as слово-ер from the old names of the letters с and ъ) which was formerly added to utterances, producing such combinations as да-с, прошу-с. It was restricted to towns and to the colloquial usage of speakers of the standard language. Closely linked to V address, it emphasized social distance. Although already in decline in the second half of the nineteenth century, it survived into the twentieth and only disappeared finally in the wave of change following 1917 (Černyx 1949).

Pre-Revolutionary address included the pseudo-kinship terms батюшка 'father' (diminutive), отец мой 'my father', матушка 'mother' (diminutive), мать моя 'my mother'. Apart from батюшка and матушка in a restricted use to address priests and their wives, they have all become increasingly rare in the last half century. The use in address of the ritual kinship terms крестный 'godfather', крестная 'godmother', кум and кума, which survived into the early part of this century, is now a thing of the past. A recent change in the use of true kinship terms is the decline of utterances by nephews and nieces such as Спасибо, тетя 'Thank you, aunt', Скажи, дядя 'Tell me, uncle'. They are now always accompanied by names, as Спасибо, тетя Маша, Скажи, дядя Ваня. Дядя and тетя alone are used by children to adult *strangers*.

The strongly power-marked form of address человек and the condescending любезный, both used mainly to servants, disappeared totally and quickly after the October Revolution.

Other aspects of speech etiquette

In addition to address forms, the norms of certain other typical sequences in specific settings have changed since 1917.

The commonest formulas expressing thanks, for example, are nowadays спасибо, большое спасибо, благодарю (вас/тебя). Благодарствуйте and мерси, though they survived the Revolution (the latter until the 1930s), are now obsolete. Certain other sequences of thanks are now used mainly by the older generation: покорно (or покорнейше) благодарю, я вам (очень, крайне, глубоко, чрезвычайно) признателен(-льна), примите мою благодарность (признательность) (Akišina and Formanovskaja 1973: 76).

In contemporary Russian apology is usually expressed by извини(те) or прости(те). Also widely used (and widely objected to) is извиняюсь—a form commonly believed to have originated during the First World War, though really it is much older (Mazon 1920: 54; Karcevskij 1923: 17, 42; Azov 1923; Krysin and Skvorcov 1965). Although it would probably no longer be described as 'very vulgar' (Karcevskij 1923: 42), it is still not entirely acceptable as standard and is not given in Akišina and Formanovskaja (1973). Along with мосье, мерси, etc., the French form пардон (once in use in privileged circles) (Volkonskij 1913: 207) has become totally defunct. Pre-Revolutionary виноват(а) is now archaic but may be heard from old people. It also has a specialized function in the armed forces (Akišina and Formanovskaja 1970: 121). (The same is true of слушаюсь, literally 'I obey', used before the Revolution by servants, waiters, etc.)

Other typical formulas which have fallen out of use or at least become rare and restricted to older speakers are:

Invitation: покорно/покорнейше прошу; пожаловать + infinitive; милости прошу (милости просим, remarkably, is still current); извольте; извольте + infinitive. The phrase чего изволите? formerly used by servants and waiters and described by Ovsjannikov (1933: 313) as 'a lackey's phrase, indicating obsequiousness and grovelling', is now defunct.

Request: сделайте милость; сделайте (мне) одолжение, не откажите в любезности, не сочтите за труд, окажите любезность are typically used by the older generation (Akišina and Formanovskaja 1973: 56).

Introduction: рекомендую(сь).

Leavetaking: разрешите откланяться, позвольте откланяться and честь имею (used by older generation only, according

to Akišina and Formanovskaja 1973: 40); храни тебя созда-
тель, желаю здравствовать (Trofimenko 1973: 21).

Greeting: доброго здоровья (Akišina and Formanovskaja
1970: 24).

It is easier to identify archaisms than innovations, since innovation, to a large extent, has meant the functional extension of
formulas which existed before the Revolution. It seems likely,
in fact, that the number of elements in the etiquette structures
before 1917 was greater than it is today. Choice between the
elements, like that between address forms, depended on social
factors, some of which have now disappeared. Among the
obviously new formulas, however, we may mention привет
(greeting) and пока (leavetaking). The latter, though known
before the Revolution, has only subsequently become widely
accepted and used (Jakobson 1921: 27; Azov 1923; Seliščev
1928: 74).

Finally, it should not be forgotten that the Russian speech-
etiquette and address systems were changing before 1917,
albeit slowly. Kantorovič recalls, for example, that even before
the Revolution it had become usual to address domestic servants with V, though T was then still the normal mode of
address to a yard-keeper (дворник), a cabman, or a peasant at
a market (1966: 67). The Revolution accelerated the existing
trend, however, and we have now reached a stage where
etiquette demands the use of V to every adult stranger.

8

ORTHOGRAPHY

THE aspects of language change we have described so far in this book are only to a limited extent subject to the control of language planners. So far as pronunciation, stress, morphology, syntax, and vocabulary are concerned, language planning is largely a matter of assessing the changes that have already occurred and of deciding to what extent the codified standard should be adjusted to keep up to date (Haugen 1966a: 52). It is really a question of resolving conflict between standard and non-standard. Orthographical change is a different thing entirely, however, for orthographical change occurs exclusively through planning.

Orthography is also unlike the aspects of language dealt with so far in that it is concerned essentially with (*a*) the question of correctness, and (*b*) writing. Change in phonology, morphology, syntax, and vocabulary, on the other hand, takes place in all languages, whether they have writing and standardized forms or not. Nevertheless, when we are dealing with a standardized written language, such as Russian, and particularly with questions of change and standardization, the problems of orthography are similar to those of change in the levels of language proper. The standard/non-standard dialectic affects orthography as much as it affects them, for while there is no such thing as non-standard orthography, non-standard spelling clearly occurs as the mistakes made by those (particularly schoolchildren) who have not yet mastered the rules. If the rules are often broken this may mean that they are more difficult to learn than they really need to be and that there may be a case to be made out (as in the case of mistakes in pronunciation, grammar, or vocabulary) for changing the rules. The desire to eliminate non-standard (i.e. incorrect) spelling is usually the motive behind spelling reform, and pressure towards reform often comes from those who are most aware of the problems encountered in learning to spell, i.e. from school-teachers, particularly those working with younger children. This has certainly been the case in Russia in the twentieth century.

Teachers of one kind or another were behind the pressure for reform which began to build up in the nineteenth century (Šapiro 1951: 191) and eventually resulted in the spelling reform of 1917–18. No doubt their primary objective was to make things easier for their pupils, but before long the question of reform became linked with the broader question of reducing illiteracy.

Despite Peter the Great's important reform of 1708–10 introducing the 'civil alphabet' (гражданский шрифт), spelling remained chaotic throughout the eighteenth and most of the nineteenth century. The main step towards standardization before 1917 was the publication in St. Petersburg in 1885 of the first edition of Ja. K. Grot's manual *Русское правописание*, which, though it gained acceptance in schools, had no official authority, and was not universally recognized. It was, however, the nearest thing there was to an official orthographic code.

By the beginning of the twentieth century there were a number of organizations working for reform, prominent among which was the section of Russian language teachers of the Pedagogical Society at Moscow University (Šapiro 1951: 191; Černyšev 1947: 170). The section's special committee dealing with this question included among its members the subsequently famous linguistic scholar F. F. Fortunatov.

Even when it is obvious that a spelling system is inefficient and there is general agreement that change is necessary, it is often difficult even for experts to decide exactly what form change should take. There are few languages for which a purely phonemic system (i.e. one in which each symbol corresponds to a single phoneme) is suitable. It is always quite likely, as in the case of Russian, that certain phonological and morphological issues will be in conflict, and that the most efficient system will therefore be a compromise, a morphonological system. If Russian spelling were to follow the phonological principle alone, it would produce a host of new difficulties by raising morphological doubts in the minds of its users. For example, the preposition в in Russian constitutes one morpheme, but it has two realizations as [v] or [f], depending on whether the sound immediately following is voiced or not, e.g. в доме [ˡv domˌı] 'in the house', but в саду [f sʌˡdu] 'in the garden'. Now if we were to follow the phonological principle exclusively we should have to write в before voiced sounds and ф before unvoiced sounds. We should have two symbols for one morpheme, and users of Russian, when writing, would have the problem of choosing between them. Generally, an efficient spelling system is one in which the sound system is represented as closely as possible in writing without upsetting the graphic representation of the grammatical system.

The inefficiency of the pre-1917 orthography was largely due to a superfluity of symbols. There were three cases of simple duplicates (phonologically speaking), viz. ѣ and e, и and i, ѳ and ф. The choice between the members of any of these pairs had no phonetic significance, and the occasions on which the ѣ/e and и/i choices were meaningful on other levels (e.g. в поле (accusative) 'into the field': в полѣ (prepositional) 'in the field'; мир 'peace': мір 'world') were so rare as to be negligible. The hard sign ъ, which was written at the end of every word ending in a hard consonant (except palatals, where the choice between ъ and ь was determined morphologically), e.g. столъ, лѣсъ, was also superfluous, since its mere absence could also indicate hardness.

Many of the opponents of change were in positions of power. They included the Minister of Internal Affairs D. S. Sipjagin who, at the same time as the Pedagogical Society was making proposals for the abolition of ѣ and ъ, intended actually to prohibit the printing of books in an orthography omitting these letters (Černyšev 1947: 170). Although no such prohibition ever came into force (partly thanks, no doubt, to the objections voiced by Academicians A. A. Šaxmatov and A. I. Sobolevskij in the name of the Academy of Sciences), the Society's application for the formation of a special commission to examine the question of spelling reform was rejected by the Ministry of National Education in February 1903 (Šapiro 1951: 191). The Academy, however, continued to show an interest in the matter and decided to set up a Commission on the Question of Russian Orthography. The Commission, which consisted of representatives of the Academy, schoolteachers, journalists, and writers, met on 12 April 1904 and agreed unanimously that simplification of the orthography was desirable (Černyšev 1947: 174–5). They then went on to discuss the desirability of abolishing certain letters and, having put the fate of each such letter individually to the vote, decided by large majorities in favour of the abolition of ѳ, ъ, и or i, and ѣ.[1] The Commission then set up a sub-commission under the chairmanship of Fortunatov to work out questions of simplification not connected with the exclusion of letters. The first meeting of the sub-commission took place the following day and in May that year the *Предварительное сообщение Орфографической подкомиссии* (*Preliminary Communication of the Orthographic Sub-Commission*) was published in St. Petersburg. The sub-commission had obviously wasted no time; but meanwhile the subject of reform had begun to be aired in the press. The campaign against reform was led by the newspaper *Новое время* (Černyšev 1947: *passim*), and after publication of the Preliminary Communication the debate became somewhat heated. Not only were there a large number of people of power and influence who were opposed to change of any kind in the orthography, but there was also a large body of opinion in favour of only very restricted reform. This was the position of many members of the Academy, including the distinguished Slavist Vatroslav Jagić. The fact that the opposition had several prominent writers in their ranks, including Lev Tolstoj, undoubtedly strengthened their morale (Černyšev 1947: 217–18; Il'inskaja 1966: 87–8). V. I. Černyšev, who was himself a member of the original Commission and closely connected with the work of the sub-commission, estimated that the only really devoted and active supporters of reform at that time were Šaxmatov and Fortunatov (Černyšev 1947: 227–8).

And so the movement for reform temporarily lost momentum, especially after the work of the sub-commission was interrupted by the political upheaval of 1905–6 (Šapiro 1951: 193). The one section of Russian society in which considerable numbers never lost sight of the need for simplification of the orthography was the teaching profession. In 1907 a group of members of the State Duma who were also teachers wrote asking the Academy of Sciences not to postpone for too long its work on the spelling

[1] The voting figures are given in Černyšev (1947: 182).

question and expressing the view that the complexity of the existing orthography was 'a considerable obstacle to the spread of literacy among the popular masses'. But their request had no effect (Černyšev 1947: 230).

The sub-commission resumed its work in December 1910, and its proposals were published in May 1912 in St. Petersburg as *Постановления Орфографической подкомиссии* (*Resolutions of the Orthographic Sub-Commission*). They took for granted the proposals made in 1904 to abolish ѳ, ъ, ѣ, and either и or i, and included the following further recommendations:

(1) The letter i to be abolished.

(2) The hard sign to be retained in the body of words after prefixes, e.g. подъезд, объем.

(3) The soft sign to be abolished at the end of words after the absolutely hard consonants ж and ш, e.g. рож (not рожь 'rye').

(4) The soft sign to be abolished at the end of words after the absolutely soft consonants ч and щ, e.g. ноч (not ночь 'night').

(5) To retain the spelling -ться for infinitives of reflexive verbs (despite the fact that the т is hard).

(6) To consider 'desirable but not obligatory' the use of ё.

(7) The letter o to be written consistently after ж, ц, ч, ш, щ, in stressed syllables, e.g. чорный 'black'. (Since these consonants are not affected by the soft/hard distinction, the use of o in some words (e.g. шовъ 'seam') and e (ё) in others (e.g. шелъ 'went') was (and still is) of no phonetic significance.)

(8) The prefixes воз-, из-, низ-, раз-, без-, чрез-, and через- to be written with c before all voiceless consonants, e.g. бесполезно (not безполезно 'useless'). (The existing rule affected only воз-, из-, низ-, раз-, which were written with з before voiced consonants and с before voiceless consonants except с itself; без-, чрез-, через- were always written with з. Grot, though confirming this practice in his rules, considered it would have been better to write the -з- forms in all cases.[1])

(9) The masculine and neuter genitive singular endings to be written -ого, -его (replacing -аго, -яго). (It was decided to retain the existing spelling of masculine nominative and accusa-

[1] See Vinogradov (1965: 231).

tive singular adjectives, e.g. добрый 'good', синий 'blue', rather than write -ой, -ей, consistently for all adjectives regardless of stress.)

(10) To write -ые, -ие, consistently in the nominative and accusative plural of all adjectives and participles (replacing -ыя, -ія in the neuter and feminine).

(11) To write и (not ѣ) in они and одни in all plural genders and cases.

(12) To write ee (not ея) as the genitive of она. (Up to now ee (её) had been written only in the accusative.)

(13) To simplify the rules for the division of words at the end of a line.

These proposals received no official recognition, and it was not until the beginning of 1917 that the question of reform was once again brought to the fore by the Всероссийский съезд преподавателей русского языка средней школы (All-Russian Congress of Teachers of Russian in Secondary Schools), which met in Moscow from 27 December 1916 to 4 January 1917 with 2,090 members present. The Conference sent an official letter to the Academy of Sciences (dated 10 February 1917), stating that 'for everyone who actually works in a school or is at least closely connected with one, there is not the slightest doubt that orthographic reform cannot be put off any longer . . .' (Černyšev 1947: 235).

It might well be thought that in the context of the events of February 1917 spelling reform did not stand very high in the scale of priorities. That the teachers thought otherwise may be seen from their letter, in which they declared: 'The members of the Congress are convinced that the difficult circumstances of the time we are living through not only cannot constitute an obstacle to the realization of reform, but on the contrary demand a drastic elimination of everything that up to now has prevented the broad development of popular education' (Černyšev 1947: 235).

On 27 February 1917 the monarchy fell. The letter from the teachers' Congress was considered by the Academy at its General Meeting held on 29 March. Meanwhile the Provisional Government had been formed. The Academy reacted to the letter in the by now time-honoured way of appointing yet another commission to examine the question, but this time things proceeded rapidly. The new commission summoned a larger Assembly for Considering Simplification of the Orthography. Sixty-three people were invited to attend the meeting of the Assembly on 11 May, but only thirty of them were actually present. Šaxmatov, as chairman,[1] told the Assembly that the commission was proposing the acceptance of a considerably modified reform, including the retention even of ѣ and i. His own views were much more radical, and he was doubtless delighted to discover that the Assembly had no intention of accepting modified reform and to see it proceed to pass a set of resolutions which largely coincided with the proposals made by Fortunatov's sub-commission in May 1912. The proposals of the Assembly of 11 May 1917 were as follows:

(1) Replacement of ѣ by e.

(2) Replacement of ѳ by ф.

(3) Exclusion of ъ at the end of words and of both parts of compounds such as контр-адмирал, but its retention in the body of words as the separative sign.

(4) Replacement of i by и.

(5) Acknowledgement of ё as 'desirable but not obligatory'.

(6) The replacement of з by с in the prefixes из-, воз-, вз-, раз-, роз-, низ-, без-, чрез-, через-, when immediately followed by voiceless consonants, including с itself, but retention of з elsewhere.

(7) Replacement of -аго, -яго by -ого, -его in genitive singular of adjectives, participles, and pronouns.

(8) Replacement of -ыя, -ія by -ые, -ие in nominative and accusative plural of neuter and feminine adjectives, participles, and pronouns.

(9) Replacement of онѣ by они in the nominative plural of the feminine personal pronoun.

(10) Replacement of однѣ, однѣхъ, однѣмъ, однѣми, by одни, одних, одним, одними, respectively.

(11) Replacement of ея by ee (её) in the genitive singular of она.

(12) Simplification of rules governing division of words at the end of a line.

(13) Acceptance of either spelling for words of the type встороне/в стороне, сверху/с верху.

---

[1] His co-reformer, Fortunatov, had died in 1914.

The only new points in these proposals were:

(1) Exclusion of ъ in the body of compound words like контр-адмирал.

(2) Retention of existing spellings with e or o after ж, ч, ц, ш, щ.

(3) Retention of ь in all positions.

(4) Acceptance of either spelling of words like с верху/сверху.

(5) Addition of роз- and вз- to prefixes written with с before voiceless consonants.

Šaxmatov asked the Academy to communicate these proposals to the Ministry of Popular Education, which had already expressed its willingness to adopt them for use in schools (Černyšev 1947: 240–1), but the Academy with supreme lack of concern postponed consideration of the question until autumn. Deputy Minister O. P. Gerasimov, who had himself been a member of the Assembly, was not prepared to wait for the Academy and simply asked Šaxmatov to forward precise details of the proposals. He then had the Ministry issue a circular, dated 17 May 1917 and addressed to the trustees of school areas, giving details of the reformed orthography and directing that the heads of schools take immediate measures to put the reform into effect from the beginning of the new school year. On 22 June the Ministry confirmed the circular and gave further instructions.

The Minister of Education immediately came under attack in the press. Among his opponents was a group of civil servants in his own ministry, who claimed that there were more important educational issues than spelling reform. The Minister, A. A. Manujlov, was supported by Professor (later Academician) P. N. Sakulin, who had taken a prominent part in the discussion in the Assembly on 11 May. In an article published in *Русские ведомости* Sakulin recalled that the reactionary ministers of education of the past would never have supported this reform, 'just as they did not support anything which tended towards the well-being of the masses' (Černyšev 1947: 243–5). By August Manujlov was Minister of Education no longer, and, as the proposed reform had been associated with him personally, rumours sprang up that it was not to be implemented after all. The Ministry denied this, but the proposals continued to be attacked in the press and their success was still not really assured when, on 25 October, the Provisional Government was overthrown and Soviet power established.

Up to now only the Ministry of Education had accepted the reform and ordered its implementation in schools. The Provisional Government had made no decision as to its implementation anywhere else. This ambiguous situation was cleared up by the Bolsheviks. On 23 December 1917 the People's Commissariat of Education issued a decree signed by A. V. Lunačarskij that 'all state and government institutions and schools without exception should carry out the transition to the new orthography without delay', and that 'from 1 January 1918 all government and state publications, both periodical (newspapers, magazines) and non-periodical (books, scientific works, collections, etc.)' should be printed in the new orthography. In schools the reform was to be introduced gradually, beginning from the youngest classes. There was to be no compulsory re-education of those who had already learned the old rules. For those at school already only violations of rules common to both old and new systems were to be considered mistakes.[1]

The rules in Lunačarskij's decree were no different from those put forward by the Assembly of 11 May, except that now вз- was omitted from the rule regarding the spelling of prefixes, but a new decree of the Soviet of People's Commissars, issued on 10 October 1918, made two minor changes: there was no mention of ё or of allowing compound adverbs to be written as one word or two. (Strangely enough, вз- was now reintroduced.) What these two points had in common was their ambiguous nature: the decision to remove them was probably due to the belief that it would be better if all the rules were categorical and admitted no facultative variants.

The terms of the Decree of 10 October 1918 were thus as follows (Černyšev 1947: 248–9):

(1) The letter ѣ to be replaced by е.

(2) The letter ѳ to be replaced by ф.

(3) To abolish ъ at the end of words and the components of compound words, but to retain it within the body of words as the separative sign.

(4) The letter i to be replaced by и.

(5) To write из-, воз-, вз-, раз-, роз-, низ-, без-, чрез-,

---

[1] The full text of the decree is given by Černyšev (1947: 247–8).

через- with з before voiced consonants and с before voiceless consonants including с.

(6) To write -ого, -его (for -аго, -яго) in the genitive singular of masculine and neuter adjectives.

(7) To write -ые, -ие (for -ыя, -ія) in the nominative and accusative plural of feminine and neuter adjectives.

(8) To write они (for онѣ) in the nominative plural of the feminine personal pronoun.

(9) To write одни, одних, одними (for однѣ, однѣх, однѣми) in the feminine plural.

(10) To write ее in the genitive singular (for ея).

(11) In dividing words to observe only the following rules: a consonant (whether alone or in a group of consonants) immediately before a vowel should not be separated from the vowel, nor should a group of consonants at the beginning of a word be separated from a following vowel. The letter й before a consonant should not be separated from a preceding vowel.

Apart from a few minor adjustments, the orthography as amended by this Decree has remained in use from 1918 up to the present day. Proposals for further reform have been made from time to time, however, and there is still a great deal of dissatisfaction with certain details of the existing system. Nevertheless, there can be no doubt that the reform of 1917–18 was of great social significance and opened up the way for the Soviet Government's campaign against ignorance and illiteracy. It is said that the language planner's hands are 'least tied when he can plan a language from the ground up, say in a wholly illiterate society' (Haugen 1966*b*: 16), but although the literacy rate was extremely low by European standards, Russia was by 1917 far from being wholly illiterate. Nevertheless, conditions for reform, if not ideal, were at least good, for the great majority of Russians were not going over to a new spelling system but learning to write for the first time. The fact that they were now able to learn the use of an orthography with relatively few inconsistencies was of great advantage to both learners and teachers. Among the minor benefits of the reform was the saving in print and paper: new editions of large literary works were found to be pages shorter than they had been before 1918.

Bearing in mind the general rule that the closer the fit between graphological and phonological systems the better, provided it is not so close as to affect the fit between graphology and morphology (cf. p. 202 above), we can see that the Russian spelling system was much improved after 1917. Grapheme and phoneme were certainly closer than they had been before, while the relationship between grapheme and morpheme had been seriously affected only in one case—Rule 5.[1] While this rule removed a phonological inconsistency, it might have been better, in the wider context of prefixes as a whole, to have allowed the morphological principle to prevail here. No concession to the phonological principle is made in the case of other prefixes (e.g. от- is never written од-, although before most voiced consonants it is so pronounced, as in отдать [ʌd'dat̪]), and the desirability of using з forms in all positions had been pointed out by Grot (cf. p. 204 above). On the other hand, the reform still left untouched certain inconsistencies in the relationship between sound and symbol, whose amendment would not have affected morphology, such as the use of г (pronounced [v]) in the genitive singular of adjectives and pronouns.

The Decree of 1918 (and for that matter the earlier proposals for reform too) only enumerated changes to be made. There was still no single code of orthographic rules. But by now it was at least clear that Grot's guide had been superseded. In fact, the new orthography was to remain uncodified until 1956.

The elliptical style of the 1918 Decree, especially the fact that it includes no examples, suggests that it was intended to be read together with the Decree of December 1917 (and hence with the proposals of 11 May 1917 too). Rule 3, for example, deprived of the example контр-адмирал does not make clear what is meant by the term 'compound words' (сложные слова). And Rule 9, though it was obviously intended to change the spelling of all plural cases, enigmatically omitted the dative. Now if these omissions are not simply mistakes (which, despite the fact that the Decree was drawn up in turbulent times, seems unlikely), they must mean that the additional information in the December decree was taken for granted. If this is so, one cannot but wonder whether the

[1] The morphological uses of ѣ (cf. p. 202) were of negligible advantage.

points concerning ё and the facultative division of compound adverbs were really meant to fall into abeyance. In practice, however, it was assumed that they were, and the other inconsistencies were ignored.

Another point which does not become clear from a reading of the various sets of proposals and decrees is the question of the letter v, called йжица. Some accounts of the reform tell us that it is thanks to the Soviet decrees that this letter disappeared.[1] Yet neither of them mentions it. Nor do we find mention of it in any earlier proposals unless we go back as far as the commission which met in April 1904, when Fortunatov stated: 'this letter is nowadays usually not used, and even Grot . . . stated positively that ижица might be considered to have been removed from the Russian alphabet; so now there is no longer any need to put the question of removing this letter' (Černyšev 1947: 177). From 1904 onwards all those concerned with spelling reform appear to have assumed that the question of ижица had already been settled.

The 1918 Decree followed its predecessors in abolishing the hard sign except in its special function as the separative sign within the body of words. In this role it represents the phoneme /j/ immediately after a prefix ending in a consonant and before a vowel, e.g. съесть [sjesĻ] 'to eat'. It thus duplicated one of the functions of the soft sign, which, as separative sign, represents /j/ between any other consonant and a vowel, e.g. пью [p̡ju] 'I drink'. The proposals made by the Moscow Pedagogical Society in 1901 included the total abolition of ъ and the exclusive use of ь as separative sign. And there was a majority in favour of abolishing ъ (without qualification) in the Commission of 1904. The result of the eventual compromise decision to retain it after prefixes was that in texts written in the new orthography it had extremely low frequency—a fact which emphasized its anomalous status. The practice, which grew after 1918, of replacing it with the apostrophe (e.g. с'есть 'eat', под'езд 'entrance', and sometimes inverted as под'езд) may well have gained support from the belief that the letter ъ ought really to have been abolished altogether, and that to avoid its use was to follow the true spirit of the reform (Polivanov 1927: 185). (The choice of this particular symbol to replace the hard

[1] e.g. Vinogradov (1965: 53).

sign was not new. There had been experimental printing with
the apostrophe in the nineteenth century.) But there was
another, more concrete, reason for the introduction of the
apostrophe in the 1920s. Certain printers hostile to the Bolsheviks deliberately continued printing in the old orthography.
The reaction of the Soviet authorities was to confiscate the
types and matrices for the letters ъ, ѣ, ѳ, v, and i.¹ The fact that
ъ still had a use (albeit vastly restricted) was either overlooked
or ignored.

Towards the end of the 1920s, however, ъ began to be
restored in printed publications, but meanwhile people had
grown used to the apostrophe and some objected to the restora-
tion of what they regarded as a pre-Revolutionary letter
(Il'inskaja 1966: 92). The 1920s also saw the disappearance of
the apostrophe and full stops used with acronyms (for examples,
see p. 80 above) and the development of the present practice
of writing them closed-up, e.g. MXAT, MXATa.

Attempts to retain the old orthography in Russia were very
short-lived indeed. During 1918, however, both systems were
being used in print, and there were even a few cases of printers
adopting only part of the new rules, i.e. dropping ъ, but otherwise retaining the old system.² Outside Russia, on the other
hand, certain *émigré* groups have continued to use the old
orthography intact even to the present day, and there are said
to have been attempts to revive the old spelling in German-
occupied Russian territory during the Second World War
(Istrin 1963: 154).

But if attempts to retain the old orthography after 1917 were
negligible, efforts to change spelling still further were more
determined. In 1929 a new Orthographic Commission was
formed, and a new plan for orthographic reform was put forward the following year (Černyšev 1947: 250–1). Among the
new proposals were:

(1) Replacement of ъ by ь as the only separative sign, e.g.
съезд 'congress'.

¹ *Практика...*, 1932: 66. The confiscation is said to have been carried
out by a detachment of armed sailors who went round the Petrograd
printers' shops (Il'inskaja 1966: 92; Suprun 1969: 15).
² Trockij's pamphlet *Международное положение и Красная Армия*,
Moscow, 1918, for example, was printed in this way.

(2) To write ы (not и) consistently after ж, ш, ц, e.g. жырный 'fat'.

(3) To replace г by в in the genitive singular of adjectives pronouns, and participles, e.g. доброво, ево.

(4) To write -ыи, -ии (not -ые, -ие) in the nominative and accusative plural of adjectives, e.g. добрыи, синии.

(5) To write the present and perfective future endings of all stem-stressed verbs (including present participles) as: -ишь, -ит, -им, -ите, -ут (-ют), -ущий (-ющий), -имый; e.g. делаишь, любют, возют.[1]

These proposals had no effect in practice, but certain points they raised (some of which had been raised before) were to be considered again later. During the 1930s committees continued to work on minor adjustments, ironing out inconsistencies, and the preparation of a consolidated code of spelling rules, but there were no practical results. The work was interrupted by the Second World War: there were no meetings between 1940 and 1954 (Bukčina *et al.* 1969: 14).

The lack of a set of rules permitted the survival of certain inconsistencies. The use of double letters in loanwords, for example, varied a great deal (Panov 1965: 154–5). Eventually, in 1956, *Правила русской орфографии и пунктуации* (*Rules of Russian Orthography and Punctuation*) was published in Moscow, codifying the existing orthography and introducing a few minor adjustments in the interests of great uniformity. It was the first complete set of spelling rules to be published since Grot's manual in 1885. The 1956 rules, which had the approval of the Academy of Sciences of the U.S.S.R. and other official bodies, took into account the opinions expressed in a public discussion on spelling which had taken place in the columns of the main teachers' specialist publications in 1954. The year 1956 also saw the publication by the Academy of a comprehensive *Орфографический словарь русского языка* (*Orthographical Dictionary of the Russian Language*) composed in accordance with the Rules.

Among the new rules intended to counter inconsistency was one demanding that after prefixes (except меж- and сверх-) ending in a consonant ы not и should be written, e.g. предыстория 'pre-history'. The problem arises from the fact that the

---

[1] In 1930 the pronunciation любют, возют, etc. was still standard (see p. 41, above).

final consonants of these prefixes remain hard even when used to
form compounds whose root begins with the phoneme /i/. The
и in a spelling such as предистория, therefore, is not consistent
with the grapho-phonological rule that и (unlike ы) indicates
that the consonant immediately preceding it is soft. The rule
demanding the use of ы thus maintains the fit between sound
and symbol at the expense of the morphological principle.
Foreign prefixes контр-, пан-, суб-, транс-, etc. (e.g. субинс-
пектор 'sub-inspector') and stump-compounds (e.g. Госиздат
'State Publishing House') are specifically excluded from this
rule. It has been pointed out that in practice the native prefixes двух-, трех-, and четырех- and certain foreign prefixes
not mentioned in the 1956 Rules are also excluded (Es'kova
1964: 6). There has always been some uncertainty as to
whether и or ы should be written in this position, and the more
loanwords beginning with /i/ appeared and were used in compounds, the greater the problem became. In the 1930s there
was utter inconsistency, for there was no rule in existence. By
1964, however, it was possible to state that, although spellings
with и contrary to the 1956 rule were still occurring in print,
those with ы were gaining ground. Against this, it has to be
admitted that the new type was already gaining ground before
1956 and had been used sporadically even before 1917 (Es'kova
1964: 10–11).

The 1956 Rules brought a little more order to the problem of
whether to write е or о after ж, ч, ш, щ by abolishing alternations of the type чорт/черти 'devil(s)', жóлудь/желудéй
'acorn(s)' (henceforth черт, желудь) (*Правила* . . ., 1956: 7–9).
They also cleared up certain inconsistencies in the use of
the hyphen in compound adjectives and adverbs (*Правила...*,
1956: 41–2, 47). Among the problems they have not been
very successful in settling is the question of where to use э in
foreign words (Bukčina 1974: 44–6).

But the general question of reform was scarcely affected by
the 1956 Rules, which were consolidatory rather than innovatory, and in 1962 a new Orthographic Commission was set up
under the auspices of the Russian Language Institute of the
Academy of Sciences of the U.S.S.R. Its proposals, which were
published in 1964 both in the press and in a separate *Предложения по усовершенствованию русской орфографии* (*Proposals for*

the Improvement of Russian Orthography) aroused widespread interest, and their appearance was followed by serious public discussion of them in the columns of certain newspapers and journals, as well as on radio and television. They were, of course, only proposals, and the Commission's objective in publishing them was merely to test public opinion. Nevertheless, there was a certain amount of confusion at the time which resulted in a few cases of school-teachers taking steps to put the proposals into practice (Bukčina *et al.* 1969: 5).

Letters numbering over 10,000, expressing opinions on the proposals, were received by newspapers and journals and by the Russian Language Institute direct. They were subsequently all passed to the Institute, where they were studied and catalogued. Preliminary conclusions arising from this work were published in 1969 (Bukčina *et al.* 1969). The largest professional group among the authors of the letters was that of teachers, and the overwhelming majority of them were in favour of further reform and of the new proposals (Bukčina *et al.* 1969: 19–20). Writers also constituted a clearly defined professional group among those who wrote in, but in contrast to the teachers they were nearly all opposed to the proposals and, indeed, to reform of any kind. This picture of the distribution of support and opposition is a familiar one.

In the kind of public discussion which took place in 1964 writers are always likely to have influence out of all proportion to their numbers, for they are widely thought to be specialists in the linguistic field.[1] And so it was in this case. Among the prominent opponents of reform were the writers Vera Inber, Tixon Semuškin, Semen Kirsanov, and Leonid Leonov. The latter's outspoken opposition, in particular, made a great impact.

Not surprisingly, the writers' views on the relationship between sound and symbol show a fair degree of confusion. But letters from members of other professions show that the objections made by writers carried great weight with them, and the fact that the 1964 proposals remained proposals and nothing more was probably a result more of the opposition of the writers than of any other single cause.

[1] Lest it be thought that all writers have always opposed orthographic reform, it is worth recalling that Čexov appears to have favoured it (Il'in-skaja 1966: 88–9).

The reformists at least learned that in any future attempts they might make it would be useful, if not essential, to have the support of writers of stature. By a decision of the Presidium of the Academy of Sciences of the U.S.S.R. dated 5 February 1965 K. A. Fedin, L. M. Leonov, A. T. Tvardovskij, and M. V. Isakovskij became members of the Orthographic Commission (Bukčina *et al.* 1969: 23).

The 1964 proposals were as follows:

I. New Rules

(1) To use only ь as the separative sign, e.g. подьезд (for подъезд). And to omit the separative sign altogether after сверх-, меж-, двух-, трех-, четырех-, пан- транс-, контр-.

(2) To write и consistently after ц. The choice of и rather than ы was made in order to conform to the pattern established for the other consonants not forming part of hard/soft pairs, viz. ж, ч, ш, щ.

(3) After ж, ч, ш, щ, ц to write consistently о where the syllable is stressed, and е where it is not, e.g. жолтый (for желтый 'yellow'). But to write еще 'still, yet' with е (ё). Some foreign words would continue to be written with о in unstressed positions. It was pointed out that this simple rule (which had been tested experimentally in schools) would replace fourteen rules in the 1956 code.

(4) Not to write ь after ж, ч, ш, щ, e.g. доч (for дочь 'daughter'). This was not to affect the use of ь as the separative sign, e.g. instrumental singular ночью.

(5) To abolish а/о vowel-alternation in root syllables, e.g. возрост (for возраст 'age') because о appears in the same root when stressed, e.g. рост 'growth'. But плавец (for пловец 'swimmer') because of плавать 'swim'. It was proposed to leave и/е alternations.

(6) To replace the two suffixes -инский, -енский with a single -инский, since -енский never bears the stress. To retain -енский only where considerations of word-formation make it desirable, e.g. Фрунзенский (derived from Фрунзе 'Frunze').

(7) To replace the two suffixes -иц, -ец with one, viz. -ец.

(8) To abolish double letters in certain foreign words, e.g. тенис (for теннис 'tennis'), and to produce a complete list

(which would be fairly short) of words in which double letters might be retained.

(9) To write -нн- in participles with prefixes, e.g. написан-ный 'written', and -н- in those without, e.g. писаный 'id.'

(10) To further simplify the rules for the use of the hyphen.

(11) To permit -ие (as well as -ии) in the prepositional singular of nouns with nominative singular in -ий and -ие, and in the dative and prepositional singular of nouns with nominative singular in -ия, e.g. о Василие (as well as о Василии 'about Vasilij'), на линие (as well as на линии 'on the line').

(12) To write у (not ю) consistently after ж and ш. Therefore жури (not жюри 'jury'), etc.

(13) To write only о or е before the suffix -нька in diminutives, e.g. паенька (not паинька 'good child').

(14) To write достоен (for достоин 'worthy') and заец, заечий (for заяц 'hare', заячий 'id. (adjective)') to conform to the general derivation pattern exemplified in спокоен (спокойный 'peaceful'), европеец 'European' (genitive европейца).

(15) To write деревяный 'wooden', оловяный 'tin', стекляный 'glass' (instead of existing spellings with -нн-). These are the only three such adjectives.

II. Amendments to Existing Rules

(1) To permit either ы or и in compounds such as предысторический 'pre-historical'. The Commission stated that it found it impossible 'not to consider the wishes of specialists' (i.e. presumably specialists whose terminology is affected).

(2) Simplified rules were put forward on where to write words together, separately or with a hyphen, on the use of capitals, on the division of words, and on punctuation.

The Commission also published details of its deliberations on those rules from the 1956 code for which it proposed no change. These included:

(i) On ё the Commission stated: 'Despite the desirability of "obligatory ё" the experience of many years shows that in practice this letter does not catch on.'

(ii) The proposed replacement of -ьо- and -йо- in foreign words by ё, e.g. маёр for майор.

(iii) Spellings with э in foreign words.

(iv) The question of the prefixes ending in з. A possible revival of the pre-1917 practice was rejected.

Also rejected were proposals (*a*) to go over to the Latin alphabet,[1] (*b*) to replace и by i, and (*c*) to change the shape of certain letters.

Although no actual changes have resulted from the 1964 proposals, the reactions they provoked from the public have provided Soviet language planners with a store of useful information on beliefs, attitudes, and patterns of misunderstanding as to the relationship between sound and symbol. For example, the proposal to write и consistently after ц aroused more opposition than any other (Bukčina *et al.* 1969: 58). The normal function of the graphemic opposition и/ы is to indicate the presence or absence of palatalization in the preceding consonant, but since the /ts/ phoneme does not form part of a palatalized/non-palatalized pair, the graphemic distinction has no phonetic meaning. The letters received show, however, that many of their authors believe that it *does* have phonetic meaning. A certain Ju. P. Tixonov of Kujbyšev even claimed, in a letter, now with the Russian Language Institute, that цыган 'gypsy' and циган were two different words with different meanings (Bukčina *et al.* 1969: 59). A less serious correspondent wrote: 'I don't want to eat огурци and хлебци. I want to eat огурцы (cucumbers) and хлебцы (loaves). Believe me, they'll taste better that way' (Bukčina *et al.* 1969: 60). It is true that in the speech of the older generation of intellectuals a half-soft [ts] may be encountered in loanwords, and soft [tsʲ] does occur in some dialects, but the confusion in the minds of these correspondents clearly stems from the spelling alone.

Objections of another kind were made by those who believed that a change in the spelling would result in a change in pronunciation. Spelling pronunciations are not unknown to Russian, of course,[2] but the consistent use of и after ж and ш has had no influence whatever on the articulation of these

---

[1] This proposal had also been made in 1919 and 1929–30 (Il'inskaja 1966: 93; Makarova 1969).

[2] Even pre-Revolutionary ея and the adjectival ending -ыя had some influence on the pronunciation of educated Petersburgers (Polivanov 1927: 181; «Почта...» 1968: 105–6).

consonants, and there is therefore no reason to think that it would affect щ (Bukčina *et al.* 1969: 61–2).

Objections to the proposal to abolish ь after ж, ч, ш, and щ also arise from the confusion of sound and symbol. Some correspondents claimed that they could distinguish between a hard and soft ж and a hard and soft ч, depending on whether or not ь is written after them (Bukčina *et al.* 1969: 70–80). There is, of course, nothing in the sound system of Standard Russian to support this belief.

Throughout the period we have surveyed, most of the opposition to spelling reform has been based on prejudice and misunderstanding of the linguistic facts. The main supporters of reform have been linguists and school-teachers, the former because they were aware of inconsistencies between the graphic and phonic systems, the latter because they were familiar with the day-to-day difficulties of pupils learning to read and write. The main opposition (as in other spheres) has come from writers, largely no doubt as a result of their attachment to what they regard as an important tradition of their craft. Some of the opposition before the Revolution stemmed from general conservatism: the belief that anything which benefited the masses or changed the established order would inevitably harm those in power. The political symbolism of both orthographic change and opposition to change may be seen in the continuing use of the old system in *émigré* groups and in attempts by the Germans to reintroduce it during the Second World War (cf. p. 212, above).

The Reform of 1917–18 was a decisive move in the campaign to abolish illiteracy. It removed many of the difficulties encountered in learning to read and write Russian by both native speakers and foreigners. Despite further minor amendments made in 1956 the system is still capable of being improved, as the 1964 proposals showed, though the inconsistencies as they stand are not serious.

The main difficulty in introducing spelling reform is persuading those who already can read and write to accept and use the new system. Nowadays, when virtually everyone who is capable of literacy is literate, this problem would be far greater than it was in 1917, simply because the number of people who need persuading is far greater. For this reason, sociological factors, including widespread myths and beliefs about the spelling system, must and are being taken into account by Russian language planners. For the issues are not purely linguistic, and if (as has been suggested) it is 'perhaps more difficult to hear and assess one's own speech accurately than to learn the existing orthographic rules' (Bukčina *et al.* 1969: 47), there may be good extra-linguistic reasons for retaining a system which linguistically is imperfect.

REFERENCES

AASAMAA, I., 1974, *Как себя вести*, 4. edition, Tallinn. (Translated from Estonian original, 1970, Tallinn.)

AGEENKO, F. L., and ZARVA, M. V., 1960, *Словарь ударений для работников радио и телевидения*, ed. K. I. Bylinskij, M.

AKIŠINA, A. A., and FORMANOVSKAJA, N. I., 1970, *Русский речевой этикет*, M.

—— 1973, *Речевой этикет (в таблицах и упражнениях)*, M.

ALEKSEEV, D. I., 1961, «Склонение буквенных аббревиатур», in *Вопросы теории и методики изучения русского языка*, Kujbyšev, pp. 62–82.

ALTAJSKAJA, V. F., 1960, «Переходные явления в лексике русского языка послеоктябрьского периода», *RJaŠ*, 5: 14–20.

ANDREEV, N. D., 1963, «Об одном эксперименте в области русской орфоэпии», *VKR*, 4: 49–52.

ASTAF'EVA, N. I., 1974, *Предлоги в русском языке и особенности их употребления*, Minsk.

AVANESOV, R. I., 1947*a*, «Работа над русским произношением в школе», *RJaŠ*, 3: 1–22.

—— 1947*b*, «Вопросы образования русского языка в его говорах», *Вестник Московского государственного университета*, 9.

—— 1961, «О нормах русского литературного произношения» *RJaŠ*, 6.

—— 1972, *Русское литературное произношение*, 5. edition. M. (Earlier editions: 1. (1950), 2. (1954), 3. (1958), 4. (1967).)

—— 1975, «Ива́нов или Иванов́», *RR*, 5: 151–2.

—— and ORLOVA, V. G., 1965, eds., *Русская диалектология*, 2. edition, M.

—— and OŽEGOV, S. I., 1959, eds., *Русское литературное произношение и ударение. Словарь-справочник*, M.

AZOV, V., 1923, «Открытое письмо Академии наук, Наркому Просвещения Луначарскому, Акцентру, Губполитпросвету, Сорабису, Управлению Актеатров, месткомам частных театров и всем грамотным людям», *Жизнь искусства*, 43: 8.

BALAXONOVA, L. I., 1967, «Расческа, гребень, гребенка», *RR*, 6: 92–3.

BARANNIKOV, A. P., 1919, «Из наблюдений над развитием русского языка в последние годы войны», *Ученые записки Самарского университета*, выпуск 2: 64–84.

BARANNIKOVA, L. I., DANILOVA, Z. A., ČERNEVA, N. P., 1970, «Факторы, определяющие выбор личных имен», in Nikonov (1970: 177–82).

BARING, M., n. d., *What I Saw in Russia*, London.

BARINOVA, G. A., 1966, «О произношении [ж̅'] и [ш̅']», in Vysotskij *et al.* (1966: 25–54).

—— IL'INA, N. E., KUZ'MINA, S. M., 1971, «О том, как проверялся вопросник по произношению», in Vysotskij *et al.* (1971: 315–42).

—— and PANOV, M. V., 1971, «О том, как кодировался фонетический вопросник», in Vysotskij *et al.* (1971: 302–14).

BELODED, I. K., 1964, «Теоретические проблемы изучения украинской литературной речи», *Известия Академии наук СССР, Отделение литературы и языка*, том 23, выпуск 6: 476–7.

BELYK, N. A., 1970, «Некоторые правовые и социологические вопросы антропонимики», in Nikonov (1970: 9–23).

—— 1974, «Юридическая служба «Известий». Имя, отчество, фамилия», *Izvestija*, 17 May 1974.

BOBRAN, M., 1974, 'Czasownikowa pojedyncza bezprzyimkowa wariacyjna rekcja silna w języku polskim i rosyjskim', *Slavia Orientalis*, 23: 443–50.

BOLLA, K., PÁLL, E., PAPP, F., 1970, *Курс современного русского языка*, Budapest.

BONDALETOV, V. D., 1970, «Ономастика и социолингвистика», in Nikonov and Superanskaja (1970: 17–23).

—— and DANILINA, E. F., 1970, «Средства выражения эмоционально-экспрессивных оттенков в русских личных именах», in Nikonov and Superanskaja (1970: 194–200).

BONDARKO, L. V., 1973, Review of Vysotskij *et al.* (1971), *VJa*, 2: 135–9.

—— and VERBICKAJA, L. A., 1973, «О фонетических характеристиках заударных флексий в современном русском языке», *VJa*, 1: 37–49.

BORKOVSKIJ, V. I. and KUZNECOV, P. S., 1965, *Историческая грамматика русского языка*, 2. edition, M.

BORUNOVA, S. N., 1966, «Сочетания [ш'ч'] и [ш̄'] на границах морфем», in Vysotskij *et al.* (1966: 55–71).

BRAGINA, A. A., 1973, *Неологизмы в русском языке*, M.

BROMLEJ, S. V., 1973, «Противопоставленность I и II спряжений в русских говорах и литературном языке», in *Исследования по русской диалектологии*, ed. Ju. S. Azarx *et al.*, M., pp. 155–75.

BROWN, R. and GILMAN, A., 1972, 'The pronouns of power and solidarity', in *Language and Social Context*, ed. P. P. Giglioli, Harmondsworth, pp. 252–82. (Reprinted from *Style in Language*, ed. T. A. Sebeok, Cambridge, Mass., 1960, pp. 253–76.)

BUKČINA, B. Z., 1970, «Строп–стропа», *RR*, 1: 120.

—— 1974, « «Правила русской орфографии и пунктуации» (1956 г.) и орфографическая практика», *Известия Академии наук СССР, Серия литературы и языка*, том 33, № 1: 44–52.

—— KALAKUCKAJA, L. P., ČEL'COVA, L. K., 1969, *Письма об орфографии*, M.

BULAXOVSKIJ, L. A., 1952, *Курс русского литературного языка*, том 1, 5. edition, Kiev.

—— 1954, *Русский литературный язык первой половины XIX в.*, 2. edition, M.

BUTORIN, D. I., 1964, «Употребление в распределительном значении количественных числительных с предлогом *по*», *VKR*, 5: 144–9.

—— 1966, «Об особых случаях употребления винительного падежа прямого объекта в современном русском литературном языке», in Kačevskaja and Gorbačevič (1966: 125–36).

—— 1969, «Компонент и компонента», *RR*, 5: 121.

ČERNYŠEV, V. I., 1915, *Правильность и чистота русской речи*, 2. edition, выпуск 2, Pg.

—— 1947, «Ф. Ф. Фортунатов и А. А. Шахматов — реформаторы русского правописания», in *А. А. Шахматов 1864–1920. Сборник статей и материалов*, ed. S. P. Obnorskij, M.–L., pp. 167–252.

ČERNYX, P. JA., 1929, I. *Современные течения в лингвистике*. II. *Русский язык и революция*, Irkutsk.

—— 1948, «Заметки об употреблении местоимения *вы* вместо *ты* в качестве формы вежливости в русском литературном языке XVIII–XIX веков», *Ученые записки Московского государственного университета*, выпуск 137, Труды кафедры русского языка, книга 2: 89–108.

—— 1949, «К истории форм вежливости в русском языке. О частице с», *Доклады и сообщения филологического факультета Московского государственного университета*, выпуск 8: 58–65.

Численность, размещение, возрастная структура, уровень образования, национальный состав, языки и источники средств существования населения СССР по данным Всесоюзной переписи населения 1970 года, 1971, M.

CORBETT, G. G., 1976, 'Address in Russian', *Journal of Russian Studies*, 31: 3–15.

ČUKOVSKIJ, K., 1963, *Живой как жизнь. О русском языке*, 2. edition, M.

ČUMAKOVA, JU. P., 1970, «К вопросу о формах личного имени в русской диалектной речи», in Nikonov and Superanskaja (1970: 200–5).

DAL', V. I., 1863–86, *Толковый словарь живого великорусского языка*, Pb.

DANILINA, E. F., 1969, «Категория ласкательности в личных именах и вопрос о так называемых «сокращенных» формах имен в русском языке», in Nikonov and Superanskaja (1969: 145–61).

DENISON, N., 1968, 'Sauris: a trilingual community in diatypic perspective', *Man* (new series), 3 (4): 578–92.

DERJAGIN, V. JA., 1968, «Уважаемый товарищ!» *RR*, 5: 139–40.

DRAGE, C. L., 1967*a*, 'Changes in the regressive palatalization of consonants in Russian since 1870', *Zeitschrift für Phonetik, Sprachwissenschaft und Kommunikationsforschung*, 20: 181–206.

—— 1967*b*, 'Factors in the regressive palatalization of consonants in Russian', *Zeitschrift für Phonetik, Sprachwissenschaft und Kommunikationsforschung*, 20: 119–42.

—— 1968, 'Some data on modern Moscow pronunciation', *Slavonic and East European Review*, 46: 353–82.

DURNOVO, N. N., SOKOLOV, N. N., UŠAKOV, D. N., 1914, *Диалектологическая карта русского языка в Европе*, Pg. (Reproduced as supplement to Avanesov and Orlova (1965).)

ERVIN-TRIPP, S., 1972, 'On sociolinguistic rules: Alternation and co-occurrence', in *Directions in Sociolinguistics*, ed. J. J. Gumperz and D. Hymes, New York, etc., pp. 213–50.

ES'KOVA, N. A., 1964, «Графическая передача фонемы «и» в начале морфемы, не являющейся флексией или суффиксом, после твердой согласной предшествующей морфемы», in *О современной русской орфографии*, ed. V. V. Vinogradov *et al.*, M., pp. 5–17.

—— 1967, «О недостаточности действующего правила употребления так называемой буквы *ё*», *VKR*, 8: 73–84.

FAKTOROVIČ, T. L., 1966, «*Вратарь*», *Этимологические исследования по русскому языку*, выпуск 5: 145–7.

FILIN, F. P., 1973, «О структуре современного русского литературного языка», *VJa*, 2: 3–12.

FRIEDRICH, P., 1966, 'Structural implications of Russian pronominal usage', in *Sociolinguistics. Proceedings of the UCLA Sociolinguistics Conference 1964*, ed. W. Bright, The Hague–Paris, pp. 214–59.

—— 1972, 'Social context and semantic feature: The Russian pronominal usage', in *Directions in Sociolinguistics*, ed. J. J. Gumperz and D. Hymes, New York, pp. 270–300.

GANIEV, Ž. V., 1966, «О произношении сочетаний «стк», «здк», «ндк»», in Vysotskij *et al.* (1966: 85–95).

GLOVINSKAJA, M. JA., 1966, «В защиту одного приема фонетического обследования», in Vysotskij *et al.* (1966: 163–72).

—— 1971, «Об одной фонологической подсистеме в современном русском литературном языке», in Vysotskij *et al.* (1971: 54–96).

—— IL'INA, N. E., KUZ'MINA, S. M., PANOV, M. V., 1971, «О грамматических факторах развития фонетической системы современного русского языка», in Vysotskij *et al.* (1971: 20–32).

GORBAČEVIČ, K. S., 1966, «*Премировáть или премúровать*», *VKR*, 7: 211–13.

—— 1971, *Изменение норм русского литературного языка*, L.

—— 1973, ed., *Трудности словоупотребления и варианты норм русского литературного языка*, L.

—— 1974, «Вариантность ударения в формах инфинитива», *RJaŠ*, 5: 9–13.

GORNFEL'D, A. G., 1922, *Новые словечки и старые слова*, Pb.

GORŠKOV, A. I., 1969, *История русского литературного языка*, M.

GRAUDINA, L. K., 1964*a*, «О нулевой форме родительного множественного у существительных мужского рода», in Mučnik and Panov (1964: 181–209).

—— 1964*b*, «Развитие нулевой формы родительного множественного у существительных—единиц измерения», in Mučnik and Panov (1964: 210–21).

—— 1966, «Опыт количественной оценки нормы (форма род. ед. *чая–чаю*)», *VKR*, 7: 75–88.

GRIGOR'EV, V. P., 1961, «О нормализаторской деятельности и языковом «пятачке»», *VKR*, 3: 3–20.

GROT, N. JA., 1891–5, *Словарь русского языка*, Pb.

GRUZBERG, L. A., 1974, «Лексика обращений в народно-разговорной речи», in *Живое слово в русской речи Прикамья*, выпуск 4, ed. A. A. Bel'skij *et al.*, Perm', pp. 50–61.

GVOZDEV, A. N., 1958, *Современный русский язык*, часть 1, M.

HALLE, M., 1959, *The Sound Pattern of Russian*, The Hague.

HAUGEN, E., 1966*a*, 'Linguistics and language planning', in *Sociolinguistics. Proceedings of the UCLA Sociolinguistics Conference 1964*, ed. W. Bright, The Hague–Paris, pp. 50–67.

—— 1966*b*, *Language Conflict and Language Planning. The Case of Modern Norwegian*, Cambridge, Mass.

—— 1969, 'Language planning, theory and practice', in *Actes du Xe Congrès international des Linguistes*, Bucharest, pp. 701–11.

Iскоvič, V. A., 1961, «*Никитич или Никитович*», *VKR*, 3: 229–32.

—— 1968, *Языковая норма*, M.

—— 1971, «Современные аббревиатуры», *RR*, 2: 74–9.

—— 1972, «Новые тенденции в образовании аббревиатур. (О путях включения аббревиатур в систему языка)», in *Терминология и норма*, ed. V. P. Danilenko, M., pp. 88–101.

—— 1974, «Очерки синтаксической нормы. 1–3», in Zolotova (1974*b*: 43–106).

Il'inskaja, I. S., 1966, ed. *Орфография и русский язык*, M.

—— and Sidorov, V. N., 1955. «О сценическом произношении в московских театрах. (По материалам сезона 1951/52 г.)», *VKR*, 1: 143–71.

Isačenko, A. V., 1954, 1960, *Грамматический строй русского языка в сопоставлении с словацким*, Parts I and II, Bratislava.

Istrin, V. A., 1963, *1100 лет славянской азбуки*, M.

Istrina, E. S., 1948, *Нормы русского литературного языка и культура речи*, M.–L.

Ivančikova, E. A., 1966, «О развитии синтаксиса русского языка в советскую эпоху», in Pospelov and Ivančikova (1966: 3–22).

Ivanova, T. A., 1967, «Именительный множественного на -*á* (*podá, tenopá, гоcпиталя́*) в современном русском языке», in Meščerskij *et al.* (1967: 55–78).

Ivanova-Luk'janova, G. N., 1971, «Ленинградское [ш'ч']», in Vysotskij *et al.* (1971: 249).

Jachnow, H., 1973, 'Zur sozialen Implikation des Gebrauches von Anredepronomen (mit besonderer Berücksichtigung des Russischen)', *Zeitschrift für slavische Philologie*, 37: 343–55.

Jakobson, R., 1921, *Vliv revoluce na ruský jazyk*, Prague.

Janko-Trinickaja, N. A., 1964, ««Проблема номер один». (Числительное в роли несогласованного определения)», in Mučnik and Panov (1964: 303–10).

—— 1966*a*, «Кратный именительный в функции определения», in Pospelov and Ivančikova (1966: 174–85).

—— 1966*b*, «Наименование лиц женского пола существительными женского и мужского рода», in Zemskaja and Šmelev (1966: 167–210).

—— 1967, «*И уважаемый... и уважаемая...* (По поводу заметки A. K. Панфилова)», *VKR*, 8: 240–4.

Jazvickij, E. V., 1969, *Говорите правильно. Эстетика речи*, L.

Jiráček (Iraček), I., 1969, «Ударение существительных с суффиксом -*аж* в современном русском литературном языке», *Русский язык за рубежом*, 2: 92–4.

Jones, D., and Ward, D., 1969, *The Phonetics of Russian*, Cambridge.

Kačalovskij, E., 1975, «Кодекс петровцев» *Литературная газета*, N° 24, 11 June 1975, pp. 10–11.

Kačevskaja, G. A., and Gorbačevič, K. S., 1966, eds., *Нормы современного русского литературного словоупотребления*, M.

Kalakuckaja, L. P., 1970, «О склонении имен собственных (морфологический тип на -*a* неударное)», in Kostomarov and Skvorcov (1970: 218–42).

KALININ, A. V., 1971, *Лексика русского языка*, 2. edition, M.

KANTOROVIČ, V. JA., 1966, «*Ты» и «Вы*». (*Заметки писателя*), M.

—— 1974, «*Ты» и «Вы*». *Вчера и сегодня, в условиях научно-технической революции*, M.

KARCEVSKIJ. S. I., 1923, *Язык, война и революция*, Berlin.

KASVIN, G. A., 1949, «Основы настоящего времени глаголов 2-го спряжения», in *Материалы и исследования по русской диалектологии*, том 3, M.–L.

KIPARSKY, V., 1963, *Russische historische Grammatik*. Band I. *Die Entwicklung des Lautsystems*, Heidelberg.

KLINSKAJA, L., 1957, «К вопросу обогащения словарного состава языка», *RJaŠ*, 3: 22–7.

KOGOTKOVA, T. S., 1970, «Литературный язык и диалекты», in Kostomarov and Skvorcov (1970: 104–52).

KOLESOV, V. V., 1967, «Развитие словесного ударения в современном русском произношении», in Meščerskij *et al.* (1967: 96–118).

KOLOMIJEC', V. T., 1973, *Розвиток лексики слов'янських мов у післявоєнний період*, Kiev.

KONDRATENKO, G. I., 1970, «Наблюдение за употреблением личных имен в Брянской области», in Nikonov (1970: 115–17).

KONDURUŠKIN, S. S., 1917, *Толковый словарь (пособие при чтении газет)*, Pg.

KOROTKOVA, T. A., 1970, «Динамика личных имен свердловчан», in Nikonov (1970: 110–15).

KOSTOMAROV, V. G., 1959*a*, «Откуда слово *стиляга?*», *VKR*, 2: 168–75.

—— 1959*b*, «Словесные сорняки», *Литература и жизнь*, 16 December 1959, p. 2.

—— 1965, «Культура языка и речи в свете языковой политики», in *Язык и стиль*, ed. T. A. Degtereva, M., pp. 3–55.

—— 1971, *Русский язык на газетной полосе. Некоторые особенности языка современной газетной публицистики*, M.

—— and LEONT'EV, A. A., 1966, «Некоторые теоретические вопросы культуры речи», *VJa*, 5.

—— and SKVORCOV, L. I., 1970, eds., *Актуальные проблемы культуры речи*, M.

KOŠUTIĆ, R., 1919, *Граматика руског језика* I, 2. edition, Pg.

KOTELOVA, N. Z., and SOROKIN, JU. S., 1971, *Новые слова и значения*, M.

KOŽIN, A. N., 1961, «Русский язык в дни Великой Отечественной войны», *Ученые записки Московского областного педагогического института*, том 102, выпуск 7: 630–48.

KŘÍŽKOVÁ, H. (KRŽIŽKOVA, E.) 1968, «Предикативная функция прилагательных и существительных и структура предложения», *Československá Rusistika*, 13, 210–19.

KRYSIN, L. P., 1964, «О словах *хлебороб* и *хлопкороб*», *RJaŠ*, 2: 24–7.

—— 1965, «Иноязычная лексика в русской литературной речи 20-х годов», in Zemskaja and Šmelev (1965: 117–34).

—— 1968, *Иноязычные слова в современном русском языке*, M.

—— 1973, «К социальным различиям в использовании языковых вариантов», *VJa*, 3: 37–49.

References   227

—— 1974, ed., *Русский язык по данным массового обследования*, M.

—— and Skvorcov, L. I., 1965, *Правильность русской речи. Словарь-справочник*, 2. edition, M.

Kudrjavskij, D. I., 1912, *Введение в языкознание*, Jur'ev (Derpt).

Kuz'mina, S. M., 1963, «Борис Годунов» на сцене Центрального детского театра», *VKR*, 4: 144–53.

—— 1966, «О фонетике заударных флексий», in Vysotskij *et al.* (1966: 5–24).

Kuznecova, L. N., 1963, «Орфоэпические заметки о Центральном детском театре», *VKR*, 4: 138–44.

Kuznecova, O. D., 1970, «Балка и овраг», *RR*, 1: 117–18.

—— 1971, «Задира, забияка», *RR*, 5: 96–8.

Labov, W., 1966, *The Social Stratification of English in New York City*, Washington, D.C.

Lakoff, R., 1973, 'Language and woman's place', *Language in Society*, 2: 45–80.

Lapteva, O. A., 1968, «Внутристилевая эволюция современной русской научной прозы», in Vinokur and Šmelev (1968: 126–85).

Ljustrova, Z. N., and Skvorcov, L. I., 1972, *Мир родной речи. Беседы о русском языке и культуре речи*, M.

Lopatin, V. V., 1973, *Рождение слова*, M.

Makarova, R. V., 1969, «Нужна ли латинизация?» *RR*, 4: 123–4.

Mazon, A., 1920, *Lexique de la guerre et de la révolution en Russie (1914–1918)*, Paris.

Meromskij, A., 1930, *Язык селькора*, M.

Meščerskij, N. A., 1967*a*, *Развитие русского языка в советский период*, L.

—— 1967*b*, «О некоторых закономерностях развития русского литературного языка в советский период», in Meščerskij *et al.* (1967: 5–30).

—— Korotaeva, È. I., Gruzdeva, S. I., Moiseev, A. I., 1967, eds., *Развитие русского языка после Великой Октябрьской социалистической революции*, L.

Miljutin, V., 1918, «Как произошло название «народный комиссар»», *Izvestija*, 6 November 1918, p. 3.

Mirtov, A. V., 1941, *Лексические заимствования в русском языке в Средней Азии*, Taškent–Samarkand.

—— 1953, «Из наблюдений над русским языком в эпоху Великой Отечественной войны», *VJa*, 4.

Mis'kevič, G. I., 1967, «Комсомолия, пионерия», *RR*, 4: 6–8.

Mizin, O. A., 1975, «Обращения в произведениях В. И. Ленина», *RR*, 2: 29–35.

Mučnik, I. P., 1961, «Двувидовые глаголы в русском языке», *VKR*, 3: 93–115.

—— 1963*a*, «Категория рода и ее развитие в современном русском языке», in Mučnik (1963*b*: 39–82).

—— 1963*b*, ed., *Развитие современного русского языка*, M.

—— 1964, «Неизменяемые существительные, их место в системе склонения и тенденции развития в современном русском литературном языке», in Mučnik and Panov (1964: 148–80).

MUČNIK, I. P. (*cont.*), 1971, *Грамматические категории глагола и итени в современном русском литературном языке*, M.

—— and PANOV, M. V., 1964, eds., *Развитие грамматики и лексики современного русского языка*, M.

MULLEN, J., 1967, *Agreement of the Verb-predicate with a Collective Subject*, Cambridge.

NAKHIMOVSKY, A. D., 1976, 'Social distribution of forms of address in contemporary Russian', *International Review of Slavic Linguistics*, 1 : 79–118.

NATANSON, È. A., 1966, «Термины профессионально-просторечного словообразования и их классификация», in *Проблемы лингвистического анализа*, pp. 174–85.

NICHOLSON, J. G., 1968, *Russian Normative Stress Notation*, Montreal.

NIKOLAEV and PETROV (no initials given), 1903, *Светский хороший тон и умение жить и вести себя дома, в семье и обществе*, ed. O. P. Svetlov, 2. edition, M.

NIKOLAEVA, T. M., 1972, «К вопросу о назывании и самоназывании в русском речевом общении», in *Страноведение и преподавание русского языка иностранцам*, ed. E. M. Vereščagin and V. G. Kostomarov, M., pp. 134–50.

NIKONOV, V. A., 1970, ed., *Личные имена в прошлом, настоящем, будущем. Проблемы антропонимики*, M.

—— 1974, *Имя и общество*, M.

—— and SUPERANSKAJA, A. V., 1969, eds., *Ономастика*, M.

—— 1970, eds., *Антропонимика*, M.

OBERMANN, M., 1969, *Beiträge zur Entwicklung der russischen Sprache seit 1917*, Meisenheim am Glan.

Общевоинские уставы вооруженных сил СССР, 1971, M.

«Ответы на вопросник по норме», 1965, *VKR*, 6: 211–17.

OVSJANNIKOV, V. V., 1933, *Литературная речь*, M.

OŽEGOV, S. I., 1955, «Очередные вопросы культуры речи», *VKR*, 1: 5–33.

—— 1972, *Словарь русского языка*, 9. edition, ed. N. Ju. Švedova, M. (1. edition (1949), 2. revised edition (1952), 4. revised edition (1960)).

PANFILOV, A. K., 1965, *«Уважаемый товарищ или уважаемая товарищ?»*, *VKR*, 6: 189–95.

PANOV, M. V., 1963, «О стилях произношения (в связи с общими проблемами стилистики)», in Mučnik (1963*b*: 5–38).

—— 1964, *И все-таки она хорошая!*, M.

—— 1967, *Русская фонетика*, M.

—— 1968, ed., *Русский язык и советское общество*, 4 vols., M.

—— 1971, «О том, как кодировался вопросник по произношению», in Vysotskij *et al.* (1971: 294–301).

PARIKOVA, N. B., 1966, «О южнорусском варианте литературной речи», in Vysotskij *et al.* (1966: 125–35).

PAVLOVSKAJA, L. K., 1967, «Сложносокращенные слова», *RR*, 6: 16–19.

PAŽIN, V. N., 1969, *Как себя вести*, L.

PEN'KOVSKIJ, A. B., 1967, «О некоторых закономерностях усвоения орфоэпических норм (г смычное и ɣ фрикативное)», *VKR*, 8: 61–72.

PIROGOVA, N. K., 1967, «О нормах и колебаниях в ударении (на материале глагола)», *Научные доклады высшей школы, Филологические науки*, 3 : 14–22.

«Почта «Русской речи» », 1968, *RR*, 1 : 104–20.

POLIVANOV, E., 1927, «К десятилетию орфографической реформы», *Родной язык в школе*, сборник 5 : 180–9.

POPOV, A. S., 1964, «Именительный темы и другие сегментированные конструкции в современном русском языке», in Mučnik and Panov (1964 : 256–74).

—— 1966, «Изменения в употреблении номинативных предложений», in Pospelov and Ivančikova (1966 : 74–94).

POPOVA, Z. D., 1974, «Просторечное употребление падежных форм и литературная норма», in Zolotova (1974*b* : 176–86).

POSPELOV, N. S., and IVANČIKOVA, E. A., 1966, eds., *Развитие синтаксиса современного русского языка*, M.

Практика газетной корректуры, 1932, L.

Правила русской орфографии, 1956, M.

PROKOPOVIČ, N. N., 1966, «О процессах структурного преобразования словосочетаний в современном русском языке», in Pospelov and Ivančikova (1966 : 127–46).

PROTČENKO, I. F., 1961, «Формы глагола и прилагательного в сочетании с названиями лиц женского пола», *VKR*, 3 : 116–26.

—— 1964, «О родовой соотносительности названий лиц (из наблюдений над лексикой советской эпохи)», in Mučnik and Panov (1964 : 106–37).

—— 1973, *Проблемы развития лексики и словообразования русского языка в советскую эпоху. (Социолингвистический аспект)*, автореферат, M.

—— 1975, *Лексика и словообразование русского языка советской эпохи. (Социолингвистический аспект)*, M.

RAY, P. S., 1963, *Language Standardization. Studies in Prescriptive Linguistics*, The Hague.

RED′KIN, V. A., 1966, «К дублетности ударения в русском языке», *VKR*, 7 : 95–105.

REFORMATSKIJ, A. A., 1966, «[ɣуc′]», *VKR*, 7 : 119–121.

RODIONOV, N., 1950, «Об одном неудачном словаре», *Культура и жизнь*, N° 16, 11 June 1950, p. 4.

RØED, R., 1966, *Zwei Studien über den prädikativen Instrumental im Russischen*, Oslo.

ROGOŽNIKOVA, R. P., 1966, «Активизация в современном русском языке подчинительных конструкций с союзами *раз* и *поскольку*», in Pospelov and Ivančikova (1966 : 61–73).

ROJZENZON, L. I., 1966, «Заметки по русской лексикографии», *Этимологические исследования по русскому языку*, выпуск 5 : 104–20.

—— and AGAFONOVA, N., 1972, «К методике составления этимологического словаря русского языка», *Этимологические исследования по русскому языку*, выпуск 7 : 175–9.

ROTHSTEIN, R. A., 1973, 'Sex, gender, and the October Revolution', in *A Festschrift for Morris Halle*, ed. S. R. Anderson and P. Kiparsky, New York, etc.

ROZENTAL′, D. È., 1964, *Культура речи*, 3. edition, M.

230   *The Russian Language since the Revolution*

ROZENTAL', D. È. (*cont.*), 1971, *Справочник по правописанию и литературной правке для работников печати*, 2. edition, M.

—— and TELENKOVA, M. A., 1972, *Practical Stylistics of Russian*, M.

RYBNIKOVA, M., 1925, *Книга о языке*, 2. edition, M.

ŠAFIR, JA. M., 1924, *Газета и деревня*, 2. edition, M.

—— 1927, *Вопросы газетной культуры*, M.–L.

ŠANSKIJ, N. M., 1963– , *Этимологический словарь русского языка*, M.

ŠAPIRO, A. B., 1951, *Русское правописание*, M.

—— 1952, «Ударение в кратких прилагательных», *Доклады и сообщения Института языкознания*, l.

Сборник указов и постановлений временного правительства, выпуск № 1, 27 февраля–5 мая 1917г., 1917, Pg.

ŠČETININ, L. M., 1968, *Имена и названия*, Rostov-na-Donu.

—— 1970, «Историческая динамика употребления русских личных имен на территории бывшей Области войска донского и Ростовской области за 1612–1965 годы», in Nikonov and Superanskaja (1970: 248–52).

SELIŠČEV, A. M., 1928, *Язык революционной эпохи*, M.

—— 1939, «О языке современной деревни», *Труды Московского института истории, философии и литературы*, том 5: 66–123.

SHAPIRO, M., 1968, *Russian Phonetic Variants and Phonostylistics*, Berkeley–Los Angeles.

SIMINA, G. JA., «Фамилия и прозвище», in Nikonov and Superanskaja (1969: 27–34).

Систематический сборник узаконений и распоряжений Рабочего и Крестьянского Правительства, 1919, M.

SJÖBERG, A., 1964, *Synonymous Use of Synthetical and Analytical Rection in Old Church Slavonic Verbs*, Stockholm.

ŠKLOVSKIJ, V., 1925, «Ваши пожелания нашей художественной литературе?...», *Журналист*, № 5: 29–31.

SKOBLIKOVA, E. S., 1959, «Форма сказуемого при подлежащем, выраженном количественным сочетанием», *VKR*, 2: 91–116.

SKVORCOV, L. I., 1972, «Профессиональные языки, жаргоны и культура речи», *RR*, 1: 48–59.

Словарь Академии Российской, по азбучному порядку расположенный, 1806–62, Pb.

Словарь церковно-славянского и русского языка, 1847, Pb.

«Словарь произношений и ударений», 1971–2, *RR*, 1971, 4: 151–3, 5: 140–1, 6: 111–12; 1972, 1: 145–6, 2: 147–8, 3: 149–50, 4: 147–8, 5: 147–8, 6: 109–10.

Словарь современного русского литературного языка, 1950–65, 17 vols., M.

ŠMELEV, D. N., 1961, «Стилистическое употребление форм лица в современном русском языке», *VKR*, 3: 38–59.

ŠMELEVA, I. N., 1966, «Стилистические сдвиги в лексике современного русского языка», in Kačevskaja and Gorbačevič (1966: 24–42).

SOLOUXIN, V., 1964, «Давайте поищем слово» *Неделя*, № 4, 19–25 January 1964: 23.

ŠOR, R. O., 1926, *Язык и общество*, M.

—— 1929, «О неологизмах революционной эпохи», *Русский язык в советской школе*, N⁰ 1: 50–6.

«Современное сценическое произношение», 1967, *RR*, 1: 37–46.

ŠPIL'REJN, I. N., REJTYNBARG, D. I., NETSKIJ, G. O., 1928, *Язык красноармейца. Опыт исследования словаря красноармейца московского гарнизона*, M.–L.

STONE, G., 1973, 'Language planning and the Russian standard language', *Transactions of the Philological Society*, 1972 (1973): 165–83.

SULERŽICKIE, M. and D., 1967, «Морская терминология и редакторская практика», letter to the editor, *RR*, 2: 65–9.

SUPERANSKAJA, A. V., 1959, «О произношении современной студенческой молодежи», *VKR*, 2: 157–62.

—— 1965*a*, «Род заимствованных существительных в современном русском языке», *VKR*, 6: 44–58.

—— 1965*b*, «Склонение собственных имен в современном русском языке», in *Орфография собственных имен*, ed. A. A. Reformatskij, M., pp. 117–46.

—— 1968, *Ударение в заимствованных словах в современном русском языке*, M.

—— 1969, *Структура имени собственного. Фонология и морфология*, M.

—— 1970, «Личные имена в официальном и неофициальном употреблении», in Nikonov and Superanskaja (1970: 180–8).

—— 1973, *Общая теория имени собственного*, M.

SUPRUN, A. E., 1957, «К употреблению родительного и именительного падежей множественного числа прилагательного в сочетаниях с числительными *два, три, четыре* в современном русском языке», *Ученые записки Киргизского государственного педагогического института*, выпуск 3.

—— 1963, «Среднеазиатская лексика в русском языке», *Этимологические исследования по русскому языку*, выпуск 4: 145–59.

—— 1969, *Русский язык советской эпохи*, L.

ŠVEC, A. V., 1971, *Разговорные конструкции в языке газет*, Kiev.

ŠVEDOVA, N. Ju., 1966, *Активные процессы в современном русском синтаксисе*, M.

—— 1970, ed., *Грамматика современного русского литературного языка*, M.

TEKUČEV, A. V., 1974, *Преподавание русского языка в диалектных условиях*, M.

THELIN, N. B., 1971, *On Stress Assignment and Vowel Reduction in Contemporary Standard Russian*, Uppsala.

TIMOFEEV, B., 1963, *Правильно ли мы говорим? Заметки писателя*, 2. edition, L.

TOBOLOVA, M. P., 1974, «Ударение в стихах», *RR*, 5: 42–7.

TROFIMENKO, V. P., 1973, *Формулы речевого этикета в разговорной речи. (На материале произведений А. П. Чехова)*, автореферат, Rostov-na-Donu.

TRUBECKOJ (TRUBETZKOY), N., 1934, 'Das morphonologische System der russischen Sprache', *Travaux du Cercle Linguistique de Prague*, 5.

—— 1958, *Grundzüge der Phonologie*, 3. edition, Göttingen.

ULUXANOV, I. S., 1968, «История слов *горожанин–гражданин*», *Этимологические исследования по русскому языку*, выпуск 6: 166–78.

—— 1972, *О языке древней Руси*, M.

Уровень образования, национальный состав, возрастная структура и размещение населения СССР по республикам, краям и областям по данным Всесоюзной переписи населения 1959 года, 1960, М.

Ušakov, D. N., 1935–40, ed., *Толковый словарь русского языка*, 4 vols., М.

—— 1968, «Московское произношение», *RR*, 2: 43–9.

Ušakov, N. N., 1957, «Морфологические недочеты в окончаниях имен существительных и их предупреждение», *RJaŠ*, 5: 73–80.

Устав внутренней службы рабоче-крестьянской армии, 1918, n.p.

Uxanov, G. P., 1966, «Типы предложений разговорной речи, соотносительно со сложными синтаксическими единствами (предложения с препозитивной придаточной частью)», in Pospelov and Ivančikova (1966: 23–52).

Vinogradov, V. V., 1965, ed., *Обзор предложений по усовершенствованию русской орфографии (XVIII–XX вв.)*, М.

—— Istrina, E. S., Barxudarov, S. G., 1960, eds., *Грамматика русского языка*, revised edition, 2 vols. in 3 books, М.

—— and Švedova, N. Ju., 1964, eds., *Очерки по исторической грамматике русского литературного языка XIXв.*, 5 vols., М.

Vinokur, T. G., and Šmelev, D. N., 1968, eds., *Развитие функциональных стилей современного русского языка*, М.

Volkonskij, S., 1913, *Выразительное слово. Опыт исследования и руководства в области механики, психологии, философии и эстетики речи в жизни и на сцене*, Pb.

Vomperskij, V., 1964, «Склоняется ли слово *эхо*?», *VKR*, 5: 178–82.

Voroncova, V. L., 1959, «О нормах ударения в глаголах на *-ить* в современном русском литературном языке», *VKR*, 2: 117–56.

—— 1967, «Ударение в глаголах на *-ировать*», *Русский язык за рубежом*, 2: 82–5.

Всесоюзная перепись населения — всенародное дело, 1969, М.

Vysotskij, S. S., Panov, M. V., Reformatskij, A. A., Sidorov, V. N., 1971, eds., *Развитие фонетики современного русского литературного языка. Фонологические подсистемы*, М.

—— Panov, M. V., Sidorov, V. N., 1966, eds., *Развитие фонетики современного русского языка*, М.

Ward, D., 1965, *The Russian Language Today*, London.

Xodakov, M. S., 1972, *Как не надо себя вести*, М.

«Заметки крохобора» 1976, *Литературная газета*, 27: 6.

Zemskaja, E. A., 1973, ed., *Русская разговорная речь*, М.

—— and Šmelev, D. N., 1965, eds., *Развитие лексики современного русского языка*, М.

—— 1966, eds., *Развитие словообразования современного русского языка*, М.

Zolotova, G. A., 1974*a*, «О характере нормы в синтаксисе», in Zolotova (1974*b*: 145–75).

—— 1974*b*, ed., *Синтаксис и норма*, М.

GENERAL INDEX

St. Petersburg pronunciation, Old (OPb) 22, 27–9, 38, 53 f.
Sakulin, P. N. 207
Šapiro, A. B., stress survey 69
SAR, stress recommendations 70 n.
Šaxmatov, A. A. 202, 203, 206, 207
schools 78
scientific style 125, 129 f.
SCRJa, stress recommendations 72
Second World War 95, 143–4, 212, 219
Seliščev, A. M. 138
Semuškin, T. 215
separative sign 212, 216
Sipjagin, D. S. 202
Slavineckij, Epifanij 31
Sobolevskij, A. I. 202
social mobility 3, 192
social variation 13–15, 82–4, 131 ff., 136, 178, 189 f.
spelling pronunciation 23, 27, 30, 38, 39, 40, 52, 54 f.
sport 162, 165
SPU, stress recommendations 65, 72
SSRLJa, stress recommendations 64, 65, 67, 70
standard language 2–3, 6, 7, 10–11, 200
standardization 24
streets, preposition with 121
stress
   and conjugation 64–8
   in noun declension 58–62
   of adjectives, short forms 68–9
Struggle against Cosmopolitanism 144, 146
students 13–14, 98
stump-compounds 78, 99 ff.
style 19, 118, 119, 121 f., 124–30, 160
   of pronunciation 26 f., 28, 35, 38, 41 f., 42, 52, 57, 65, 66, 68
Šukšin, V. M. 185
Sumarokov, A. P. 173
Superanskaja, A. V., pronuncia-

tion survey 26, 31, 34 f., 38, 39, 40, 63, 71
surnames 85 ff.
surprise, verbs of 106
surveys
   methods 7–16
   syntactic 102, 108, 116, 121, 163 f., 168–71
   see also RJaSO
Sverdlovsk 191–2

Table of Ranks 193
Tambov 189
Tambov *gubernija* 187
technological change 71 f.
theatre 23, 30, 36, 38, 40, 46, 129, 162
thematization, see topicalization
Tixonov, Ju. P. 218
Tolstoj, L. N. 50, 70, 78, 133, 203
topicalization 127 f.
towns, prepositions with 122
Trockij, L. D. 148
Trubeckoj, N. S. 50 f., 82–3
Turgenev, I. S. 78
Tvardovskij, A. T. 216

Ukraine 30 f., 32, 57
Ukrainian 158
Ul'janovsk 189
urban features 129 f., 184–7, 190, 191, 197
Ušakov, D. N. 23 f., 40
   pronunciation recommendations 23, 41, 70, 72
U.S.S.R. 149

verbal noun, use of 129 f.
verse 22, 37 f., 56, 60, 62 f., 64 n.
Vil'jams, V. R. 86
Vinogradov, V. V. 71
Vladimir (town) 189
vocative 94
voice 31
Voronež 138

RUSSIAN INDEX

характерный 14, 71 n.
-хий, pronunciation of adjectives in 37–9
хирург, gender agreement when referring to woman 169
хлебец 218
хлебороб 158
хлестать 96
хлопкороб 158
хлопоты, stress of oblique cases 60
хныкать 96
хобби 146
ходить
    ходят 23, 41 f., 54
хороший
    хороши, -о 69
хохма 156
храбрый
    храбры 69
хрипнуть 97

ц, pronunciation of 218–19
ца, pronunciation of pretonic 40
царизм 141
царь 142
це, pronunciation of pretonic 40, 54
цеика 100
цека 100
целинник 146
целовать 40, 54
    целую 40
цена
    цену 59
церковь 50, 54
цех, prepositional singular 89
ЦИК 140
ЦК 78–9
цыган 218

ч, pronunciation before a plosive 34
    pronunciation before н 34 f., 54
чаёк 88–9
частота 52
часть, stress of plural 59
чека, 100, 140
чекист 141
человек 197

через- 204, 206, 209
черт 214
    черти 36
четверг 50
четыре, adjective case after 111 f.
четырех- 214, 216
-чик 98
    feminine equivalent of 161
чин 154
чиновник 141
чистка 141
чистота 52
-чица 161
член
    -иха 165
чорт 214
чрез- 204, 206, 208
чрезвычайка 141
что 34
    чего 34
чувствительный, government of 107
чулок, genitive plural 92
чутье, government of 107

ш, palatalized 36
ша, pronunciation of pretonic 39 f., 54
-ша 159, 161, 165 f.
шаг
    шаги 39
шампунь 75
шансонетка 45 f.
шезлонг 135
Шереметьево 87
шкраб 101, 141
шортики 146
шорты 145, 146
шоссе 46 f., 48, 76
шпаргалка 156
шпион
    -иха 165
штрейкбрехер 132
штурман, nominative plural 90
Шура 180

щ, pronunciation of 26, 27–9, 53
Щелково 87
щи 27, 28